LEARNING
and
Individual Differences

MERRILL'S INTERNATIONAL PSYCHOLOGY SERIES

Under the Editorship of

DONALD B. LINDSLEY

University of California of Los Angeles

AND

ARTHUR W. MELTON

University of Michigan

LEARNING

AND

INDIVIDUAL DIFFERENCES

Edited by

ROBERT M. GAGNÉ

University of California
Berkeley

A Symposium of

THE LEARNING RESEARCH
and DEVELOPMENT CENTER

University of Pittsburgh

Charles E. Merrill Publishing Co.
A Bell and Howell Company
Columbus, Ohio

This volume is a collection of papers prepared for a symposium made possible through financial support provided under a contract with the Personnel and Training Branch, Psychological Sciences Division, Office of Naval Research.

Standard Book Number 675-09819-X

Library of Congress Catalog Card Number: 67-10538

PRINTED IN THE UNITED STATES OF AMERICA

3 4 5 6 7 8 9 10 11 12 13 14 15-76 75 74 73 72

TABLE OF CONTENTS

INTRODUCTION
to the Conference

LEARNING AND INDIVIDUAL DIFFERENCES: INTRODUCTION TO THE CONFERENCE

ROBERT M. GAGNÉ
University of California, Berkeley

The question of how people differ in the rate, extent, style, and quality of their learning is one which has concerned psychologists for a great many years. The history of investigation of this question is not characterized by smooth or continuous development. Instead, there have tended to be periods of activity followed by rather lengthy periods of inactivity. It appears that for many years the tradition of intelligence testing seems to have cast an obscuring shadow over the whole enterprise. Important practical results have indeed been achieved by measuring intelligence, which by arbitrary definition can be named "learning ability." But it is questionable whether the good effects of these practical outcomes balance the obstacles to clear thinking resulting from a passive acceptance of this unsupported and unanalyzed definition. At the present time it seems fair to say that we know considerably more about learning, its varieties and conditions, than we did ten years ago. But we do not know much more about individual differences in learning than we did thirty years ago.

It is true that there have been a few people working to bring some measure of clarification to this field which remains unpopular up to the present day (see Glaser, Chapter 1). There have been persevering attempts to make increasingly detailed analyses of the dependent variables in learning, and to relate these to a broader domain of human abilities. There have also been contributions designed to refine the methods of measurement of such variables as learning rate. Despite these efforts, we are still in the position of not being able to make definitive statements about differences in human learning abilities.

The Conference and Its Purpose

In the attempt to shed new light in this important research area, a conference was convened on April 9 and 10, 1965, at the Learning Research and Development Center, University of Pittsburgh—one of the national centers established by the U.S. Office of Education. The conference was supported by funds made available under a contract with the Office of Naval Research, Personnel and Training Branch. Its intent was to make still another try at defining the basic problem of individual differences in learning, and to delineate the assumptions and boundaries associated with research on this problem. In broad terms, the question posed to the participants was: In what sorts of ways may people be expected to differ in their learning, and how might these ways be measured as individual differences? The various answers to this question, and the discussion of them, constitute the chapters of this book.

Composition of the Conference

It will be apparent that we sought investigators with particular kinds of interests as contributors to the conference and to this volume. Primarily, we wanted people who had been studying various kinds of learning conditions and learning processes, and we hoped to encourage them to think about their work in terms of individual differences. Some of them, we found, had not systematically considered individual differences in relation to their studies of learning, but were willing to do so, and were, perhaps, intrigued by the idea. Others had already done some thinking along these lines, and welcomed an opportunity to express their views. Accordingly, we were able to gather together a group of people who had been conducting experimental studies of learning in one or another of its varieties, and who were interested in formulating and discussing the implications of their work for individual differences in learning.

Achievements of the Conference

The fact that we sought primarily investigators of learning for this conference should not be taken to imply that we considered this the only possible approach to a consideration of the basic problem. Very simply, it was thought to be an approach worth trying. In addition, it seemed to us that it had been some time since students of learning had been heard from on the subject of individual differences. The chances appeared good that modern views of learning as a process would generate some new hypotheses about the nature of individual differences in learning, their relative importance and ways of measuring them.

Several kinds of outcomes were hoped for at the time the conference was planned, and may be fairly said to have been achieved in some considerable measure. As reflected in the subsequent chapters of this volume, they may be summarized as follows:

1. New interpretations of previously known relationships between individual differences and learning variables.
2. New formulations of the basic problem of individual differences in learning, including the suggestion of new distinctions and the identification of subproblems.
3. Suggested new methodologies for investigating the problem.
4. Suggested new varieties of individual differences in learning.

Summary of Contents

The papers and discussions of the conference proceed from general considerations of the problem, with historical overtones, to more specific descriptions of the implications generated by findings in particular fields of learning research. Each chapter contains a major paper immediately followed by the discussant's comments, with the exception of Chapters 8 and 11. The volume as a whole may be said to provide a survey of views on the problem of individual differences in learning from an important segment of the psychological research community.

In an opening presentation (Chapter 1), Glaser traces the historical roots of some of the major issues in the investigation of individual differences related to learning. In his discussion of Glaser's paper, Travers points out some of the difficulties that have been instrumental in preventing the development of a common viewpoint by investigators of learning and by psychometric scholars. Cronbach, in Chapter 2, describes a number of alternative patterns of instruction in the schools, and the different implications for individual differences which arise from them. Carroll discusses these ideas in the light of the problem of matching instructional methods to individual differences.

From a consideration of studies of verbal learning, Jenkins, in Chapter 3, stresses the relevance of those experimental variables known to affect the course of learning to the problem of identifying individual differences. Fleishman's discussion of Jenkins' paper includes the particular point that individual differences measures must possess both stability and generality across learning tasks. Chapter 4, by Anderson, presents an anlysis and evaluation of evidence relating individual differences to problem solving, and its implications for future directions of research. In his discussion of this paper, Duncan emphasizes the need to conduct studies which introduce systematic variations in task variables, and which search for interactions of such variables with individual differences.

A review of evidence on individual differences related to attention is presented by Maltzman, in the light of his own and Russian investigators' studies of the orienting reflex, in Chapter 5, Wickens' discussion of Maltzman's paper suggests some limitations to the orienting reflex as a substitute for the concept of attention.

Chapter 6 contains a broadly-oriented discussion by Jensen of the varieties of sources of individual differences variables, considered in terms of a three-dimensional schema representing learning types, procedures, and contents. Jensen recommends focusing attention on one narrow class of variables while holding others constant, as a promising research strategy. Cofer's discussion of this paper injects a caution concerning the probable generality of individual differences among a variety of learning tasks.

In Chapter 7, Glanzer describes some criteria for R-R theory, derived from a consideration of his own and other studies relating individual differences to the learning of perceptual tasks. Fitts' comments on this presentation give emphasis to the importance of process variables in illuminating perceptual performances, as well as their relation to human differences. Fleishman, in Chapter 8, reviews a body of evidence from studies which he and others have carried out on individual abilities related to the learning of motor skills.

Chapter 9, by Zeaman and House, presents a systematic review of findings relating measures of intelligence to learning by contrasting the performances of normals and mental retardates. Wischner discusses this paper with particular reference to the authors' theory that attention is a primary determiner of learning differences. In Chapter 10,

Kjeldergaard considers the desirable characteristics of computer models of human learning and thinking, and includes evidence from a recent study comparing the performances of humans and a computer program in a word-association task. Gregg's comments on this paper emphasize the idea that a computer simulation model, although representing a single individual, nevertheless takes potential sources of individual differences into account.

Chapter 11, by Melton, presents a broadly based interpretation of some of the major issues and implications of the conference presentations.

LEARNING
and
    Individual Differences

1

SOME IMPLICATIONS OF PREVIOUS WORK ON LEARNING AND INDIVIDUAL DIFFERENCES[1]

ROBERT GLASER

University of Pittsburgh

It is well documented that the German and English traditions of the nineteenth century gave rise to two apparently separate disciplines of scientific psychology represented by the correlationist psychometricians and the experimentalist "psychonomes." This history can be traced from the Titchener-Baldwin controversy in the 1890's, through to Cronbach's (1957) presidential address on "The Two Disciplines of Scientific Psychology." Rather than pointing to this general condition, my concern here is with a review of what psychologists interested in learning have done when the spectre of individual differences has visited them. I have been selective but not intentionally distorting, although there are some omissions in the interest of brevity. On the whole, the amount of work is meager. While major learning theorists have indicated their concern with individual differences, this concern, for the most part, has never risen above the threshold of serious action.

[1] Work on this paper was assisted by the literature search and suggestions of Miriam Cohen of the University of Pittsburgh.

Early Studies

I start this review with Stella Sharp (1898), a student in Titchener's laboratory at Cornell. Her article on individual psychology expressed a concern of the experimentalist about the generality of behavioral laws. She stated the law of memory as follows: "The time necessary to fix impressions in memory increases at first proportionally to the number of impressions; but, after a certain limit, the 'time of acquisition' increases more rapidly than the number of impressions." She went on to say, "This law of memory is common to all; no one can escape it; but the law does not say that the limit, beyond which the time necessary to retain the impressions is no longer proportional to the number of impressions, is fixed and common for all. This limit is a variable property of memory, and here Individual Psychology comes in and investigates the subject in its different aspects; it enquires in what measure this limit varies in different individuals, and whether it remains constant in one individual for different kinds of impressions" (p. 331).

We move on to the period of the nature-nurture controversy, during which time studies in individual differences in learning tried to resolve the question of the relative importance of heredity and environment in producing individual differences. E. L. Thorndike started a line of reasoning in his *Educational Psychology* (1914), when he pointed to experiments which showed that equal learning opportunity, that is, equalizing practice, seems to increase differences. He wrote that, "So far as they go, . . . experiments in practice have given no support to the common assumption that differences in external conditions are responsible for the bulk of the variations found among men of the same race and general social status" (p. 307). The methodology he fostered for some years runs as follows: The experimental condition is that equal amounts of practice are given to members of a group in a behavior in which they are already partly practiced and in which they display individual differences. The reasoning goes that if individual differences in the behavior are increased with respect to initial differences by the equal amount of practice, then it is concluded that individual differences are due less to previous conditions of practice than to native capacities for learning through practice. If, on the other hand, differences decrease, the results are inconclusive because there may have been differences in native capacity which practice gradually reduced; or there may have been differences in previous amounts of practice; or there may have been differences in the capacity for rapid learning in early stages which diminished in later stages. Kincaid (1925) reviewed studies on the effects of practice and individual differences and concluded that experimental investigations yield varying answers to the question of whether individual differences increase or decrease as a result of the addition of equal amounts of practice. The preponderance of evidence led to the conclusion that individual differences decrease with practice, thus leaving things inconclusive. Kincaid found little explanation for the disagreement in experimental data in such factors as task or length of practice. An obvious problem for Kincaid was that investigators failed to provide good data on original scores, a point I shall return to later.

This kind of experiment persisted, and a study with such reasoning was reported by Harter (1934) in which individuals were classified on a digit-symbol code test (considered a test of associative capacity) and then given practice. Practice established large individual differences, and it was concluded that individual differences in associative capacity are not due to learning, but rather to differences in speed of neural functioning.

Woodrow (1938) pointed out that the divergence or convergence of individual differences with practice depends upon the shape of the learning curve and the position of individuals on it as a result of their prior task-relevant experience. In addition, he indicated that changes in individual differences as a result of practice might also be a function of the fact that the way in which a task is performed changes in the course of practice. Woodrow referred to the results of a factor-analysis study showing that final scores are dependent on a different pattern of abilities than initial scores (shades of the Fleishman studies to come).

A chapter by Tryon (1942) on individual differences appeared in the second edition of Moss' *Comparative Psychology.* In this chapter, studies were presented on the stability of individual differences in animals, on the relation between behavior differences and physiological differences, on heredity vs. environment, and on intra-individual differences. With the exception of the selective in-breeding studies, this chapter is reminiscent of genetics in its early years, when it was primarily the study of the distribution of individual differences and less the study of the experimental variation of conditions which influence gene frequencies.

Correlations of Learning Variables and Psychometric Measures

We come now to a new trend seemingly begun by the classic article by Woodrow (1946) pointing out the lack of relationship between general "ability" measures, such as intelligence, and learning variables. "Ability" measures are operationally defined in terms of task accomplishments; for example, the ability to add numbers correctly, to solve puzzles, or to improve with practice in some specified performance. Learning ability is defined as a change measured simply by the difference obtained by subtracting initial from final scores, the assumption being that these are valid measures of improvement. These scores consist of such measures as amount done in a given time, time required for a unit amount, errors, and also learning rate calculated from a curve fitted to obtained data.

Woodrow's findings were that data from laboratory and classroom experiments contradict the assumption that the ability to learn, in the sense of ability to improve with practice, is identical with intelligence. Correlations between intelligence and gain were generally insignificantly positive and often close to zero. Analyses of gains in a wide variety of performances showed no general factor, but rather factors involving limited groups of performance. These group factors were not measures of learning, that is, difference measures where two tests are given, but rather were one-test performances of Thurstone-type tasks such as memory, visual-spatial ability, speed, and perceptual ability. There is abundant evidence of the importance of specific factors uncorrelated with the group factors and uncorrelated with each other.

Woodrow interpreted his results by assuming that a score at any stage of practice consists of a general factor, G, and specific factors. He further pointed out that experiments show that specific factors change with practice. As a result, there can be a high and undiminishing correlation between the general factor and scores at all stages of practice, and it is also possible for the correlation between G and gain to be negligible when gain is the result of a high degree of specificity; this specificity results from task characteristics and individual differences in performing these tasks.

The line of work generated by Woodrow is reflected today in the psychometric, correlationally-oriented studies carried out as a result of Gulliksen's active interest in the problem. This is exemplified by the work of his students, such as Stake (1961) and Duncanson (1964). Stake's thesis was designed to investigate individual differences in certain learning tasks with reference to various aptitude and achievement tests. With 240 children, Stake used 12 learning tasks including such things as word matching, maze learning, memory for words, listening comprehension, picture matching, and number-pattern memory. A battery of reference tests was given, such as the *Primary Mental*

Abilities Test, the *Otis Intelligence Test,* and the *Stanford Achievement Test.* Data for performance on each of the learning tasks were fit by the Thurstone hyperbolic learning curve, and three parameters were obtained: an asymptotic or total-errors parameter, a curvature or learning-ability parameter, and a goodness of fit or regularity of performance parameter. These parameters, the reference measures, and school grades were intercorrelated and factor analyzed. The data showed that the curvature and asymptote parameters correlated with aptitude and achievement, supporting the notion that intelligence can be defined as ability to learn. Factor analysis showed essentially four learning factors: two memory-task factors, a numerical-task learning factor, and a concentration factor. The results were interpreted to mean that no general learning ability is found other than the general aptitude measured by intelligence tests, and that the various factors obtained indicate that learning ability can be specific to a particular type of task. Interestingly enough, verbal vs. non-verbal tasks did not define separate factors, nor did rote vs. relational tasks. The use of learning-curve parameters in this study probably came from Gulliksen's (1942) early work at the University of Chicago. He found that learning-curve parameters are more sensitive to experimental conditions than the usual measures of errors, time, and number of trials to reach criterion. Gulliksen's use of curve parameters differs from Hull's notion, which I will come to shortly, of equating curve constants with individual differences.

The study by Duncanson (1964) used a smaller variety of tasks more systematically specified to obtain a picture of task interrelationships. Tasks of three types were employed: concept formation, paired associates, and rote memory. Each task employed three different types of material: verbal, numerical, and figural. Reference variables were *Kuhlman-Anderson IQ, Stanford Achievement Battery,* and tests from a kit of reference tests for cognitive factors (French, Ekstrom, and Price, 1963). Learning measures were obtained from learning curves, using Tucker's factor-analytic method employing reference curve weights to describe each person's learning performance. Duncanson's findings were the following: (1) With the important exception of the concept-formation tasks employed, learning is related to IQ, scholastic achievement, and the reference tests. (2) Learning factors, that is, a concept-formation factor and verbal and non-verbal learning factors, are independent of ability factors. There are two possible reasons for this: these factors represent abilities not included in the reference tests, and there is a difference between measures of learning and abilities measured in a static testing situation. (3) A third finding is that, again, some learning is related to other learning, and there are some sharp distinctions between some types of tasks.

This line of work from Woodrow through Gulliksen defines a present, active attempt by correlational psychologists to handle learning and individual differences. It is difficult for me to say where this kind of endeavor will lead, although I will have some comment later on.

Measuring Behavioral Change

I turn now to a related development primarily coming out of the correlational camp and also featured prominently in Woodrow's article; this is the measurement of behavioral change. Recent work (Lord, 1958; Manning and DuBois, 1962) shows that the use of raw change or crude gain, such as Woodrow used, results in spurious correlations between a measure of learning and some outside variable. Individual differences in proficiency at the beginning of practice must be taken into account. This can be done by calculating a residual gain which is final status less the portion predictable from initial status. The reasoning here is that when the learner enters with different degrees of knowledge, partial correlation is the appropriate tool, since differences in measured knowledge consist of two parts: that predictable from knowledge at some earlier point and that unpredicted from the earlier measure. This latter residual is to be correlated with outside predictors of learning.

The problems of measuring change as seen by psychologists concerned with measurement are discussed in the recent book edited by Harris (1963). Here there are some interesting leads, several of which can be merely mentioned. Bereiter (1963) raised the problem that high reliability of change scores usually requires low test-retest correlations. This implies that a test may not measure the same thing before and after learning. It is likely that the test-retest problem is spurious because change, in learning, often involves the acquisition of behavior different from that involved in the initial starting state. Also of interest are Holtzman's (1963) remarks on the need for statistical models appropriate for the single case; he focused on time-series analysis. Using time as the major ordering dimension, other concurrent variables were taken into account. The models he suggested are not unrelated to stochastic learning models, where repeated measures through time are obtained on a single individual. An interesting implication of this is that analysis of patterns and a course of action, rather than discrete responses, is a possible way for analyzing behavior that might help to produce stability of measures obtained from the individual organism.

Also related to the Woodrow trend is the work of Fleishman (summarized in Fleishman, 1965) on ability factors in the course of perceptual-motor skill learning. As an illustration of this approach with respect to individual differences, in one of his series of studies Fleishman (1955) stratified a group of subjects into ability levels based on scores achieved on selected tests, and then plotted the performance curves of the sub-groups over practice. When the group was stratified on the basis of scores on a test of verbal fluency, the sub-group learning curves tended to converge through practice. In contrast, when stratified on measures of reaction time and speed of arm movement, the curves tended to diverge as practice continued. The interpretation to be made is that individual differences at later stages of learning this task depend on abilities different from those at early stages of learning. This finding by Fleishman further underscores the importance of experimental work on behavioral change which studies the influence of task variables, particularly as they change in the course of learning.

Effects of Individual Differences on Learning Functions

To turn now to another approach, the *Psychological Review* article by Hull (1945) on the place of innate individual and species differences in a natural science theory of behavior is a landmark in the history of concern with the individual differences problem in learning. Hull's thesis was that the study of behavior has two tasks: the first is deriving the primary laws as displayed by the model or average organism under given conditions; the second is the problem of innate behavioral differences under identical conditions. Most neglected, said Hull, is the relationship between the two approaches. Hull was primarily concerned with individual differences that are innate and constitutional; he acknowledged environmental and historical sources of individual differences, but they were not his main concern. His approach, however, was applicable to both sources. As is known, he adopted the point of view of the natural sciences, of physics in particular. A scientific law is expressed in terms of an equation of a particular form, and the empirical constants in the equation are determined by observed conditions so that they vary with individual events but do not change the general form of the law. Hull's notion was that individual differences find expression in these empirical constants. He gave as an example an equation for the difference limen of an organism, containing constants that imply individual differences referring to his theoretical constructs such as excitatory potential, generalization gradients, and oscillatory variation.

A keen illustrative study following this approach was published ten years later by Zeaman and Kaufman (1955). Their problem was to identify given empirical individual differences with a theoretical source expressed as an equation parameter. In a perceptual-motor task of quickly writing letters of the alphabet upside down and backwards, wide individual differences appeared. The assumption was made that the number of letters printed per trial best corresponded to amplitude as the appropriate performance measure to employ as a dependent variable; an equation was written which included constants for reaction potential, oscillatory potential, inhibition, etc. Different curves were then generated considering the effect of equating individual differences with different theoretical parameters; the theoretical expectations were worked out in terms of what would happen to starting differences during practice if they were accounted for by the different parameters. The empirical curves obtained represent what would happen if the source of individual differences resulted from conditioned inhibition. Massed and spaced practice conditions which influence generalized conditioned inhibition were experimented with to support this interpretation, the dependent variable being the preservation and loss of starting differences of groups of individuals under massed and spaced practice. The experimental technique employed was to select different sub-groups on the basis of starting scores, vary the number and kind of practice trials, observe the relative changes in mean score of these groups during the course of practice, and compare these changes with those that would be produced by individual differences in the theoretical variables. The hypothesis tested is that differences on the first trial scores reflect differences related to the theoretical variables which will influence learning. Findings of other studies on psychomotor performance (Reynolds and Adams, 1954) and verbal learning (Noble, Noble, and Alcock, 1958) generally concur with Hull's notion that individual differences affect the constants of a functional relationship rather than its form.

The approach just described is similar to the approach taken by Spence (1956; 1960) in his work on eyelid conditioning employing the *Manifest Anxiety* or *A-Scale*. The reasoning begins with Hull's basic assumption that $E = H \times D$, that is, the excitatory potential which determines response strength is a multiplicative function of the learning factor, H, and the generalized drive factor, D. This drive level, D, is equated with a persisting response in the organism, aroused by the aversive stimulation of an acquired emotional drive. It is further assumed that individuals differ characteristically in the magnitude of this persisting emotional response to noxious stimulation. If individual differences in emotional responsiveness could be assessed, the multiplicative schema would lead to the prediction that highly emotional subjects would exhibit a higher level of performance under aversive forms of conditioning than less emotional subjects. The A-scale was developed for this purpose, i.e., to extend the notion of D, as a function of the strength of the emotional response of an organism to noxious stimulation, to an individual difference variable. The work reported in this section represents a large part of the amount of the attention paid by major learning theories to individual differences.

Relation of Individual Learning Measures to Group Measures

Another active area expressing the general concern about individual differences has been study of the relationship between individual and group curves. The literature on this topic usually begins by citing the article by Merrell (1931) in *Human Biology* on the relationship of individual growth to average growth. After examining data, Merrell wrote the following (p. 68):

> The average of a series of individual growth curves may differ in certain fundamental characteristics from the separate curves. Therefore when observations on any biological form are taken on different individuals of varying ages and the description of growth is given in terms of the averages of these observations, the form of the growth of these averages cannot be assumed to be characteristic of the growth of the individual organism. The curves may differ as to the number of major cycles in their growth and as to the degree of skewness.
> The extent of these differences depends upon the variability of the individuals.

The Vincent curve (Hilgard, 1938) was an early procedure proposed for averaging individual curves that took into account differential rates of learning, its only use being to reveal the form of the learning function when individual curves do not differ in form. Sidman (1952) pointed out that, for individual curves that are the exponential growth functions predominantly used in learning theory, if individual differences occur in asymptotes and in the rate of approach to asymptotes, the average curve cannot be described by this kind of equation.

About the same time, Hayes (1953) suggested the backward curve in which individual curves are displayed horizontally so that their final points coincide before an average curve is computed. Such a curve indicates the course of learning only in the immediate region of the criterion.

Estes (1956) reviewed the problem of inference about the learning of a single organism from curves based on group data. His principal point was that valid treatment of average curves depends upon the familiar procedures of statistical inference. The defensible case for the average curve is the testing of hypotheses about individual functions; a requirement for this is to recognize the effects of averaging, so that unwarranted inferences are not drawn from the mean curves. Given a specified theoretical assumption about the form of an individual curve, the characteristics of the average curve can be deduced and these deductions tested against obtained data. The testing of quantitative theories against average data is usually concerned either with the form of the functional relationship or with parameter values for the population of organisms sampled. With this in mind, Estes proceeded to classify functions into three classes: (1) Those unmodified by averaging. In such cases the mean curve for the group has the form of the individual functions, and the parameters of the mean curve are simply the means of a corresponding individual parameter. (2) Functions for which averaging complicates the interpretation of parameters but leaves the form unchanged. (3) Functions modified in form by averaging. The most familiar example in this third case is the "exponential growth" curve encountered in many learning theories.

The procedure suggested by Estes in handling the individual-average curve problem is to state the hypothesis under test for the individual curve and then to derive the properties that should hold for the average curve if the hypothesis is correct. In an early article on statistical learning theory, Estes and Burke (1953) presented an equation representing the predicted course of conditioning for a single organism and then derived the curve showing the mean course of conditioning for a group of organisms with like θ parameters but varying in initial response probability.

Tucker (1958; 1960) pointed out, as Estes also recognized, that conformity of observed and predicted average curves is only partial confirmation of the theoretical individual curves, since the same average curve can be obtained from a variety of basic functions; thus, conformity of observed and predicted average curves indicates only that the investigator has selected one of a variety of possible basic functions for his theoretical curve. Tucker proposed that factor analysis can be used for the determination of a family of learning curves underlying obtained individual learning curves. The questions asked in analyzing the data in a particular learning study are, how many reference learning curves are needed to account for the observed performances, and what are the forms of the reference curves.

Another approach to this problem is to develop techniques which will produce lawful *individual* functions and to present the data without averaging. This essentially was the procedure adopted by Skinner and described in detail by Sidman (1960) in his book on the tactics of scientific research. A fundamental proposition of this position is similar to Hull's, i.e., variation among individuals derives from differences in the parameters of the functional relations between behavior and its controlling conditions. The argument is that if attention is paid to the variables that produce the spread about the mean values of experimental groups and these variables are introduced into the expression of the lawful relation being investigated in the experiment, then the experimental data obtained provide much more information and permit more generality. Another side of the Skinner story is the attempt to display the uniformity of results over the wide range of diverse species. It seems that the uniformities displayed must be primitive or pure laws indeed and require the necessary parameters involving individual and species differences. Toward the end of this chapter, a resolution of the individual-group curve problem is suggested by the use of limiting parameters in generally applicable laws of learning.

Initial State Measures Related to Individual Differences in Learning

In working with individual data, Skinner emphasized the notion of a behavioral baseline. The manipulation and control of individual behavior requires a stable measure of the behavior of the organism prior to experimental manipulation. With such a measure, behavioral transitions that occur in learning can be studied with precision. These behavioral baselines are individual difference phenomena resulting from prior organism history. Much of the prevalent experimentation in psychology ignores the concept of a behavioral baseline and the measurement of initial state, or it is ruled out of existence by assuming a zero baseline level, a chance baseline level, or by randomizing its effect. The properties of behavioral acquisition are functions of the initial state or the prior state of behavior, so that the investigation of individual differences in learning requires techniques for assessing, generating,

and maintaining stable baseline behavior from which transitions in the
course of learning can be studied. The special virtue for the use of a
stable baseline is that it can be used as a substitute for a control group.
The individual's initial state is a control, and individual difference factors are eliminated by the requirement for establishing a stable baseline in a single subject.

It is of interest to examine the concept of measures of initial state
a bit more by pointing to some other experimental findings. When individual differences are assessed in terms of initial state measurements
relevant to acquisition rather than generalized psychometric measures,
interesting things begin to happen. First, it should be pointed out that,
in a study by Noble, Noble, and Alcock (1958), where the *Primary
Mental Abilities* battery was used to predict individual differences in
trial-and-error learning, it was found that prediction was higher for
total correct scores than for initial correct scores. This suggests that the
usual psychometric variables are correlated with whatever happens at
the end of learning and are correlated to a lesser degree with initial
acquisition performance. This suspicion is confirmed when one looks
at Fleishman's data (1965) on the prediction of perceptual-motor skill
learning. Using a battery of tests primarily developed for prediction
purposes in the Air Force, he found that the percentage of variance
accounted for in tracking performance increases with practice, with
about 10 per cent accounted for at the beginning of practice and
slightly less than 25 per cent at the end of practice. Interesting results
are obtained when initial state is measured in terms of hypothesized
correlates of acquisition rather than of final performance. This can be
exemplified by some verbal learning studies. Cieutat, Stockwell, and
Noble (1958) showed that subjects classified on initial learning as fast
and slow learners are differentially sensitive to differences in meaningfulness in paired-associate learning. They also showed a task interaction; difficult material produces divergent slopes for fast vs. slow subjects, and easier material produces convergent slopes. Mandler and
Huttenlocher (1956) showed that initial individual differences in associative fluency are positively correlated with speed of learning. Plenderleith and Postman (1956) investigated discriminative and verbal habits
in incidental learning. Their analysis of the task showed two characteristics of subjects which should be related to success in incidental
learning: (1) the subject's ability to maintain a multiple set, i.e., to discriminate and categorize stimulus materials along more than one dimension; and (2) the ability to differentiate responses to stimulus items.
Tasks were set up to measure these two kinds of behavior, and the
results show significant correlations between these individual skills and

the degree of incidental learning. The concept of initial state as a parameter in learning functions and work such as just described suggests a line of experimental investigation which generally has been neglected.

General Laws and Limiting Conditions

At this point, I am up to date enough to have covered what I interpret to be the approaches that have been made to individual differences in the study of learning. What are the implications? It seems to me that they are the following: First, the widespread inattention to individual differences seems to indicate that psychologists have been uniquely optimistic in their expectations for the generality of behavioral laws. In the pursuit of these laws, the assessment of ranges of generalization and of limiting conditions has been by-passed. If we recognize learning as a process of transition from an initial state to an arbitrary terminal state, then with respect to the individual differences problem, we should take a lesson from other natural sciences. We must recognize limitations in the applicability of a scientific law. It is through the specification of limiting conditions that our hypothesized or theoretically derived relationships obtain concreteness.

The specific limiting conditions (or "boundary conditions") employed in physics are not unlike those required to account for individual differences in behavioral laws. For example, in order to predict the future behavior of a physical system, it is necessary not only to know the equations governing changes of the system, but also to have knowledge of its state at a particular time. It is not unusual in physics, or in psychology for that matter, to refer to initial conditions or an initial state which is in existence at some time chosen as initial time. Individual differences can be interpreted as initial states which must enter into a description of behavioral change.

A second kind of limiting condition that enters into physical theory refers to conditions which extend over a continuous interval of time. The following example from Lindsay and Margenau (1936, pp. 55-56) is illustrative:

> . . . consider a fiber which is twisted from its normal equilibrium configuration by the application of torque. When released it displays the familiar phenomena of elastic fatigue and hysteresis. This means that a knowledge of the state of twist and angular velocity of the fiber at any instant is not sufficient for a prediction of its state and motion at any subsequent time. Rather we need for this purpose the

whole history of the fiber since first it began to move at all; that is, we must know its *heredity*. The name hereditary mechanics has been given to the field of problems into which there enter what are essentially boundary conditions extending over continuous intervals of space and time and demanding integrals for their representation.

The point is, then, that individual differences can be conceptualized as limiting or boundary conditions, and that laws of learning need to consider the assessment of constants referring to initial state and "coefficients of heredity" in the sense implied above. There probably are many problems in the determination of laws of learning which are intensified because of ignorance of appropriate limiting conditions. There also is the nagging concern that there is a dearth of pure laws in psychology to which we can begin to attach limiting conditions.

Implications

It follows from this that postulated individual differences need to be incorporated into our learning theories. A major inadequacy of the factor analytic-psychometric approach that I described earlier is the lack of a theoretical framework for the selection of reference tests and learning measures. Another concern about the psychometric bias is the preoccupation with ways of getting around error variance rather than investigating the conditions which influence it. An attack on individual differences requires sustained exploration of variability so that it becomes controllable for experimental and theoretical endeavors. If the individual differences variable is to be incorporated into our work on learning, we need to be more skeptical about intrinsic variability and get on with the matter of exploring the factors contributing to variation. (Related to this is the fact that the notion of general intelligence is obviously no longer a useful scientific concept for characterizing initial state in learning studies. It leads, for example, to concern with culture-fair tests which neglect and obscure individual differences rather than determine initial patterns of ability which interact with learning (Ferguson, 1954).

In the study of individual differences in learning, the requirement for assessing initial state means that we need to be more active in postulating initial properties of the learner which interact with learning. One approach is the way this has been done by Hull and Spence. This also requires a technology for the assessment of a stable initial baseline as carried out by Skinner.

With increased attention to initial baselines, our experimental methodology can change. It seems, in particular, that if we expect individual differences to qualify behavioral laws, then our experimental subjects may need to be intensively screened and classified prior to experimentation as is done in experimental genetics, a science primarily concerned with the investigation of variation (Hirsch, 1962).

The need for "hereditary or historical mechanics" implies that in measuring change over the course of learning we need to push on with techniques for the analysis of patterns and sequential dependencies. Indices of runs of behavior and courses of learning are required to increase the stability of measures of individual performance.

Finally, in summing up the matter of laws of learning and individual differences, I recommend the position that the conceptualization required is no different from that used in other natural sciences: limiting conditions pertaining to individual differences are found to be closely associated with behavioral laws. These form a significant part of the law and of its application. These limiting conditions enable the law to be used so that it can describe and predict behavioral events. Ignorance of these limiting conditions forces our laws into frustrating generalities. A caution to be exercised is that exclusive attention to the nature of limiting conditions, like exclusive attention to individual differences, may blind us to the nature of the underlying functional relationships. Some versatility is required to keep both things in mind.

REFERENCES

Bereiter, C. Some persisting dilemmas in the measurement of change. In C. W. Harris (ed.), *Problems of measuring change.* Madison: University of Wisconsin Press, 1963, pp. 3-20.

Cieutat, V. J., Stockwell, F. E., and Noble, C. E. The interaction of ability and amount of practice with stimulus and response meaningfulness (M, M′) in paired-associate learning. *J. exp. Psychol.,* 1958, *56,* 193-202.

Cronbach, L. J. The two disciplines of scientific psychology. *Amer. Psychologist,* 1957, *12,* 671-684.

Duncanson, J. P. *Intelligence and the ability to learn.* Princeton, N. J.: Educational Testing Service, 1964.

Estes, W. K. The problem of inference from curves based on group data. *Psychol. Bull.,* 1956, *53,* 134-140.

Estes, W. K., and Burke, C. J. A theory of stimulus variability in learning. *Psychol. Rev.*, 1953, *60*, 276-286.

Ferguson, G. A. On learning and human ability. *Canad. J. Psychol.*, 1954, *8*, 95-112.

Fleishman, E. A. The description and prediction of perceptual-motor skill learning. In R. Glaser (ed.), *Training research and education.* New York: John Wiley & Sons, Inc., 1965, pp. 137-175.

Fleishman, E. A., and Hempel, W. E. The relation between abilities and improvement with practice in a visual discrimination reaction task. *J. exp. Psychol.*, 1955, *49*, 301-312.

French, J. W., Ekstrom, R. B., and Price, L. A. (eds). *Manual for kit of reference tests for cognitive factors.* Princton, N. J.: Educational Testing Service, 1963.

Gulliksen, H. An analysis of learning data which distinguishes between initial preference and learning ability. *Psychometrika*, 1942, *7*, 171-194.

Harris, C. W. (ed.). *Problems in measuring change.* Madison: University of Wisconsin Press, 1963.

Harter, R. S. A study of individual differences in associative capacity. *Pedagogical Seminary*, 1934, *44*, 139-152.

Hayes, K. J. The backward curve: A method for the study of learning. *Psychol. Rev.*, 1953, *60*, 269-275.

Hilgard, E. R. A summary and evaluation of alternative procedures for the construction of Vincent curves. *Psychol. Bull.*, 1938, *35*, 282-297.

Hirsch, J. Individual differences in behavior and their genetic basis. In E. L. Bliss (ed.), *Roots of behavior.* New York: Harper & Row, Publishers, 1962, pp. 3-23.

Holtzman, W. H. Statistical models for the study of change in the single case. In C. W. Harris (ed.), *Problems of measuring change.* Madison: University of Wisconsin Press, 1963, pp. 199-211.

Hull, C. L. The place of innate individual and species differences in a natural-science theory of behavior. *Psychol. Rev.*, 1945, *52*, 55-60.

Kincaid, Margaret. A study of individual differences in learning. *Psychol. Rev.*, 1925, *32*, 34-53.

Lindsay, R. B., and Margenau, H. *Foundations of physics.* New York: John Wiley & Sons, Inc., 1936.

Lord, F. M. Further problems in the measurement of growth. *Educ. psychol. Measmt.*, 1958, *18*, 437-451.

Mandler, G., and Huttenlocher, Janellen. The relationship between associative frequency, associative ability and paired-associate learning. *Amer. J. Psychol.*, 1956, *69*, 424-428.

Manning, W. H., and DuBois, P. H. Correlational methods in research on human learning. *Percept. mot. Skills*, 1962, *15*, 287-321.

Merrell, Margaret. The relationship of individual growth to average growth. *Hum. Biol.*, 1931, *3*, 37-70.

Noble, C. E., Noble, Janet L., and Alcock, W. T. Prediction of individual differences in human trial-and-error learning. *Percept. mot. Skills*, 1958, *8*, 151-172.

Plenderleith, M., and Postman, L. Discriminative and verbal habits in incidental learning. *Amer. J. Psychol.*, 1956, *69*, 236-243.

Reynolds, B., and Adams, J. A. Psychomotor performance as a function of initial level of ability. *Amer. J. Psychol.*, 1954, *67*, 268-277.

Sharp, Stella E. Individual psychology: A study in psychological method. *Amer. J. Psychol.*, 1898, *10*, 329-391.

Sidman, M. A note on functional relations obtained from group data. *Psychol. Bull.*, 1952, *49*, 263-269.

Sidman, M. Tactics of scientific research. New York: Basic Books, Inc., Publishers, 1960.

Spence, K. W. *Behavior theory and conditioning.* New Haven: Yale University Press, 1956.

Spence, K. W. *Behavior theory and learning.* Englewood Cliffs, N. J.: Prentice-Hall, Inc., 1960.

Stake, R. E. Learning parameters, aptitudes, and achievements. *Psychometric Monogr.*, 1961, No. 9.

Thorndike, E. L. *Educational Psychology*, Volume III. New York: Teachers College—Columbia University, 1914.

Tryon, R. C. Individual differences. In F. A. Moss (ed.), *Comparative psychology.* New York: Prentice-Hall, Inc., 1942, pp. 330-365.

Tucker, L. R. Determination of parameters of a functional relation by factor analysis. *Psychometrika*, 1958, *23*, 19-23.

Tucker, L. R. *Determination of generalized learning curves by factor analysis.* Princeton, N. J.: Educational Testing Service, 1960.

Woodrow, H. A. The effect of practice on groups of different initial ability. *J. edu. Psychol.*, 1938, *29*, 268-278.

Woodrow, H. A. The ability to learn. *Psychol. Rev.*, 1946, *53*, 147-158.

Zeaman, D., and Kaufman, H. Individual differences and theory in a motor learning task. *Psychol. Monogr.*, 1955, *69* (Whole No. 391).

LEARNING MEASURES AND PSYCHOMETRIC VARIABLES

ROBERT M. W. TRAVERS

Western Michigan University

The lack of preoccupation with individual differences on the part of experimental psychologists appears to stem largely from the fact that laboratory scientists typically experiment with strains of species which have been bred by random mating, resulting in a highly uniform product. The human species, unfortunately, does not represent a uniform product suitable for laboratory experiment, for men are not bred by random assignment to their mates. Man's selective mating practices have resulted in the emergence of a species with large individual differences in the nervous systems that the members inherit—differences which are further compounded by differences in training conditions during the child-rearing stage. The result is a species which lacks the qualities one would want to find in one suitable for laboratory experimentation. Man's failure as a laboratory strain is to some extent the story of Glaser's paper. The tradition of the laboratory has been generally that of avoiding strains of organisms (or samples of other materials) which have uncontrolled sources of variability built into them. The sources of variability such as are measured by aptitude tests represent a class of variable which the laboratory scientist simply avoids. It is hardly surprising that the laboratory psychologist has not readily incorporated such variables into his study of learning. The problem can be avoided, as Glaser suggests, simply by screening and selecting human subjects for laboratory studies so that they begin to acquire some of the properties of a laboratory bred strain, but this is simply avoidance behavior on the part of the experimentalist.

The development of research in the area outlined in Glaser's paper has followed a typical pattern. Most of the work has had the outcome of discovering and rediscovering the nature of the difficulties involved in research of this kind. We have now rediscovered several times that gain scores on complex learning tasks, such as learning a foreign language or learning to maintain a piece of equipment, are quite meaningless in that there are not only large individual differences in initial level of learning, but the achievement measuring instruments do not generally have the scale properties which permit a comparison of gains in different parts of the scale. Much research of the past produced zero correlations between tests and measures of gain on learning tasks simply because the measures have not satisfied the conditions necessary for making a meaningful comparison. Neither do the statistical techniques suggested by DuBois (1965) solve many of these problems. When the acquisition conditions do provide comparable measures of gain, then, I suspect, one may find relationships between learning and scores on individual differences measures. For example, measures of acquisition in tasks involving verbal serial learning and verbal paired-associate learning typically show under some conditions substantial correlations with measures of intelligence, scholastic aptitude, and academic performance. However, the fact that some studies show such relationships, but others do not, suggests that the conditions under which relationships can be expected have not yet been determined. As an example of what might happen, I would hypothesize that in a serial-learning task involving nonsense syllables, typical measures of success at such a learning task would be related to intelligence test scores when the syllables were presented at a fairly rapid rate to adults, say a rate of one syllable per second, but that at much slower rates the relationship would disappear. This hypothesis is derived from evidence which indicates that measures of intelligence are related to the rate at which the individual can process information. The same kind of hypothesis might apply also to typical paired-associate learning, but in the typical paired-associate experiment, the time intervals are held at what has come to be a standard of 2.0 seconds. At this rate of presentation one would hardly expect a relationship between measures of learning and scores derived from intelligence tests.

Another factor that interferes with any relation which may exist between measures of acquisition and typical psychometric variables is found, I believe, in the nature of some of the tasks administered in studies of the relationship of learning to abilities. Only a few tasks are useful for developing aptitude tests and only a few have been valuable for developing laboratory studies of learning. I have the impression that relatively few learning tasks have been the sources of most of our knowledge of learning phenomena. Certainly the knowledge derived about animal learning from classical conditioning studies of the salivary response, the leg flexion response, studies of maze learning, and studies of behavior in Skinner boxes far outweighs the knowledge derived from sources using other tasks. Research on human learning has produced even fewer learning tasks which have had a long history of yielding significant knowledge. The tasks of rote learning, paired-associate learning, eyelid and PGR conditioning are notable for the extensive knowledge derived from them, but the number of other tasks which have had as productive a history is small.

Experimental data which fit well with other sources of information appear to come typically from situations involving tasks which the particular species takes to readily (cf. Breland and Breland, 1961). Rats placed in alleys move along them without any training. Hungry pigeons typically peck at any odd-shaped marks on a box in which they are placed before any training is provided. Such activities form the basis of learning tasks which have been used to produce a large amount of extraordinarily consistent knowledge. I doubt whether such a body of knowledge would have arisen if psychologists had become involved in training pigeons to run mazes or training rats to peck. The selection of tasks which creatures are well prepared to perform, either by nature or nurture, seems to be an important prerequisite for the development of a consistent body of knowledge about learning. For much the same reason, humans readily undertake and adapt well to learning situations involving verbal learning such as are found in typical serial-learning or paired-associate learning studies. They spend much of their lives performing this general category of task and settle down readily to such tasks in the laboratory. In contrast, many of the learning tasks included in studies of learning and human abilities are tasks lacking any history of having yielded useful information. The tasks used by Woodrow (1946) were mainly of this character. They would be considered today to be unpromising for the study of learning, let alone for the study of individual differences and learning. If we are to discover consistent relationships between measures of acquisition and psychometric variables, much more careful attention must be applied to the characteristics of the learning tasks.

The scores which have commonly been derived from experimental learning settings have not always been those which one would expect to have a high relationship to abilities as they are commonly measured. For example, most learning scores derived from paired-associate learning tasks represent a combination of achievement on the different phases of learning which the task involves. I would expect that learning in the hook-up phase would be highly related to measures of intelligence, but that learning in the response-discrimination phase would not be. Learning curves derived from typical paired-associate learning situations do not permit this kind of analysis. Current efforts to provide analyses of the learning involved in certain common verbal tasks offer promise that some of the variables that may be identified may well approximate those which have been identified in the study of individual differences. Again, I would expect that measures of individual differences might show very little relationship to learning on many tasks, but substantial relationships to performance on new tasks involving transfer. I suspect that many aptitude variables are highly related to specific transfer processes and may represent conditions very similar to those developed in the experimental development of learning sets.

Finally, the point must be made that the thinking of experimental psychologists and the thinking of those engaged in the study of individual differences shows little interaction and, in the absence of such interaction, one would hardly expect that the two areas would develop with a set of common variables. The furrow plowed by the experimental psychologist can rarely be expected to cross the furrow plowed by the psychometrically-oriented psychologist. The two furrows aren't even in the same field.

REFERENCES

Breland, K., and Breland, M. The misbehavior of organisms. *Amer. Psychologist*, 1961, *16*, 681-684.

DuBois, P. H. The design of correlational studies in training. In R. Glaser (ed.), *Training research and education*. New York: John Wiley & Sons, Inc., 1965, pp. 63-86.

Woodrow, H. The ability to learn. *Psychol. Rev.*, 1946, 53, 147-158.

2

HOW CAN INSTRUCTION BE ADAPTED TO INDIVIDUAL DIFFERENCES?

LEE J. CRONBACH
Stanford University

Adapting education to the individual has meant many things in educational discussions; these tend to be jumbled together, perhaps because this topic has never been subjected to logical or philosophical analysis. I shall use the rubrics in Table 1 to distinguish methods of adaptation and thereby to structure this discussion. In due time I shall amplify each of these and examine the social and pedagogical concepts on which it rests.

Two preliminary remarks are called for. First, these adaptations are by no means mutually exclusive; they can combine in various patterns, and no doubt all of them have a place in the ideal educational system. Second, it is category 3b that is most interesting for this conference, since all the other devices alter administrative arrangements rather than instructional technique. This is the approach that calls for a new psychological theory of aptitude. An aptitude, in this context, is a complex of personal characteristics that accounts for an individual's end state after a particular educational treatment, i.e., that determines what he learns, how much he learns, or how rapidly he learns. I presume that an individual has greater aptitude for learning, say, to multiply from one method of teaching than from another method that is equally good on the average. Aptitude, pragmatically, includes whatever promotes the pupil's survival in a particular educational environment, and it may have as much to do with styles of thought and personality variables as with the abilities covered in conventional tests.

TABLE 1

PATTERNS OF EDUCATIONAL ADAPTATION TO
INDIVIDUAL DIFFERENCES

Educational goals	*Instructional treatment*	*Possible modifications to meet individual needs*
Fixed	Fixed	1a. Alter duration of schooling by sequential selection.
		1b. Train to criterion on any skill or topic, hence alter duration of instruction.
Options	Fixed within an option	2a. Determine for each student his prospective adult role and provide a curriculum preparing for that role.
Fixed within a course or program	Alternatives provided	3a. Provide remedial adjuncts to fixed "main track" instruction.
		3b. Teach different pupils by different methods.

Adaptation Within a Predetermined Program

It was in the early years of this century that individual differences became a primary topic in educational theory. Until that time, there was largely a fixed curriculum starting with the common branches of knowledge, and proceeding through an academic high school program and a college liberal arts program. Individual differences were taken into account chiefly by eliminating students. Less successful students (and those from poorer families) dropped out all along the way.

When ability tests became available they were used by schools—to put it bluntly—to decide which pupils should be allowed to drop by the wayside or to vegetate in an undemanding "slow" classroom, and which should proceed briskly, be indoctrinated with high aspirations, and go on to higher education. Those mental tests have prospered which show predictive validity for success in the predetermined curriculum.

The social theory behind 1a, the selection system, is that every child "should go as far in school as his abilities warrant." This assumes a point of diminishing returns in education, reached early by some persons, late by others. Such an assumption supports a periodic weeding-out of the less responsive pupils.

There is some logic to the opposite position: that certain common learnings should be attained, that everyone should stay in school until he masters them, and hence that we should train to criterion on the central educational outcomes. Such a procedure has never been followed in any pure form, since it would extend the education of some youngsters until they are oldsters. But it is clearly more humane than the Procrustean keep-pace-or-fall-out policy, and in modified form it is widely practiced. We saw it in the old policy of keeping a child in the first grade until he could read his primer, and we see it in today's non-graded primary unit that some children complete in two years and some in four. It appears in the claim that linear programmed instruction brings all learners to criterion on its fixed content, each at his own rate. Homogeneous grouping likewise has been premised on adjusting the pace of instruction, with some sections spending time on the more fundamental subskills and others going ahead. Adjusting pace or time implies changing the amount of exercise given to a particular connection, to use the appropriately Thorndikean terminology.

The most interesting psychological point about this approach is that it invokes a construct of "rate of learning." This concept is distinctly arguable. Woodrow (1946), you may recall, spent twenty years compiling evidence that rate of learning is entirely inconsistent from one task to another, and that there is no justification for identifying mental test score with ability to learn. His position is in harmony with the interpretations of John Anderson (1939) and Humphreys (1960). While the evidence does not support the idea of a general capacity to learn, sophisticated studies can perhaps salvage the concept of ability to learn as distinct from past learning.

My working hypothesis is that, when several intellectual tasks are to be learned under much the same instructional conditions, there will indeed be some individual consistency in time needed to reach the criterion. If the several tasks all lie in the same field—foreign language, say, or mathematics—the consistency will be much stronger. Research steps in the right direction have been taken by several studies in Gulliksen's laboratory (Allison, 1960; Stake, 1961; Duncanson, 1964; see also Jensen, 1962, and Mackay and Vernon, 1963). I shall not be satisfied, however, until we get data on learning rates under instructional conditions; present studies have invariably measured learning rates under conditions of practice unguided save for knowledge of results. My hypothesis implies that the person's learning rate will vary, depending on the nature of the instruction; I therefore expect that adapting instructional *technique* will in the long run be more important than merely altering the duration of exposure.

Adaptation by Matching Goals to the Individual

When the high school began to serve all youngsters—that is, when the nation began fifty years ago to regard dropouts as undesirable rather than as good riddance—the influx of unselected students called for a radical alteration of program. In Thorndike's laboratory, Margaret Cobb (1922) found, for example, that there is considerable risk of failure if a pupil with a mental age below 15-6 enrolls in high school algebra. Extrapolating, she wrote: "Probably in 90 cases out of 100, it is unwise to guide the average or less intelligent than average child into the present academic high school . . . He should be encouraged to try some other type of training" (p. 549). Consequent to such thinking, schools introduced vocational and homemaking curricula, and new courses were designed. The course in algebra, for example, was replaced for the less able student by a course in general mathematics. This solution is more than a decision about education; it is a decision about the role the individual is to play as an adult.

There are dangers, however, in setting differentiated goals. Differentiation of mathematics courses meant that the discipline of mathematics was kept an arcane possession of a selected class, while the lower classes were drilled on formulas useful to shopkeepers. Today the theme in mathematics teaching (and similarly in other subjects) is to give every pupil an understanding of the same basic discipline, even though some pupils go farther and deeper. Cobb had carefully qualified her report as applying to algebra as customarily taught, but the educational profession lost sight of the qualification and for thirty years ignored the possibility that algebra can be taught by a considerable variety of techniques. In startling contrast to the easy way out that reserved algebra to bright adolescents, there are now many primary-grade curricula teaching what is unmistakably algebra.

Goals are also modified when the student is allowed to select his major field of study or to choose among elective courses. This is, of course, necessary and will continue. The only comment pertinent in this discussion is to note the rather small success of differential aptitude tests in predicting which academic subjects the person will learn most easily (McNemar, 1964). We haven't the faintest evidence, for example, what constitutes mathematical aptitude, save for the obvious fact that a person who has mastered one mathematical fact or process has an advantage in learning the next process in a hierarchy. According to most studies, the complex of abilities the British call *v:ed* makes for success in all fields of academic work. Two rationalizations for this fact are available. Concepts in the end require a verbal or at least a symbolic form, and hence call for verbal skills. Secondly, our academic subjects are all taught by much the same verbal abstract methods. This second condition is not obviously necessary, and we can hope to reduce the dependence of success on the *v:ed* complex.

Adaptation by Erasing Individual Differences

Most tactics the school uses are intended to minimize the nuisance of individual differences so that it can go on teaching the same unaltered course. This is true also of remedial instruction, which adds onto the common program rather than redesigning it. Remedial work takes it for granted that the classroom work is largely a fixed program. Many a pupil needs help that the standard program does not give him, and supplementary instruction is therefore provided, with the intention of repairing the gaps in skill and putting him back on the pace. That is to say, remedial instruction attempts to erase individual differences.

Some remedial treatments are developed by breaking the subject matter into component processes, classifying the pupil's errors, and providing special explanations or drill. Under the Thorndikean view of every multiplication combination as a separate bond, the diagnostic process was to take an inventory of combinations mastered and not mastered and then to direct practice to the weak bonds. We see similar thinking today, considerably elaborated, in Gagné's (1962) discussion of hierarchies of information and skill. It takes still another form in branched programmed instruction, where there is a continuous diagnosis of misconceptions or gaps in recall, and an appropriate remedial loop follows each significant error. It is also seen in the assignment of a short linear program covering a single topic or subskill for independent study when the teacher finds a pupil weak in that respect. This type of hole-patching is not very interesting psychologically, and its value may be quite limited.

What is monitored in a branched program is subject-matter mastery, in the narrowest sense. The programs check on the learner's ability to give the response as taught. But education is aiming at transferrable responses, both cognitive and affective. Unless these broader outcomes are monitored the program may do harm rather than good. It ought to be possible to teach a historical unit on the years 1856-1861 and ask questions at these various levels, among others: (1) Does the student know the facts about what Lincoln did that Buchanan didn't? (2) Has the student arrived at a sensible opinion about the responsibilities of an elected leader in dealing with a controversial matter? (3) Can the student give a fair-minded evaluation of partisan comments, both contemporary and retrospective? Since each of these is an objective of teaching history, a poor performance on any one of these outcomes would call for remediation; three distinct remedial loops would be needed. I doubt that anyone has been designing remedial loops for the important transfer outcomes. To recognize multiple outcomes, moreover, we will need new program structures allowing for multidimensional monitoring and branching.

The "compensatory education" now being proposed for young disadvantaged children is remedial. It is hoped that appropriate stimulation will develop the intellectual skills and attitudes that constitute normal readiness for primary school. There is knowledge about readiness for reading and its development on which these activities can draw. Also needed is a theory, presently lacking, about the process of information intake and study. Recent, observations on encoding, mediation, and use of feedback are carrying us in the right direction (Bloom, Davis and Hess, 1965, pp. 45-48).

A distinction needs to be made regarding the scale of adaptation. Branched programming is a microadaptation; a new decision is made every few minutes. The decision to put a six-year-old into lessons that generate reading readiness, instead of giving him a primer, is a microadaptation; the decision prescribes several weeks of treatment. The choice of scale merits a good deal of thought. The finer scale is more responsive, but not necessarily superior, since each microdecision is made with less information. Microdecisions keep such a multiplicity of treatments in play that it becomes impossible to evaluate every branching rule with care. Macrotreatments, being fewer, can be designed on the basis of theory and can be empirically validated.

Adaptation by Altering Instructional Method

The teacher adapts instructional method to the individual on both the micro and macro scales. He barely acknowledges the comment one pupil makes in class discussion, and stops to praise a lesser contribution from another who (he thinks) needs special encouragement. He turns away one pupil who asks for help—"You can find the answer by yourself if you keep at it"—and walks the length of the classroom to offer help to another, because he has decided to encourage independence of the former pupil and to minimize frustration of the latter. On the larger scale, he not only allows options for a term paper, but may custom-tailor a project for the student with special abilities or limitations.

The significant thing about these adaptations is their informality. The teacher picks up some cues from the pupil's test record and his daily work, and other cues from rather casual observation of his social interactions. The teacher forms an impression of the pupil from the cues, usually without an explicit chain of reasoning. He proceeds on the basis of the impression to alter the instruction; the adaptation too is intuitive, without any explicit theory. No doubt the decisions tend to be beneficial, but there is reason to think that intuitive adaptations of this kind will be inefficient and occasionally may be harmful.

When we encourage a teacher to adapt in this way to individual differences, we are asking him to function as a clinician. Clinical procedures are advantageous under certain circumstances. The reading specialist or speech specialist is a clinician who selects from a wide repertoire of instructional methods. But to guide his adaptations he has been taught an explicit theory of the subject matter, worked out through a generation or more of careful observation, whereas theories are not available for most school subject matter. Diagnosis in reading and speech is aided by special tests, such as the *Illinois Test of Psycholinguistic Abilities* (McCarthy and Kirk, 1961) which charts an elaborate profile of encoding and decoding skills; no such formal devices are in regular classroom use. The selection of exercises for a clinical case is guided by the transmitted experience of previous clinicians, but the classroom teacher has no such dependable guide.

It is very likely that teachers overdifferentiate. I know no research on impressionistic adaptation of instruction, but something can be learned from studies in which counselors have been asked to predict a student's grade average. Various biases appear in the estimates, but the most significant finding (Cronbach, 1955, pp. 182-183) is that the counselors overdifferentiate; they tend to expect too much from the persons who tested high, and too little from those who tested low. A regression line is an actuarial formula that starts with the group average and ranks differential information as a correction factor, giving the latter just as much weight as it deserves. The greater the accuracy and pertinence of the differential information, the greater its weight. The judges in the study cited gave considerably more weight to differential information than the regression formula did. Certain reasonable assumptions, entered into a decision-theoretic model, lead us to the conclusion that the poorer the differential information, the less the teacher should depart from the treatment that works best on the average (Cronbach, 1955, p. 181; Cronbach and Gleser, 1965, p. 62). Modifying treatments too much produces a worse result than treating everyone alike.

To systematize the process of adaptation, and hence reduce error, calls for a theory whose propositions would state the conditions of instruction best for pupils of certain types, both conditions and types being described in terms of fairly broad dimensions (cf. Jensen, 1962). I doubt that we can develop a separate rationale for each area and level of the curriculum, but I have hopes for the more general theory applicable at many levels and in many areas. Such a theory deals with aptitude-treatment interactions.

Aptitude information is not useful in adapting instruction unless the aptitude and treatment interact—more specifically, unless the regression line relating aptitude to payoff under one treatment crosses the regression line for the competing treatment (Cronbach and Gleser, 1965). An aptitude measure that validly predicts success within both treatments may have no value in deciding which treatment to give Johnny. If two treatments are about equally good on the average, the decision about Johnny requires a predictor that correlates with payoff under one treatment and does not correlate under the other treatment; (or, what is less likely, that correlates negatively with payoff under the second treatment). This implies that general ability is likely to be a poor basis for differentiating instruction, because it correlates with success in most instruction.

I doubt that the dimensions manipulated in conventional studies of learning are the ones most likely to be important in instruction. In instruction the stimulus material develops progressively, whereas in the practice conditions of the conventional experiment the stimuli remain essentially unchanged from trial to trial. Educational content has a meaningful structure; hence, a learner can reach the point of judging his own response without external feedback, indeed, of judging a response before he utters it. Variables having to do with logical organization and with dependency on the teacher should loom considerably larger in research on instruction than they have in past research on learning.

There are many hints of interactions in the literature, but I am not able to synthesize these findings. Few variables have been given the concentrated attention that produces consistent findings. When there are two or more studies involving more or less the same aptitude and treatment dimensions, they not uncommonly disagree. I shall confine myself to some remarks on three types of variables.

General ability. Of all individual differences, the one that comes first to the educator's mind is general mental ability. We naturally think that teaching very bright students calls for methods unlike those that fit average students. I do not believe, however, that there are any well-established interactions of instructional method with mental age, within any age group.

One reason is that a truly general aptitude would correlate with performance no matter what the instructional method. The attainment score under any of the treatments should show an uptrend with increase in aptitude; while there may be some difference in slope, from treatment to treatment the differential effect will be small. Early in the work on programmed instruction, it was thought that linear, small-step programs would succeed with everyone, so that the regression of attainment on ability would have essentially a zero slope. Such a horizontal regression would be likely to cross the upsloping line for a conventional treatment. Stolurow (1964) reports one such interaction: learning from a set of irregularly-sequenced exercises correlated with general ability, but when the same exercises were formed into a well-sequenced program, the correlation vanished. The sequence, Stolurow says, does for the poorer students what the good ones can do for themselves. Results with quite the opposite implications are reported by Schramm (1946, p. 33), however. When regular classwork in English was compared with the programmed *English 2600*, the abler students achieved better with the program, and the below-average students suffered from the change. Other studies of programmed instruction only confuse the picture further.

Puzzlement of a different sort is introduced by the Osler studies (Osler and Fivel, 1961; Osler and Trautman, 1961). These studies used the usual concept-attainment procedures. Older children tend to do better. Within an age group, the brighter children did conspicuously better than average children when the concept was presented by means of simple, schematic stimuli. Common sense leads us to think that bright children ought to be better able to handle complex stimuli, but when meaningful stimuli were used, the bright children were very much handicapped, and indeed, did slightly worse than average children. We cannot generalize that lessons for brighter children ought to use simplified stimuli, but we can at least hesitate before offering them lessons richer in detail. What is especially noticeable in the Osler studies is that some of the results are more strongly related to IQ than to

MA; that is to say, the difference between MA and CA tells more about the child's process of concept attainment than his ability level does.

Something rather similar is implied in the study of G. L. Anderson (1941). He studied about 300 fourth-graders taught arithmetic by either a meaning or a drill method for an entire year. Outcomes were projected onto two pretests, one of general ability and one of past arithmetic achievement. The Johnson-Neyman method (Johnson and Neyman, 1936) which Anderson applied not only established the presence of an interaction of method with individual differences for ten outcome measures (out of eleven investigated), but also divided the pretest space into regions where each method was superior. Anderson presents a number of charts showing those dividing lines, in a space defined by the ability test and the compass arithmetic pretest. I have made a composite in Figure 1. Since the two scales have nearly the same standard deviations it has not been necessary to put a metric onto my figure. Each line on the chart is the dividing line for one of Anderson's posttest scores; the persons below and to the right tended to achieve better under the meaning method than under the drill method. Where the line is nearly horizontal, the interaction was determined almost entirely by the arithmetic test; where the line is nearly vertical, the mental test is the significant predictor of differential success. Where the line makes a 45° angle with the horizontal, the significant differential information is the difference between the two scores. Most lines are in about this position. Hence the person who has "overachieved" in the past will profit most from the drill method, and the underachiever, whose mental test standing places him higher than his past achievement, does best under the meaning method. For only one of the outcome measures did the mental test considered alone give a noteworthy interaction. Too often psychologists have tried to find correlates of the mental test score and to use the mental test score as a basis for adapting instruction. This study turns attention to the difference between the mental test score and that on other variables. Anderson's study implies that the difference can be valid for selecting an educational treatment when the mental test itself is not.

Modes of presentation. Though we might uncover interactions by hit-and-miss exploration in which results under one instructional treatment after another are projected onto a mass of differential information, another experimental strategy is more promising. I suggest that we set out to invent interactions. Specifically, *we ought to take a differential variable we think promising and design alternative treatments to interact with that variable.* Until the present time, the differential psy-

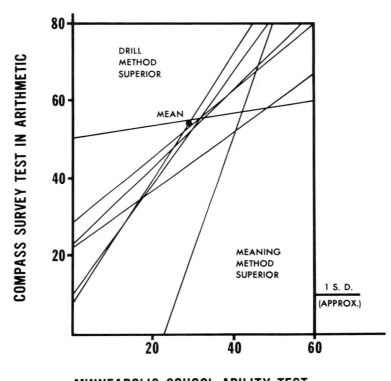

MINNEAPOLIS SCHOOL ABILITY TEST

Figure 1. Pretest patterns favorable to learning from drill or meaningful instruction. Each line is a "line of non-significance" determined by Anderson for one class of elementary school children and its control group, using the Johnson-Neyman method. This is best interpreted as showing the location where the regression plane for the Neyman method intersects the regression plane for the drill method. In each comparison, pupils below or to the right of the line tended to do better on the Johnson-Neyman method than the drill method, while those above or to the left of the line tended to do better on the drill method.

chologist has let the institution tell him the treatments for which he is predicting success, and he has designed tests or batteries to make that prediction. I suggest that we now let the institution specify only the criterion—not the treatment—and that the psychologist select an aptitude variable and design treatments expected to interact with it.

One place to begin is with the abilities that have emerged repeatedly in factor analysis. We can accept the position of Ferguson (1954) and Gagné (1960) that spatial ability, for example, ought to transfer to the mastery of tasks calling for spatial transformations of data. As I said earlier, spatial tests have had very little power to predict learning, but this may be because instruction is so largely verbal. Demonstrative geometry remains in the school curriculum not to teach theorems about triangles but to develop understanding of and skill in proof. Other mathematical and logical systems provide equally rigorous illustrations of proof. Suppose, then, that we develop a mathematics course calling for reasoning about figures, with maximum demand placed on spatial abilities. We develop a second course calling for reasoning about, say, number theory. Pupils high on suitable spatial measures would take one course, those high on certain numerical or logical measures would take the other. With ingenuity, we might create a third course, equally good as mathematics, for pupils weak on both of these aptitudes and high on a third. Here we would begin to capitalize on the principle that guides military classification: if you define distinct tasks and sort persons on differential aptitudes rather than general aptitude, a far larger proportion of the population turns out to be successful. A proposal like this was outlined by Gagné (1960), when he suggested that the addition of signed numbers be taught to eighth-graders using either spatial, verbal, or symbolic concepts. Primary abilities, he surmised, would differentially predict success in the three treatments. To the best of my knowledge his study has not been carried out.

Constructive vs. defensive motivation. The interaction that is most thoroughly documented at present involves attitudes having to do with confidence, willingness to risk failure, and motivation for self-directed achievement. J. W. Atkinson (1964) reviews many studies of need for achievement and motive to avoid failure (or anxiety). For the sake of brevity I shall speak of the student high on achievement motivation and low on anxiety as "constructively" motivated and the one with the opposite pattern as "defensively" motivated, setting aside the intermediate patterns which generally give intermediate results. This person variable interacts with perceived risk or difficulty, a treatment variable. The constructives show their best persistence when led to think they are dealing with problems where there is moderate risk. The defensives are most persistent when led to think the chance of success is very low (Feather, 1961). Consistent with this, Kogan and Wallach (1964, p. 192) find defensives rigid when in difficulty, and unwilling to withdraw from a blind alley. Given simple instructions to get to work and to do a task, constructives achieve well; adding pressure lowers their score (Atkinson and Reitman, 1956). The same pressure—a cash prize, pacing, and stern supervision—improves the work of the defensives. Telling the low-anxious student that he has done poorly improves his work, while favorable comment improves the work of the defensives (Mandler and Sarason, 1952). These studies are of enhancement of performance through short-term treatment, and do not bear directly on learning from instruction. Three other studies were conducted in the classroom.

Atkinson and O'Connor (1963) find that homogeneous grouping enhances the school learning of constructives, and has no appreciable effect on defensives. A larger study by Grimes and Allinsmith (1961) compared primary reading achievement under a structured phonics program with achievement under a less structured whole-word approach. Self-rated anxiety and rated compulsivity were used as differential variables, with the results in Table 2.

TABLE 2
MEAN OVER- OR UNDER-ACHIEVEMENT[a] OF PUPILS OF VARIOUS TYPES UNDER TWO METHODS OF INSTRUCTION (GRIMES & ALLINSMITH, 1961)

| *Compulsiveness* | *High* | *High* | *Low* | *Low* |
Anxiety	*High*	*Low*	*High*	*Low*
Structured Instruction	1.24	.42	.08	.08
Loosely Structured Instruction	−.22	.16	−.68	−.14

[a] Expressed in years of overachievement, using regression of achievement test on IQ to define expectation.

While the structured treatment produced better results for all groups, there was a marked interaction; structure was particularly helpful to the defensive pupils in the left column. Unfortunately, this was not a well controlled study, and one cannot say which of many differences between the structured and unstructured classes produced the results.

These studies give considerable support to the hypothesis that defensive pupils will learn most if the teacher spells out short-term goals, gives a maximum of explanation and guidance, arranges feedback at short intervals to keep the pupil from getting off the track—in general, if the teacher maximizes opportunity for dependence. The constructives, on the other hand, should face moderately difficult tasks where intermediate goals are not too explicit; feedback should be provided at intervals, for the purpose of teaching them to judge themselves rather than for motivational support. Perhaps these are the pupils most apt to profit by a shift from didactic teaching to learning by discovery.

There is one study not consistent with my hypothesis. Flanders (see Amidon and Flanders, 1961; Flanders, 1965) compared a "direct" style of teaching geometry by lecturing and criticism with an "indirect" style in which the teacher praises and draws out the students. The published data are not very complete, but there is a highly significant tendency for dependent students to do best under the indirect treatment. Independent students do equally well under either treatment. In a counterpart experiment in social studies, there was no interaction. Another treatment variable, clarity of short-term goals, was also studied, but produced no significant effects. This seems to suggest that dependent students should *not* be kept on the track by spelling out goals and applying prompt corrective feedback, but Flanders' final conclusion (1965, p. 99) is that there is no interaction. I note also that it is quite possible that Flanders made his indirect teacher supportive and his direct teacher unsympathetic and antagonistic. I would expect the dependent student to respond to supportive, warmly-toned direct teaching.

If further research confirms such hypotheses as the foregoing, wisdom will be required in educational applications. If defensives learn fastest under conditions of dependency, we probably want to arrange strongly supporting conditions for the schoolwork we take most seriously. But it would be shortsighted to restrict these pupils so that they remain defensive. Some part of the school program ought to be designed to increase their self-assurance; only this will release their full potential (Sears and Hilgard, 1964). A similar comment is to be made about verbal ability. It is all very well to put across a particular subject by a method that makes few demands on verbal ability, but it would be a disaster to keep the low-verbal child in a verbally impoverished environment. We have two coordinate problems: capitalizing on the existing aptitude pattern and modifying that pattern. The school need not deal with both at the same moment, but neither should be neglected.

My conception of strategy for adapting instruction has much in common with Cooley's (1964) proposal for "programmed experiences" in guidance. He suggests that students can be diagnosed quasi-mechanically with the aid of a computer, which can use empirically validated rules to suggest activities appropriate to the student's interests and abilities. It might, for example, list books on careers the student should consider, or recommend a second course in algebra.

It seems likely to me that even with the sort of multivariate testing a computer can provide, we will have to build up adaptations slowly, on the basis of only a few differential variables. While in principle a unique instructional diet could be matched to the student's idiosyncratic intellectual metabolism, nothing is to be gained by introducing unvalidated modifications. And it will be a long time before we have adequately validated rules of adaptation that take into account even a half-dozen differential variables. As I see it, our greatest hope for fitting the school to the individual lies in the development of theory that finally marries the differential and experimental approaches to learning.

REFERENCES

Allison, R. B. Learning parameters and human abilities. Unpublished doctoral dissertation, Princeton University, 1960.

Amidon, E., and Flanders, N. A. The effects of direct and indirect teacher influence on dependent-prone students learning geometry. *J. educ. Psychol.*, 1961, 52, 286-329.

Anderson, G. L. A comparison of the outcomes of instruction under two theories of learning. Unpublished doctoral dissertation, University of Minnesota, 1941.

Anderson, J. E. The limitations of infant and preschool tests in the measurement of intelligence. *J. Psychol.*, 1939, 8, 351-379.

Atkinson, J. W. *The psychology of motivation.* Princeton: Van Nostrand Co., Inc., 1964.

Atkinson, J. W., and O'Connor, P. Effects of ability grouping in schools related to individual differences in achievement-related motivation. Final report. Office of Education Cooperative Research Program, Project 1283, University of Michigan, 1963. Available in microfilm from Photoduplication Center, Library of Congress, Washington, D. C.

Atkinson, J. W., and Reitman, W. Performance as a function of motive strength and expectancy of goal attainment. *J. abnorm. soc. Psychol.*, 1956, 53, 361-366.

Bloom, B. S., Davis, A., and Hess, R. *Compensatory education for cultural deprivation.* New York: Holt, Rinehart & Winston, Inc., 1965.

Cobb, Margaret V. The limits set to educational achievement by limited intelligence. *J. educ. Psychol.*, 1922, *13*, 546-555.

Cooley, W. W. A computer-measurement system for guidance. *Harv. educ. Rev.*, 1964.

Cronbach, L. J. Processes affecting scores on "understanding of others" and "assumed similarity." *Psychol. Bull.*, 1955, *52*, 177-194.

Cronbach, L. J., and Gleser, G. C. *Psychological tests and personnel decisions.* Second edition. Urbana: University of Illinois Press, 1965.

Duncanson, J. P. Intelligence and the ability to learn. Unpublished doctoral dissertation, Princeton University, 1964.

Feather, N. The relationship of persistence at a task to expectation of success and achievement related motives. *J. abnorm. soc. Psychol.*, 1961, *63*, 552-561.

Ferguson, G. A. On learning and human ability. *Canad. J. Psychol.*, 1954, *2*, 95-112.

Flanders, N. A. Teacher influence, pupil attitudes, and achievement. Cooperative Research Monograph No. 12, Washington: U. S. Office of Education, 1965.

Gagné, R. M. Ability differences in the learning of concepts governing directed numbers. In *Research problems in mathematics education.* Cooperative Research Monographs, No. 3, 1960, 112-113.

Gagné, R. M. The acquisition of knowledge. *Psychol. Rev.*, 1962, *4*, 355-365.

Grimes, J. W., and Allinsmith, W. Compulsivity, anxiety, and school achievement. *Merrill-Palmer Quarterly*, 1961, *7*, 248-271.

Humphreys, L. G. Some investigations of the simplex. *Psychometrika*, 1960, *25*, 313-323.

Jensen, A. R. Reinforcement psychology and individual differences. *Calif. J. educ. Res.*, 1962, *4*, 174-178.

Johnson, P. O., and Neyman, J. Tests of certain linear hypotheses and their application to some educational problems. *Statist. res. Mem.*, University of London, 1936, *1*, 57-93.

Kogan, N., and Wallach, M. *Risk taking.* New York: Holt, Rinehart & Winston, Inc., 1964.

Mackay, G. W. S., and Vernon, P. E. The measurement of learning ability. *Brit. J. educ. Psychol.*, 1963, *33*, 177.

Mandler, G., and Sarason, S. B. A study of anxiety and learning. *J. abnorm. soc. Psychol.*, 1952, *47*, 166-173.

McCarthy, J., and Kirk, S. A. *Illinois test of psycholinguistic abilities.* Urbana: Urbana Institute for Research on Exceptional Children, 1961.

McNemar, Q. Lost: Our intelligence. Why? *Amer. Psychologist*, 1964, *12*, 871-882.

Osler, Sonia F., and Fivel, Myrna W. Concept attainment. I. The role of age and intelligence in concept attainment by induction. *J. exper. Psychol.*, 1961, *62*, 1-8.

Osler, Sonia F., and Trautman, Grace E. Concept attainment. II. Effect of stimulus complexity upon concept attainment at two levels of intelligence. *J. exper. Psychol.*, 1961, *62*, 9-13.

Schramm, W. *Four case studies of programed instruction.* New York: Fund for the Advancement of Education, 1964.

Sears, Pauline S., and Hilgard, E. R. The teacher's role in the motivation of the learner. *Yearbook, Nat'l. Soc. Study of Educ.*, 1964, *63*, I, 192-209.

Stake, R. E. Learning parameters, aptitudes, and achievements. *Psychometric Monographs*, No. 9, 1961.

Stolurow, L. M. Social impact of programmed instruction: aptitudes and abilities revisited. In J. P. DeCecco (ed.), *Educational technology.* New York: Holt, Rinehart & Winston, Inc., 1964, 348-355.

Woodrow, H. A. The ability to learn. *Psychol. Rev.*, 1946, *53*, 147-158.

INSTRUCTIONAL METHODS AND INDIVIDUAL DIFFERENCES

JOHN B. CARROLL
Harvard University

To me, the most interesting and laudable aspect of this paper is its insistence that the best way for the schools to adapt to individual differences is to reduce their effect by differentiated instructional techniques. Cronbach is correct, I think, when he says that the school as an institution should be free only to select educational goals, i.e., to identify the criterion of success, whereas it is the task of the psychologist to devise or select instructional methods that interact with pupil differences so that the achievement of all pupils *seeking a given educational goal* will be significantly greater than what it would be if a *single* "best" method were employed. He is further correct in identifying the selection of instructional methods as the only really "interesting" psychological problem in this field. He has carefully reviewed the meager literature on the interaction of individual differences and instructional methods in order to persuade us that the study of this problem is indeed feasible and promising. If this is true, certainly we need have no worry about keeping the next generation of educational research workers busy. Matching instructional method to individual difference variables will demand a highly insightful analysis of both kinds of variables: it will demand the intertwining of the methods of experimental psychology and of psychometrics such as has rarely been seen heretofore.

I am glad that the long-neglected Johnson-Neyman technique has been mentioned; what with modern computer technology, the mathematical awesomeness of the technique, that has probably inhibited its use, can be overcome. But even without the use of the Johnson-Neyman technique, much can be done with simpler techniques. I wonder how many psychologists have realized that every time a multiple regression equation contains both significant positive and significant negative regression weights, the predictive effectiveness of some sort of *difference* expression of the form $(\Sigma X_a - \Sigma X_b)$ is implied. (Here *a* and *b* refer respectively to a set of predictors with positive weights and a set of predictors with negative weights.) Thus, ordinary multiple regression techniques can be used to search for the kind of differences, e.g., the differences between verbal and quantitative ability, that Cronbach hopes may control the choice of instructional methods.

I was particularly pleased to note that Cronbach attaches great significance to the concept of "rate of learning," and states that it is deserving of intensive research investigation, particularly in its interaction with instructional method. In my own thinking, rate of learning is specific to a learning task; it is not a general parameter that applies to all learning tasks. Nevertheless, factor-analytic techniques such as those employed by Stake (1961) and others may help in identifying a set of common parameters by which to describe the learning rates for diverse learning tasks. If we assume that a given instructional technique has the effect of defining a learning task, then factor-analytic techniques may help us define the parameters of instructional techniques, up to now defined only in terms of crude, *a priori* classification.

Let me raise a few questions about the general outlook of Cronbach's paper. In the first place, I predict that the study of instructional methods and individual differences is going to be extremely difficult and frustrating, even if it is "most interesting" psychologically. Cronbach has already pointed to the inconsistency and inconclusiveness of the available research literature. It is, then, possible that research will never be able to come up with a sufficiently solid set of conclusions to justify being adopted in educational practice. Or, it may turn out that even though differentiation of instructional method is possible in an actuarial sense, the net gains are not of impressive magnitude. In many cases, the cost of differentiating instruction may be too high to suit the practical school administrator, particularly if it involves elaborate and expensive equipment or extensive teacher retraining. "Reality testing" in this field may be painful.

In this case, we may have to fall back on some of the other ways of adapting to individual differences, ways such as 1a, 1b, 2a, or 3a (see Table 1, Chapter 2). I would suggest that although modification 3b is

the "most interesting" psychologically, there are degrees of interesting-
ness and there are plenty of interesting problems implicit in these other
expedients.

For example, I think there is somewhat more to be said in favor of
modification 3a than Cronbach seems to say. For one thing, the school
is never in control of the *total* learning history of the individual. When
a group of pupils enter a classroom, at whatever grade level, they already differ in many respects. Undoubtedly they differ in aptitude, and
by this I mean that they have different *patterns* of aptitude. But even
aside from such differences, they may simply be at different points on
the learning curve. Adaptation to this kind of individual difference
merely means starting with each pupil where he is on the learning
curve and taking him from there. Already the school recognizes such
differences by establishing varying grade levels, or courses at different
levels of advancement (e.g., elementary French, intermediate French,
advanced French). I do not know whether Cronbach means to include
this rather obvious kind of educational adaptation to individual differences in his procedure 3a; if not, perhaps it will have to be classified
as a new procedure—3c: "Teach at an appropriate level on the learning
curve." From the standpoint of research, this procedure demands highly
accurate means of diagnosing at what points the student is on one or
more relevant learning curves, and presenting appropriate levels of
instruction, even though in a sense the instructional treatment may
remain fixed (i.e., a common course of study over the whole of the
learning curve). Of course, this procedure can also be combined with
3b if instructional treatment is found also to interact with some kind
of aptitude pattern.

If we assume, with many psychologists, that aptitude is partly a
matter of the possession of prerequisite knowledges and skills, or the
lack thereof, Cronbach's 3a and 3b procedures really amount to the
same thing—i.e., determining which prerequisite skills and knowledges
are lacking in the pupil and attempting to provide instruction to fill
the gaps. I do not think such instruction is necessarily to be labeled
as mere "hole-patching." Sometimes it is a matter of finding some basic
characteristic of the individual that affects all his learning—for example,
a fundamentally wrong attitude about school, a fundamental misconcep-
tion about some aspect of the subject matter, or a specific disability
in perception that nevertheless pervades his learning. There is an entirely respectable and indeed interesting field of study in attempting
to diagnose such basic lacks and prescribing appropriate instructional
procedures or "remedies." I am not sure that even the differentiated

procedures categorized by Cronbach under 3b are not all "remedies." There is a very thin line between a teaching procedure as such, and a remedy, since all teaching procedures can be called "remedies for ignorance."

I would finally like to raise a question about the assumption that Cronbach seems to make in connection with the use of different instructional methods to achieve fixed goals. The assumption is that the same goal can indeed be reached by different instructional procedures. Perhaps we need to specify what we mean by an educational goal. The problem arises because it would seem reasonable to suggest that two people who have been treated by different procedures will at least in some respects be different by virtue of the different procedures. Suppose we follow Gagné's proposal, cited by Cronbach, that the addition of signed numbers be taught using either spatial, verbal, or symbolic concepts. It may be true that the outcome of any one of these methods might be represented by the achievement of a given score on a performance test, but are these outcomes really the same? A child who has been taught spatially will have a concept of signed numbers different from the concept attained by a child taught with a purely verbal procedure, and even though the children may have the same score on a performance test, the differences might show up in dramatic form when the two children start to study some more advanced form of mathematics, say, higher algebra. Then, Cronbach's method 3b, rather than adapting to or reducing individual differences, may actually have the effect of accentuating or increasing individual differences. This could be much more than a "sleeper" effect—one that would show up only after the passage of time. It might actually have immediate effects. Using verbal, spatial, or symbolic teaching methods might have the effect of making some children highly verbal, others highly spatial, and others highly symbolic in their thinking. The achievement of fixed, common goals may be attained, if this is true, only at the cost of *differential* achievement of other goals.

At this point, I guess, we are thrown back on the social theory involved in selecting educational goals, and I am no more able to solve this problem than Cronbach was. For after pointing to the social theories implicit in procedures 1a and 1b, Cronbach dodges the question of how the schools are to select their educational goals. The fundamental question is, do we *want* to reduce individual differences? Benjamin (1949), at Harvard some years ago, gave an eloquent plea for what he called "the cultivation of idiosyncrasy."

REFERENCES

Benjamin, H. *The cultivation of idiosyncrasy.* Cambridge, Mass.: Harvard University Press, 1949.

Stake, R. E. Learning parameters, aptitudes, and achievements. *Psychometric Monogr.*, 1961, No. 9.

3

INDIVIDUAL DIFFERENCES IN VERBAL LEARNING

JAMES J. JENKINS
University of Minnesota

From time to time those of us who march under the banner of the verbal learning army gird up our loins and, casting a broad glance over the activities of the field, we *talk* about launching an attack against our collective ignorance at the point where it is most strongly defended. We loudly deplore the lack of theoretically motivated studies of individual differences in verbal learning, and suggest that *someone* should do *something* about it. The last such session with which I was connected involved a paper by Noble and my following discussion at the first Gould House Conference (Cofer, 1961). Somehow, though, following these periodic forays, the army fails to march. The field for the most part is again deserted, and we return to more traditional, more interesting, and more productive lines of attack.

As both Noble and I pointed out five years ago, this is in part a function of the differences in temperament, training, and interest of the experimentalist and the differential psychologist (see, for example, Thorndike, 1954; Cronbach, 1957) and in part a function of the state of the field. When I berated Ben Underwood some years ago for not studying individual differences in verbal learning, he replied that it was awfully hard to get interested in a variable which simply expressed itself as variance. He added that if I could show him an interesting effect of individual differences beyond simply increasing or decreasing variance, he would be delighted to investigate it.

The Nature of the Problem

When one addresses himself seriously to answering this challenge, the data are indeed discouraging. On the one hand, we long ago ceased to believe that we would find any general learning factor extending across a variety of learning situations when we dealt with normal populations. On the other hand, within a constrained set of tasks where we do find systematic differences, the evidence suggests that variation on these specific tasks usually takes the form of a simple difference in a curve-fitting constant (see, for example, Cieutat, Stockwell, and Noble, 1958; and, quite recently, Carroll and Burke, 1965).

While it is clearly of interest to the experimental psychologist to find variables which he can employ in "screening tests" to reduce the variance of subjects' performance in his experiments (e.g., Kjeldergaard, 1962), such methodological refinements are mere conveniences which in the main contribute little to our understanding of either individual differences or learning. Certainly it is possible to screen subjects on a "work sample" and stratify them appropriately, and it is useful to do so for statistical purposes, but we would be misleading ourselves and others if we felt that this was the primary goal of research on individual differences in verbal learning. (There *are* areas of individual differences research where issues of practical importance justify such an approach, that is, where either a relatively brief evaluation or an historical resumé makes possible the prediction of the outcome of an extended training experience or performance in a critical situation far removed from the present time and scene. No criticism is leveled at such research, but it would be difficult to justify equally serious concern with particular forms of verbal learning in the laboratory.)

In spite of the discouragement in the literature, however, my feeling is that the study of individual differences in verbal learning should be of concern to us in two ways. First, it can help us to understand the nature of the psychological processes which are postulated by the investigators of verbal learning, and second, it can help us to discover and understand the structure and function of individual abilities, experiential residues, and motivational states as they are "engaged by" or employed in the verbal learning processes.

What I am arguing for here rests on a simple statement of faith at the outset; the faith that the experimental variables associated with the manipulation of performance in verbal learning (i.e., the variables that enter into the process laws) are similarly differentially represented in the skills of our subjects. This may *not* be the case, of course. It may be that all our process variables are explicable in terms of some amorphous individual variable such as a "general ability to recruit weak associations," or it may be that even the simplest process variable is compounded of fifty specific individual variables combined in different ways for different individuals and subject to shifting weights for these variables for every trial in every kind of learning task. As a beginning, however, I think we must make our bets on the statement of faith. If the faith is correct, the gain in scientific economy will be enormous. If the faith is incorrect, we will at least have chosen a systematic way to go down to defeat, and the defeat will be clear.

It might be remarked that a logically alternative statement of faith could begin at the other end and take the form that known individual differences variables will determine the major processes to be identified in verbal learning. Unfortunately, this is a less attractive alternative since there appears to be no consensus whatsoever on a taxonomy of differential variables. There is, rather, a somewhat chaotic proliferation of potential candidates for variables with little rationale for their identification and no claim for their inclusiveness (see Jenkins and Lykken, 1957). In the absence of such a taxonomy and in the presence of intensive work on significant processes in verbal learning, the choice seems to be clearly dictated.

Let me repeat, then, my conception of the task. Ideally, if we fully understood a verbal learning task (e.g., paired-associate learning), we would be able to specify in fine detail the relevant experimental variables which affect the outcomes. That is, we would be able to write sets of equations in which the proper values could be entered (for stimulus material, response material, time intervals, practice lists, etc.) to predict the outcome. The usual way to talk about such equations is to assume an amorphous, homogeneous, normal subject who is passively affected by the variables. This "subject" is approximated in practice by running groups of subjects and dealing with mean values. This amounts, of course, to treating individual differences as random error.

My faith is that if we write the best equations we can now write, we will be able to find "traits" in our subjects which will map onto many of the variables which we now must write into those equations. Such a view, if true, has broad implications for both experimental and differential research.

What Sorts of Traits?

Underwood (1964) has characterized the present state of investigation in verbal learning as the "age of analysis." He supposes, hopefully, that we may be nearing the end of this age, that the process will take us to rock bottom and we can begin to build back toward more complex behavior when we have plumbed the depths of our laboratory tasks. Let us for the moment join him in this hope and ask what potential frontiers of individual differences are suggested to us by the field as we now know it.

The most obvious candidate for an important variable from the traditional associationistic point of view is the postulated ability to form new associative bonds or habits. Surely this must be an important and enduring individual differences parameter. However, the evidence in favor of such a general variable is minimal. Carroll and Burke (1965) find, for example, that "fast" and "slow" learners, as dete:mined on a pretest (Part V of the Modern Language Aptitude Test), differ in their paired-associate learning experiment only on materials of intermediate difficulty (low-frequency English words). When confronted with high-frequency English words or, on the other extreme, with low-meaningful CVCs, the ability groups give indistinguishable performances in learning. While one may argue that these effects are artifactual, due to extreme ease and extreme difficulty as constraints on variability, their particular finding is only an instance of the more general research which suggests that individuals' learning is highly variable across different types of materials and across different learning situations (see, for example, Woodrow, 1946).

A more likely conclusion to be drawn from these data is that the ability to form new associations has no status as a general trait if divorced from material and task variables. If one follows along with the kind of analysis which has been applied to paired-associate learning, it is obvious that this should be the case.

The Analysis of Paired-Associate Learning

While details may differ and the depth of the analysis may be extended, it is clear that the task of paired-associates learning may be represented as a series of tasks which must be accomplished by the subject through the course of the learning. (For more systematic statements see, for example, McGuire, 1961; Newman, 1961; and Battig, 1962.)

Requirements of the task. The subject must understand what the task is; that is, he must understand that he is (or is not) to make an overt response to the left-hand stimulus item (such as reading it aloud if it is a word or pronounceable nonsense syllable); he must realize that the right-hand item which is paired with that left-hand item on the first presentation will uniformly be so presented; he must know that he is supposed to attend to this uniformity and that his task is to pronounce this right-hand word in the presence of the left-hand word before its symbol actually appears on the drum; etc. Perhaps, in addition to these understandings he must also get a "feel" for the time intervals, adapt to the apparatus, learn to ignore the experimenter if one is present, etc. And still beyond this, he may need to be convinced that the experiment *is* a real "honest-to-goodness" learning experiment rather than a disguised personality test or social-psychological experiment.

These variables merge into the background and often receive little attention, but surely they are important in producing the first increment in "learning to learn" and "warm up" phenomena so readily obtained in the laboratory.

Identifying stimuli. The subject must discriminate the stimuli from one another (and from the responses). To each he must respond in some consistent fashion and with sufficient strength to form a stable cue system with which the response may be associated. How this is accomplished may vary enormously depending on the particular circumstances involved. If an adequate discrimination can be achieved by using only part of the information in the "nominal stimulus," subjects may elect to attend to only some salient element (say the first letter) of the stimulus complex (see Newman, 1963). Underwood and Schulz, 1960; Jenkins, 1963.) If different sets of stimuli are available, subjects may use one set in preference to another because of its meaningfulness or other attribute even when instructed to attend to another set (Underwood, Ham and Ekstrand, 1962; Jenkins and Bailey, 1964). If the stimuli are spatial figures they may require one set of discrimination skills; if they are shades of gray, another; if they are verbal, they may be susceptible to many alternative kinds of discriminations (sound, physical shape, associative richness, specific meaning relations, etc.).

Further, the operations performed on the stimulus (fractionating, selecting one aspect rather than another, etc.) may be dependent on specific utilities of the elements for the task in hand, as, for example, in acting to "suggest" the response or serving to keep two troublesome stimuli clearly separated.

Developing responses. The subject must raise the responses to a position of ready availability. This involves integrating the sequence of sub-units to form stable, unitary, response units (if that is appropriate, as it usually is) and discriminating the responses from each other and from the stimuli. It is commonly believed that this "readying" of the responses leads to the formation of a response pool (a collection of available interrelated items, ready for use) on which differentiation and selection processes are performed.

Performing. Finally, the subject must learn the appropriate occasion for the emission of each response. In a single list this means that he must correctly discriminate the stimulus for which a specific integrated response is correct. In multiple list learning, it often implies that he "knows" which list he is in and which response pool is appropriate or which set of stimulus discriminations apply or both.

Clearly, when one undertakes to study individual differences in such a setting as the paired-associate task just described, there is a bewildering jungle of experience, abilities, and strategies with which one must cope. It is not at all hard to see why the "general factor" of learning ability has not shown its head. (Even *if* it existed, we would have no reason to expect to observe it.)

We must suppose that subjects come to our experiments with a variety of specific and non-specific bits of behavior which we must account for in describing performance. They may vary with respect to every variable mentioned in each of the numbered sections above. Beyond that host of differences, they may vary with respect to some aspects of experience which produce complex resultants—partly positive and partly negative. For example, previous experience in paired-associate learning may improve performance with respect to task variables (1) and in the learning of techniques for handling problems in (2), (3), and (4), but also produce negative transfer in terms of specific learnings or behaviors.

Still beyond all these variables may lie variables of a motivational or "personality dynamic" type which may interact with the skill and habit variables to produce still more variable outcomes (e.g., as it is suggested may be the case with "manifest anxiety").

In the face of this rather deadly and disheartening analysis, it may seem ridiculous to pursue the notion of investigating individual differences in verbal learning. Some investigators have indeed assumed this to be the case (cf. Hull, 1943, p. 194) and remarked on the seeming impossibility of the task, but such a counsel of despair is not the message in this paper. On the contrary, it is my position that we have a good deal of evidence that there are stable individual differences in verbal learning (given certain constraints), that such stabilities may furnish the motivation for further work which can be seen to hold the promise of fruitful outcome for both experimentalist and differential psychologist.

Selection of a Research Strategy

Are there stable individual differences in verbal learning? Every investigator who has bothered to look knows that to be the case. In a recent set of data we have gathered using repeated learning of nonsense syllable paired-associate lists on 16 different days, the correlations between performances on any arbitrarily chosen pair of days range from the high .40's to low .90's with values in the .70's being typical. I suspect that the data in most investigators' files look like this if the subjects have been warmed up on a practice series before the first learning task, and slightly lower if the subjects have had no warm-up. It is clear that there is some array of individual factors that are relatively stable and accessible. The rather surprising thing about our data is that they hold to this relatively high level of intercorrelation as the subjects go from their first experience with nonsense syllables and paired-associate learning through to the point where they are skilled learners, conquering lists in only half the time required by the original lists.

What is argued by such data as these is that when the task is closely constrained for form and material, the relationships may be relatively straightforward. Surely this is a hint that we ought to focus our original programs of study of individual differences on just a few types of verbal learning where we already know a good deal about the material variables and where we have good descriptions of the processes believed to be involved. We could well select the desired situation or set of situations to balance the various variables listed above, to maximize one of particular interest (as Battig, 1962, attempted to do in devising a task which seemed to load almost entirely on the development of S to R associations), to minimize those which we think will be most troublesome, etc. Surely, this part of the problem is precisely where the long experimental history will help us. The more troublesome portion, once we have decided where our interests lie, is to invent plausible individual differences variables, discover methods of independent measurement of the variables, and finally find situations in which the relationship between these differential variables and our experimental phenomena can be displayed in such a fashion as to contribute the most information to our research program.

At this point one has a set of alternatives concerning procedure. One might, for example, conduct a series of experiments modeled on the pattern of Fleishman's studies of motor skills (see Chapter 8); that is, one might seek reference tests which seem to tap a series of relatively independent factors of verbal abilities and conduct factor-analytic studies of the components of the display of individual differences in a variety of verbal learning tasks and at a variety of stages in the performance of such tasks. In a somewhat analogous but alternative fashion, one might pursue the problem in multivariate factorial designs with complex analysis of variance techniques. I think there are specific advantages and disadvantages to each procedure which may argue for one over the other, depending on the aims the investigator is most interested in pursuing and on the assumptions he makes about the effects of repeated testing and repeated learning experiences, as well as his beliefs concerning the stability of ability measures.

I must opt, however, for a still different approach which will seem to some, I am sure, archaic and primitive. I think our most instructive approach is to proceed with analyses of very specific problems and the identification of specific characteristics of the subjects which bear on the microproblems selected. I suspect that in this way we may ready ourselves for more ambitious work of the kind described above and will in the long run make such work meaningful and possible. Without this slow and tortured preliminary, however, I fear that the more general approaches are bound to yield little information.

An Example of the Research Strategy

My model for productive work of this kind is the series of studies of incidental learning performed by Leo Postman and his students and, more specifically, the pair of studies of individual differences variables in incidental learning by Plenderleith and Postman (1956, 1957). Through a set of highly specific studies (Postman and Phillips, 1954; Postman, Adams, and Phillips, 1955; Postman and Adams, 1956a, 1956b;

Postman, Adams, and Bohm, 1956), these investigators developed an associative theory of learning which focused on the difference between incidental and intentional learning. Their guiding hypothesis was that selective learning under both incidental and intentional learning is a fuction of the number and strength of *differential responses* evoked from the subjects by the stimulus materials. This idea, which is a central one in many models of verbal learning, is easily related to diverse experimental work all the way from meaningfulness to mediation. In their hands it took the form that the difference between incidental and intentional learners lies in the motivation for producing differential responses. Consequently, "intention to learn" directly affects "amplitude" (or "intensity" or "clarity") of the response produced and the frequency with which the response is rehearsed.

When serial-list materials were varied in "meaningfulness" or association value, differences between the two kinds of learning were found as expected: big differences on the low association value materials (where incidental learners presumably make few and weak differential responses) and small differences on the high association value materials (where differential responses are readily available to all).

Similarly, they discovered the results could be manipulated by varying the test method. If the test consisted of easy recognition (picking out the particular stimuli they had just seen from a set of very different materials), there were no differences between the groups as to learning, and the relation of recognition with association value disappeared for the intentional group (that is, virtually *any* differential response worked). If, on the other hand, the test was made very hard (false cues for recognition), the differences were obliterated (that is, *scarcely any* differential response was good enough). When the test was intermediate, regular differences were observed.

Predictions on the differential effects of intraserial similarity were strikingly confirmed (incidental learners actually performed better under the high similarity conditions than intentional learners, presumably due to experiencing less intraserial interference). Further predictions concerning reminiscence effects, crowding and isolation, interserial interference, and the nature of the orienting task furnished clear support for the associative model the investigators were employing and their analysis of processes involved in the tasks they were utilizing.

Throughout the experimental series the investigators were impressed with the great spead of scores on the tests of incidental learning. This they attributed to two sources: (1) the readiness of the subject to give a differential response to the stimulus items (as a result of ability, experience, or the nature of the stimulus), and (2) the ability of the sub-

jects in sustaining a multiple set. Plenderleith and Postman first tried
to investigate individual differences in incidental learning by evaluating these two dimensions with an anagram task and a symbol discrimination task. The anagram task (scrambled high-frequency words)
was chosen as a first approximation as a task which would evaluate the
subject's ability to relate nonsense stimuli to conventional, meaningful
units. The symbol discrimination task consisted of a series of slides,
exposed for one minute each, that contained varying numbers of capital
letters, lower case letters, and numbers. For eight trials the subjects
were required to report the digits only; for the remaining 13 slides
subjects were to report either digits or capital letters, but the subjects
were not told which until *after* the exposure. The subject's decrease in
accuracy of discrimination of digits was recorded as a measure of his
inability to maintain a multiple set as opposed to a single set. The
subjects were independently given both incidental and intentional
learning tasks. Intercorrelations of tasks and measures are given in
Table 3.

TABLE 3

CORRELATIONS OF SCORES IN INCIDENTAL LEARNING
AND INTENTIONAL LEARNING WITH SCORES INDICATING
(1) DECREMENT IN SYMBOL DISCRIMINATION AND (2) SO-
LUTION OF ANAGRAMS, IN 100 COLLEGE UNDERGRADU-
ATES (DATA FROM PLENDERLEITH AND POSTMAN, 1956)

| | *Measure* | | |
Measure	*Intentional Learning*	*Symbol Discrim. Decrement*	*Anagrams*
Incidental Learning	.26°	−.42°	.25°
Intentional Learning		.16	.11
Symbol Discrimination Decrement			−.21†

°p < .01
†p < .05

It is clear that incidental learning is more highly related to the test
measures than is intentional learning, exactly as the investigators had
supposed. This is presumably because the higher motivation of intentional learning obscures the differences in habits and sets. However, as
intentional learning proceeds, the task becomes more complex and the
amount of material to be kept straight at any one instant increases.
Thus, the investigators expected that the demands made on the sub-

ject might become more and more like those which the incidental learning task required. Results also seem to confirm this hypothesis, as indicated in Table 4.

TABLE 4

CORRELATIONS OF SCORES ON EACH OF FOUR TRIALS OF INTENTIONAL LEARNING WITH SCORES OF (1) INCIDENTAL LEARNING, (2) DECREMENT IN SYMBOL DISCRIMINATION, AND (3) SOLUTION OF ANAGRAMS, IN 100 COLLEGE UNDERGRADUATES (DATA FROM PLENDERLEITH AND POSTMAN, 1956)

Measure	*Trials of Intentional Learning*			
	1	*2*	*3*	*4*
Incidental Learning	.26°	.36°	.52°	.56°
Symbol Discrimination				
Decrement	.16	−.01	−.24†	−.18
Anagrams	.11	.12	.24†	.19†

N = 100 college undergraduates
°p < .01
†p < .05

Plenderleith and Postman went on in another study (1957) to define a variable of *associative potency* by which they meant the *strength* of the differential response made to an item. They reasoned that this might be measured for an item across persons by extending Marbe's Law: the more subjects making the same response, the stronger that response may be inferred to be. On the subject side, potency was assumed to be reflected in *conventionality* which was defined as the degree to which a particular subject gave popular associative responses to a particular class of stimuli. The investigators argued that recall of stimulus items could be shown to be a joint function of the potency of the item and the conventionality of the subject. They further argued that the predictive effects would be most clearly seen in incidental learning on material of low associative potency.

Their experiment required subjects to associate the four kinds of stimuli (high and low potency and nonsense syllables and meaningful words, combined 2 × 2) under instructions to learn and under no such instructions. All subjects were asked to recall the stimuli at the end of the association task. Significant effects were found in recall for: meaningfulness of materials, associative potency of the nonsense materials (but not associative potency of the meaningful words), and conventionality scores, which correlated significantly with recall on low associative potency nonsense syllables (+.48) and low associative potency real words (+.36) when these were being recalled in the incidental learning condition. Thus again the hypotheses of the investigators were confirmed.

The point to be made here is probably already clear. Individual differences can be looked at by the experimentalist as a way of adding information to his description of important constructs developed in his concern with the process of learning. At the same time the inclusion of individual differences furnishes an especially severe test of the psychological reality of the theorist's conceptions. Far from being an excursion into applied psychology (as many experimentalists are prone to think of differential psychology), it can be a demanding test of the extent to which the investigator really understands his variables and has them under control. The fusion of the "two disciplines of scientific psychology" is not merely a political or social concern. It is, rather, the most rigorous task we can set for ourselves: the development of an integrated psychology of process and status laws and their interactions—here, a psychology of the human being in the act of learning.

REFERENCES

Battig, W. F. *Analysis of processes in paired-associate learning.* Cooperative Research Project No. 730. University of Virginia, 1962.

Carroll, J. B., and Burke, M. L. Parameters of paired-associate verbal learning: Length of list, meaningfulness, rate of presentation, and ability. *J. exp. Psychol.*, 1965, 69, 543-553.

Cieutat, V. J., Stockwell, F. E., and Noble, C. E. The interaction of ability and amount of practice with stimulus and response meaningfulness (*m, m'*) in paired-associate learning. *J. exp. Psychol.*, 1958, 56, 193-202.

Cofer, C. N. (ed.). *Verbal learning and verbal behavior.* New York: McGraw-Hill Book Company, 1961.

Cronbach, L. J. The two disciplines of scientific psychology. *Amer. Psychologist*, 1957, 12, 671-684.

Hull, C. L. *Principles of behavior.* New York: Appleton-Century-Crofts, 1943.

Jenkins, J. J. Stimulus "fractionation" in paired-associate learning. *Psychol. Rep.*, 1963, 13, 409-410.

Jenkins, J. J., and Bailey, V. B. Cue selection and mediated transfer in paired-associate learning. *J. exp. Psychol.*, 1964, *67*, 101-102.

Jenkins, J. J., and Lykken, D. T. Individual differences. *Ann. Rev. Psychol.*, 1957, *8*, 79-112.

Kjeldergaard, P. K. Predicting paired-associate learning speed. *Psychol. Rep.*, 1962, *11*, 353-354.

McGuire, W. J. A multiprocess model for paired-associate learning. *J. exp. Psychol.*, 1961, *62*, 335-347.

Newman, S. E. *A mediation model for paired-associate learning.* Tech. Rep. No. 1, ONR Contract Nonr 486(08), North Carolina State College, 1961.

Plenderleith, M., and Postman, L. Discriminative and verbal habits in incidental learning. *Amer. J. Psychol.*, 1956, *69*, 236-243.

Plenderleith, M., and Postman, L. Individual differences in intentional and incidental learning. *Brit. J. Psychol.*, 1957, *48*, 241-248.

Postman, L., and Adams, P. A. Studies in incidental learning: III. Interserial interference. *J. exp. Psychol.*, 1956a, *51*, 323-328.

Postman, L., and Adams, P. A. Studies in incidental learning: IV. The interaction of orienting tasks and stimulus materials. *J. exp. Psychol.*, 1956b, *51*, 329-333.

Postman, L., Adams, P. A., and Bohm, A. M. Studies in incidental learning: V. Recall for order and associative clustering. *J. exp. Psychol.*, 1956, *51*, 334-342.

Postman, L., Adams, P. A., and Phillips, L. W. Studies in incidental learning: II. The effects of association value and of the method of testing. *J. exp. Psychol.*, 1955, *49*, 1-10.

Postman, L., and Phillips, L. W. Studies in incidental learning: I. The effects of crowding and isolation. *J. exp. Psychol.*, 1954, *48*, 48-56.

Thorndike, R. L. The psychological value system of psychologists. *Amer. Psychologist*, 1954, *9*, 787-789.

Underwood, B. J. Laboratory studies of verbal learning, in E. R. Hilgard (ed.), *Theories of learning and instruction.* Chicago: University of Chicago Press, 1964, pp. 133-152.

Underwood, B. J., Ham, M., and Ekstrand, B. Cue selection in paired-associate learning. *J. exp. Psychol.*, 1962, *64*, 405-409.

Underwood, B. J., and Schulz, R. W. *Meaningfulness and verbal learning.* Philadelphia: J. B. Lippincott Co., 1960.

Woodrow, H. The ability to learn. *Psychol. Rev.*, 1946, *53*, 147-158.

HUMAN ABILITIES AND VERBAL LEARNING

EDWIN A. FLEISHMAN

American Institutes for Research
Washington, D.C.

First, let me say how delighted I am to be able to participate in a conference on learning and individual differences. As many of you know, I have been working in this area since 1951, and I can recall when it was difficult to get a sympathetic ear, especially from experimental psychologists. In those days, which were not too long ago, individual differences were still an impertinence to the learning psychologist. There were, of course, earlier pioneering studies, especially those of Woodrow, but these never made much impression on the learning literature. A similar fate befell the systematic work on individual differences in susceptibility to associative interference, by Don Lewis (1950) and his associates, in the 1940's and '50's. There is also the more recent work by DuBois (1965), on the statistical problems in the measurement of gain; by Ledyard Tucker (1959), on classes of individual learning curves; and by Marshall Jones (1960), on simplicial analysis of learning trial matrices. The important theoretical papers bearing on learning and individual differences by George Ferguson (1954, 1956), J. P. Guilford (1961), and Lloyd Humphreys (1960), and the dissertations of Stake (1961) and Allison (1960), do not seem to have had much impact on the main stream of work on the psychology of learning. So, I feel a conference such as this may represent a real milestone and perhaps a turning point in the history of psychology of learning. It is especially gratifying to see leaders in the field of learning participating in the conference.

I think many of us who have been concerned with individual differences in learning have been impressed by the large differences in learning associated with initial ability differences of our subjects and the relatively small differences due to the treatments typically investigated. Yet, experimental psychologists have typically been disinterested in the *sources* of these individual differences and the interaction of these with treatment effects. They have ignored the work of the correlational psychologists who *have* been concerned with such sources (as has been ably pointed out by Lee Cronbach). If characteristics that vary from individual to individual are ignored, investigations of learning are limited to a fairly narrow range of topics, such as variations in internal drives or external stimuli on changes in behavior. It would appear that much current learning research is more concerned with situational variables temporarily associated with individuals than with more permanent traits of individuals related to learning. While these comments are fairly general, they do relate to the paper just presented.

I am particularly glad to be able to say a few words about Dr. Jenkins' paper, which first off, lays to rest the ghost of a general learning factor. The evidence against a general learning factor comes from a variety of sources, and I can cite just a few examples to back up Jenkins on this. It was not too long ago that intelligence was defined as "ability to learn" and many distinguished psychologists held this view. First of all, the factor analysts have shown that intelligence is not a unitary ability, that a large number of group factors can be identified. Second, r's between IQ and gain (however measured) resulting from training are often quite low. Third, improvement in one task is often uncorrelated with improvement in other tasks. Evidence from "level of performance" scores (as distinguished from "improvement" scores) also confirm these findings. And the studies by Stake and by Allison, using still a third type of learning measure (derived from learning curve parameters), have confirmed the earlier results.

Stake (1961) used an asymptote parameter, a curvature parameter, and a fit (regularity of performance) parameter. Correlations among learning tasks among parameters did not yield a unitary learning factor. Stake did get four factors. Two seemed to be rote memory learning factors; another was limited to numerical tasks, and another to sustained concentration. Allison's study (1960) also identified broad group factors, but they were defined by common ability factors on the reference tests. The design of his study allowed the learning factors to be identified in terms of functions typically dealt with by differential psychologists.

My own work (see Chapter 8) confirms a multifactor theory of learning, consistent with the independent findings above. Our studies go a bit further in showing the change in contribution of individual differences variables (in our case, pre-task abilities) at different stages of learning. They also underscore the increasing specificity of performance, which occurs at advanced levels of learning. Individual differences in learning seem increasingly a function of factors specific to the task to be learned. However, it is possible to identify more general ability factors which also contribute to performance at advanced proficiency levels. There is a need to develop more ingenious ways of identifying these "more general" factors, and our later work is attempting to do this.

It appears in Jenkins' paper, as well as in other papers presented here, that there is a need to define what an individual difference variable is. The demonstration of individual differences, along a particular variable, in a particular experiment, is not sufficient. When I talk about such variables, I refer to traits within the individual which have some *stability* and *generality*. Thus, it is meaningless to say that "susceptibility to associative interference" is an individual difference variable, just because we can show differences among subjects in such a measure, in a single experiment. We would still need to show that it is the same individuals who show such effects in different experiments. It may be that we would find that the same individuals show these effects in a given range of tasks, but not in others. This is nothing new to the differential, or correlational, psychologist and represents the factor-analytic approach when properly applied. This helps us better define the limits and generality of the individual difference variable, whose interaction with treatment effects we wish to investigate.

Jenkins mentions Underwood's comment about the lack of interesting effects of individual difference variables. I would like to refer to the curves in my later chapter where groups were stratified on different individual difference variables. By appropriate selection of variables we can show that some learning curves converge as a function of practice (e.g., the two-hand coordination performance, stratified on subjects' pre-task spatial ability), while other curves diverge (e.g., two-hand coordination performance stratified on subjects' pre-task kinesthetic sensitivity). I think these are *fascinating* results.

Jenkins points out the need for a taxonomy of known individual difference variables, with which I wholeheartedly concur. In our own perceptual-motor work I made this the first order of business. The idea was to develop a classification system of perceptual-motor abilities and to identify measures most diagnostic of the categories developed. These could then be used as anchor variables, or reference variables, in probing relations with complex tasks and interactions with learning variables. Today we use such reference tests in a great variety of learning studies.

Besides our studies of abilities related to performance at different stages of learning in a variety of different types of tasks, we have used such reference ability variables (a) to describe part-whole task relationships, (b) to predict associative interference effects, (c) to predict performance on massed versus distributed practice trials, and (d) to relate individual difference (ability) variables to variations in task difficulty, or (e) to evaluate the relation between ability variables and variation in different stimulus-response compatibilities.

Can this be done with verbal learning? I believe that it can. There is already a great deal of information on verbal and cognitive abilities and these provide a starting point. This does not rule out the generation of new hypotheses about stable, general attributes in this area. Jenkins, in his paper, suggests a few, such as "ability to form new associative bonds or habits" or "ability to recruit weak associations." One study of this type has already been done by Paul Games (1962), under Bechtoldt. I do not have time to present his data here, but will summarize briefly. Games used a series of tasks previously found to define two factors—Rote Memory and Span Memory. He then gave a series of verbal learning tasks to the same subjects. He varied methods of presentation (anticipation or free recall), constancy of order, type of task (serial or paired-associates), in line with a number of prior hypotheses.

The battery was administered to 100 students, product-moment correlations computed and factor analyzed. Two sets of factors were extracted—a set of reference factors and a set of factors confined to the experimental tests. The Rote and Span Memory factors were clearly defined as specified. The exprimental verbal learning tasks displayed substantial loadings on the Rote Memory factor, and negligible or low loadings on the Span factor. Variations in method of presentation and constancy of order had no consistent systematic effect on loadings on either factor. The only substantial change of factorial composition attributable to practice was a shift of the Repeated Span tests from the Span factor toward the Rote Memory factor. The free recall mode of response had no observable effect on loadings on these factors.

Two factors specific to the experimental tasks were rather clearly indicated, and a possible third specific factor was extracted, and interpreted as a "Letter Pairs" content factor. An additional factor was suggestive of an "Anticipation Method" factor.

Christal (1958) offers two alternative hypotheses about the Rote Memory factor. "The first is that associative memory is a rather limited and artificial factor which reflects the extent to which examinees resort to use of 'memory crutches' in a formal testing situation." According to this interpretation, there should be a systematic reduction in Rote Memory loadings for free recall measures, since the absence of the initial stimulus portion of the "memory crutch" should greatly reduce the usefulness of this device. Games found no such reduction. Christal's alternative hypothesis was that Rote Memory represents "ability to reproduce the same materials after they have been well integrated through many exposures under various conditions and various contexts." The data from Games' study are compatible with this hypothesis (as long as six trials on a verbal learning task are considered as a limited exposure). This hypothesis clearly implies that as learning progresses, loadings will shift away from the Rote Memory factor, but when this would occur is unspecified. No decrease in Rote Memory loadings from trials 1 to 6 was observed in this experiment.

According to Games, in either case, Rote Memory would seem to be the major individual difference learning parameter needed in theories of behavior in verbal learning situations. Approximately one-fifth to one-fourth of the total variance of the Letter Pairs tasks and nearly one-third of the total variance of the Serial Task can be attributed to the Rote Memory factor. Only one set of tests, the Repeated Span tests, clearly demonstrated a need for both a Span Memory individual difference parameter and a Rote Memory parameter; the former accounts largely for the initial scores, and the latter appears to be more important as learning progresses. Equally important to theoretical formulations was the fact that variations in method of presentation and the constancy of order failed to demonstrate any consistent systematic effects on loadings on either the Rote Memory or Span Memory factors.

One practical implication of this study, pointed out by Games, is that the selection of slow or fast learning subjects can be accomplished in group sessions, even in experiments that will later use individual sessions and conventional memory drum presentation. The experiment further suggests that, at least as far as individual differences are concerned, present-recall verbal learning studies may be carried out using group testing, at a saving of time and expense, and little or no loss of generality and comparability of data.

I have described this experiment at length, since it is the only one I know of in the area of verbal learning which follows the paradigm we have found so useful in the area of perceptual-motor learning. And it illustrates the types of information that can be gained with such research designs in areas of verbal learning. I want to emphasize that the individual difference variables of "Rote Memory" and "Span Memory" are relatively unsophisticated, but are derived from previous correlational studies of a variety of verbal tasks. The verbal learning psychologist who gets interested in such studies should be able to develop measures of much more sophisticated individual difference variables.

Elsewhere in his paper, Jenkins describes some possible stages that may take place during the course of paired-associate learning. These steps include "understanding what the task is," "discriminating stimuli from one another," etc. Our evidence on perceptual-motor learning indicates it is possible to gain insights about the role of different processes at different stages of learning, as we have indicated previously in this discussion and in our later chapter. Our studies clearly indicate that individual differences in verbal abilities and in abilities in the perceptual-spatial domain play a dominant role early in learning; but the importance of the type of individual difference variable decreases with practice, and motor and task-specific variables become more critical.

Another theme in Jenkins' paper is the problem of specificity of learning. Our work indicates we will have to live with a certain amount of it, since a large portion of individual differences in learning seems to be specific to the task learned. However, this does not decrease the importance of discovering what common variance there is. Our generalizations to new task situations may, in fact, depend on it.

There is also a need to investigate alternative measures of learning. Some kinds of scores (e.g., level scores, gain scores, parameter scores) may be more or less predictable than others. The experimental psychologist studying learning tends to be much more arbitrary than the differential psychologist in choosing the score assumed to be diagnostic of the performance he wishes to measure. He is also less likely to choose alternative measures to see if his conclusions are dependent on the particular measure. In the motor learning area, Bahrick, Fitts, and Briggs (1957) have shown how arbitrarily selected criterion scores can generate different learning functions.

Jenkins injects the need to look at "motivational" or personality individual difference type variables in relation to learning. I agree that this is needed. The work of Eysenck (1956) and of Taylor (1958) are some earlier examples, although confined to limited learning phenomena and a limited range of "personality" variables. The proliferation of studies using the "Taylor anxiety" scale illustrates the relative lack of sophistication of learning psychologists with this area. More recently we have been attempting to explore some "cognitive style" variables (see e.g., Witkin, 1954) as possible "personality" type variables interacting with performance at different stages of learning. One suggestive result has appeared in a recent study. We found that personality tests of "rigidity-flexibility," "anxiety," "extraversion," etc., failed to predict individual differences in associative interference, level of performance, or rate of learning at any stage of practice on a perceptual-motor task or on the same task with the display control relations reversed. Ability variables did predict these learning phenomena. However, personality tests did predict performance on the task when subjects were shifted from a distributed to a massed schedule. I mention this result to underscore Jenkins' observation that variables in this area should be explored.

Finally, Jenkins presents studies by Plenderleith and Postman as examples of studies of individual differences which might be fruitful. Interest was in accounting for incidental learning. They hypothesized two variables: "ability to sustain a multiple set" (anagrams test) and "readiness to give a differential response" (symbol discrimination test). Subjects were given an incidental and intentional learning test. The investigators found that incidental learning was predicted, but not intentional learning. I believe the differential psychologist might be of further help in interpreting these results, since the anagram and discrimination tests are probably measures of already defined ability factors. The investigators predicted that intentional learning would become more like incidental learning as practice continued and the amount of material to be kept straight was increased. Sure enough, the incidental learning task increased in its prediction of intentional learning. It should be pointed out that the finding that two other "reference" tasks *do not account* for these phenomena provides additional information about the processes involved.

These investigators went on to look at other types of measures, with meaningful results again. I did not know of these studies and was delighted to see them. I think they show the fruitfulness of using individual differences on tasks having known characteristics to probe into the process of learning other more complex tasks. These individual difference variables add information to our description of the learning process. And they provide evidence of interactions of these variables with materials to be learned.

REFERENCES

Allison, R. *Learning parameters and human abilities.* ONR Contract 694(00), NSF Grant G-642, Technical Report. Princeton, N. J.: Educational Testing Service, 1960.

Bahrick, H. P., Fitts, P. M., and Briggs, G. E. Learning curves—facts or artifacts? *Psychol. Bull.,* 1957, *54,* 256-268.

Christal, R. E. Factor analytic study of visual memory. *Psychol. Monogr.*, 1958, 72 (Whole No. 466).

DuBois, P. H. The design of correlation studies in training. In R. Glaser (ed.), *Training Research and Education.* New York: John Wiley & Sons, Inc., 1965, pp. 63-86.

Eysenck, H. H. Reminiscence, drive, and personality theory. *J. abnorm. soc. Psychol.*, 1965, 53, 328-333.

Ferguson, G. A. On learning and human ability. *Canad. J. Psychol.*, 1954, 8, 95-112.

Ferguson, G. A. On transfer and the abilities of men. *Canad. J. Psychol.*, 1956, 10, 121-131.

Games, P. A. A factorial analysis of verbal learning tasks. *J. exp. Psychol.*, 1962, 63, 1-11.

Guilford, J. P. Factorial angles to psychology. *Psychol. Rev.*, 1961, 68, 1-20.

Humphreys, L. Investigations of the simplex. *Psychometrika*, 1960, 25, 313-323.

Jones, M. *Molar Correlational Analysis.* Monograph No. 4. Pensacola, Fla.: U. S. Naval School of Aviation Medicine, 1960.

Lewis, D. *An investigation of individual susceptibility to interference.* Technical Report SDC TR 938-10. Port Washington, N. Y.: U. S. Naval Training Device Center, 1950.

Stake, R. Learning parameters, aptitudes, and achievements. *Psychometric Monogr.*, 1961, No. 9.

Taylor, J. A. The effects of anxiety level and psychological stress on verbal learning. *J. abnorm. soc. Psychol.*, 1958, 57, 55-60.

Tucker, L. Determination of generalized learning curves by factor analysis. In P. H. DuBois, W. L. Manning, and C. J. Spies (eds.), *Factor analysis and related techniques in the study of learning.* ONR Contract 816602, Technical Report No. 7. St. Louis: Washington University, 1959.

Witkin, H. A., *et al. Personality through perception.* New York: Harper & Row, Publishers, 1954.

4

INDIVIDUAL DIFFERENCES AND PROBLEM SOLVING[1]

RICHARD C. ANDERSON

University of Illinois

This paper will approach problem solving from the perspective of the psychologist, especially the applied psychologist, interested in learning or training. The question to be answered is what is there in the literature on individual differences, substantive or methodological, of value to the person concerned with developing training procedures that facilitate problem-solving performance. Much of the research on problem solving has been concerned with individual differences, conceived in terms of such constructs as rigidity, availability of function, strategy, and cognitive style. Despite some provocative ideas and data, there are grounds for arguing, as others have argued before (e.g., Duncan, 1959; Schulz, 1960), that "process-tracing" studies of individual differences within the context of problem solving have not led to a substantial corpus of knowledge. Partly for this reason, the emphasis here will be upon individual differences in problem solving in terms of dimensions established in factor analyses of aptitude tests.

In what follows, there will be a consideration of several ways in which the research on aptitude factors may bear upon investigations of the learning of complex skills, such as problem-solving skills. No

---

[1] The author is indebted to Robert Stake for reading an earlier draft of this paper and offering several valuable suggestions.

consideration will be given to customary topics such as increasing the precision of experiments by statistically controlling individual differences, or by selecting persons likely to succeed if presented with training. Instead, the attempt will be made to see whether research involving aptitude factors could have value for the development and improvement of training procedures.

Aptitude Factors and Task Analysis

Tasks can be described in terms of loadings on reference factors (or correlations with either factor scores or univocal reference tests). The pattern of loadings indicates the kinds of skills that are important for success on the task and their relative importance. It is *possible* that descriptions in these terms could be useful to the training psychologist undertaking a task analysis. Such an approach has often been advocated by factor analysts, but to the author's knowledge, few if any psychologists concerned with training have tried seriously to use the procedure for this purpose.

One of the leading advocates of task analysis by factor analysis is J. P. Guilford. He and his associates have completed an investigation in the area of problem solving that illustrates the method (Merrifield, Guilford, Christensen, and Frick, 1962). Three problem-solving tests were invented. These were included in a battery composed of reference tests for established factors and new tests to measure hypothetical factors. The results were these: No separate problem-solving factor appeared. Each of the problem-solving tests showed a sensible pattern of loadings on established factors. Finally, almost all of the true variance of the problem-solving tests was accounted for. The study supported the notion that complex problem-solving behavior is not wholly different from simpler behavior, but rather can be analysed in terms of more elemental patterns of behavior (which behavior, in this case, is still rather complex).

A second study from Guilford's laboratory (Frick and Guilford, 1957) will be described, since it involves the water-jar problem, a traditional favorite. A group version of the water-jar test was included in a battery of tests that were intercorrelated and factor analyzed. The water-jar test is supposed to measure rigidity-flexibility. As a matter of fact, the test, at least the version employed by Frick and Guilford, showed a loading of .42 on the factor General Reasoning, a loading of .45 on the factor Logical Evaluation, but a loading of only .18 on the factor Adaptive Flexibility. These are striking data.

TABLE 5

VARIMAX FACTOR MATRIX FOR DATA FROM A STUDY BY CONRY[a]

			Factors				
	I	II	III	IV	V	VI	
Tests	General Reasoning	Verbal Comprehension	Memory Span	Spatial Scanning	Perceptual Speed	Rote Memory	h^2
Predictors							
Object-Number	10	-30	03	10	16	79	76
First and Last Names	-03	24	-01	-05	07	84	77
Vocabulary	16	85	07	05	13	03	77
Advanced Vocabulary	15	90	06	-01	09	-05	85
Logical Reasoning	62	30	-12	-05	05	10	51
Inference	41	36	-03	27	-33	14	51
Nonsense Syllogism	76	09	10	-02	-07	-04	60
Auditory Number Span	-01	04	90	-01	07	-03	81
Auditory Letter Span	-05	07	87	06	07	06	78
Ship Destination	56	-02	-03	45	31	-09	62
Necessary Arithmetic Operations	68	12	-03	13	25	08	57
Finding A's	05	13	19	02	71	15	58
Number Comparisons	-22	12	-32	43	35	23	52

Locations	57	-13	-02	19	51	-12	66
Letter Sets	18	09	-01	17	59	12	44
Map Planning	13	-06	17	84	-08	08	77
Maze Tracing	10	10	-08	69	37	-09	65
Variance	22%	18%	16%	16%	15%	13%	
Criteria[b]							
Time to criterion—1st problem	-35	-08	17	-25	-10	03	(23)
Time to criterion—2nd problem	-23	-10	-07	-13	-23	-03	(14)
Cards to criterion—1st problem	-09	-06	-03	-12	-01	11	(04)
Cards to criterion—2nd problem	-21	-12	-20	-03	-09	-03	(11)

[a] Original data from a study by Conry (1965), presenting a correlation matrix in which the coefficients were rounded to two places. Decimal points omitted. The intercorrelations were analyzed by the principal components method with units in the diagonal. Factors with eigenvalues ≥ 1.00 were rotated. The factors that were rotated accounted for 66 per cent of the total variance.

[b] Loadings obtained by extension.

Apparently, less than 4 percent of the variance of the water-jar test is a function of rigidity-flexibility. A person who developed a training procedure to facilitate performance on the water-jar test by somehow increasing flexibility or eliciting flexible behavior might well come to grief, simply because flexibility is not very important for the solution of the water-jar problem.

Considering the results with the water-jar problem, one cannot help wondering whether performance on other widely used problems, such as the hatrack problem or the two-string problem, involves the behaviors each is commonly believed to involve. The two-string problem, in particular, has been used in a number of training studies, the results of which are notable chiefly for being inconsistent with one another (see Maltzman, Belloni, and Fishbein, 1964, p. 6). One of the difficulties is that the problem is psychometrically inadequate (Ray, 1955; Duncan, 1959; Anderson and Anderson, 1963). Could it also be the case that the behavior which training procedures have been designed to arrange or evoke plays a relatively unimportant role in the solution of the two-string problem? Perhaps such a state of affairs would be revealed by an analysis of the two-string problem similar to the one Frick and Guilford made of the water-jar problem.

Conry (1965) and Walsh (1963) have studied the relationship between aptitude measures and performance using a type of problem-solving task in which the subject selects instances until he can correctly name a concept. Both investigations employed the technique of canonical correlation. It seems likely to me that this technique is inappropriate when the goal is to understand the criterion task in terms of stable, meaningful dimensions. Nor does the method of including the task to be explained in a factor analysis with the reference tests for established factors seem entirely satisfactory, since this leads to a confounding of explanans and explanandum. The Conry (1965) data and the Walsh (1963) data have been re-analysed in this way: First, the correlations among the aptitude reference tests were factored. Then, loadings were obtained by extension for the measures of problem-solving performance.

Table 5 contains the re-analysis of Conry's data, which were originally obtained from 94 females enrolled in a psychology course. The first factor, General Reasoning, is the only one that shows really promising relationships with the problem-solving measures. On the whole, the aptitude factors explain disappointingly little of the variance of the problem-solving measures, perhaps for the reason that the reliabilities of the latter measures were low. Conry was not able to obtain estimates of the reliability of these scores, but some indication of reliability can be gleaned from the correlations between the two problems that were employed. The between-problems correlations were .23 and .41 for time to criterion and cards to criterion, respectively. Evidently, the reliability of any of these measures alone is fairly low.

The re-analysis of Walsh's (1963) data appears in Table 6. Her study was conducted with 53 third-graders from a suburban community. The problem-solving measure is a composite that gives equal weight to success or failure on a problem and an estimate of efficiency involving the instances the child selected. Walsh experienced some difficulty with her battery of aptitude tests. Many of the subtests of the *California Test of Mental Maturity* failed to discriminate well. As a result, scores on these subtests distributed over several weak, hard-to-interpret factors. On the other hand, most of the subtests from the *Solving Puzzles Test* discriminated very well indeed, and this may be part of the reason why these tended to load highly together on the first factor. The one thing the Walsh data do suggest is that Originality may be a factor in the performance of children on the kind of problem in which the subject selects instances until he can name a concept.

Having now reviewed some of the data bearing upon the factor structure of problem-solving tasks, let us take a closer look at the question of the value, to the psychologist interested in developing a training procedure, of a description of a task in terms of loadings on reference factors. Of course, one could not get very far by merely pondering the names of the factors with which a task is saturated. An intimate acquaintance with the skills involved in performance on the tests that define a factor is surely a prerequisite for making sense of a task in terms of factor loadings. Even with this proviso, the result of such analysis is likely to be a recipe of the form, for instance: Two parts Verbal Comprehension, one part General Reasoning, a dash of Ideational Fluency, and a pinch of Semantic Spontaneous Flexibility.

Description in terms of factor loadings seems to provide a sort of *taxonomic* task analysis. But it does not tell how to put the ingredients in the recipe together in order to get a desired complex skill. The training psychologist needs a *functional* task analysis that deals with intratask relationships among component skills and the order in which the component skills are to be performed.

Thus far the presumption has been that an adequate factor-analytic investigation can at least give, at its own peculiar level of discourse, a complete list of the essential component skills, so to speak, the necessary "ingredients" of a complex skill. However, the fact that a task

TABLE 6
VARIMAX FACTOR MATRIX FOR DATA FROM A STUDY BY WALSH[a]

Tests				Factors				
	I Fluency/ Flexi- bility	II Reason- ing I	III Origi- nality	IV Verbal Compre- hension	V Reason- ing II	VI Number	VII Right-Left Specific	h^2
Predictors								
Immediate Recall (California Test of Mental Maturity 1)	10	55	29	00	58	-05	05	74
Delayed Recall (CTMM 2)	15	-25	-10	79	25	-11	12	81
Sensing Right and Left (CTMM 3)	09	-02	07	02	14	10	82	72
Manipulation of Areas (CTMM 4)	25	60	-16	-17	04	13	28	57
Opposites (CTMM 5)	09	-10	06	08	53	63	-12	72
Similarities (CTMM 6)	07	72	17	09	07	-09	-13	59
Analogies (CTMM 7)	15	11	-07	-06	75	14	19	67
Inference (CTMM 8)	42	05	63	21	17	24	-04	71
Number Concepts (CTMM 9)	52	44	07	15	17	28	-04	60
Numerical Quantity (CTMM 10)	25	08	08	-17	02	80	28	83
Verbal Concepts (CTMM 11)	-06	17	15	79	-25	-00	-07	74

Finding Hidden Words—Flexibility (Kaya Solving Puzzles Test, Part 1)	67	46	19	-07	-03	21	-13	76
Consequence—Fluency (SPT 2)	77	11	01	13	07	02	43	81
Uses—Fluency (SPT 3)	82	09	18	07	08	07	13	74
Homophones—Organization (SPT 4)	70	03	25	21	14	20	23	71
Stories—Organization (SPT 5)	58	-08	21	-38	31	-34	03	75
Match Stick Puzzles—Flexibility (SPT 6)	-09	40	61	-16	-10	10	33	70
Finding the Rule—Flexibility (SPT 7)	71	18	-02	-07	10	12	-19	60
Doodles—Fluency (SPT 8)	63	-15	28	-39	-02	-03	07	66
Originality (Unusual Responses on SPT 2, 3, 5, 8)	33	04	77	-00	01	-06	-02	72
Variance	30%	14%	13%	12%	11%	10%	9%	
Criteria[b]								
Card Array Problems	-13	13	40	06	06	20	-05	(25)
Switching Problems	-11	07	05	-20	-01	28	-06	(14)
Chemical Problems	21	-07	35	03	17	15	02	(22)

[a] Original data from Walsh (1963). Decimal points omitted. Intercorrelations were factored by the principal components method with units in the diagonal. Factors with eigenvalues ≥ 1.00 were rotated. The factors rotated accounted for 71 per cent of the total variance.
[b] Loadings obtained by extension.

loads on several factors may very well mean that the criterion task involves *alternative* component skills rather than that each of the skills represented by the several factors is important. Referring to the factor description of the water-jar problem, for example, it may be with respect to any single individual that the skill involved in performance on the problem is General Reasoning *or* Logical Evaluation *or* Adaptive Flexibility. The factor recipe does not seem to tell the cook which ingredients are essential and which can be substituted one for another.

A description of a task in terms of factor loadings can tell what characteristics differentiate the performance of individuals on the task. But the factors that differentiate individuals are not necessarily in one-to-one correspondence with the skills that are relevant to performance on a task. The relevant behaviors that all of the members of a sample manifest, or manifest in a sufficient degree, cannot be revealed by correlational methods. By the same line of argument, the relative importance of various components of a complex task is not necessarily to be found in the magnitude of the loadings of the task on reference factors.

Finally, there is the problem of naturalistic bias in analyzing tasks in terms of factor loadings. Such a procedure indicates which skills differentiate the performance of persons who usually have no special preparation for the task at hand, and who work at the task for a short period of time. It seems reasonable to suppose that especially qualified persons—mathematicians, operations researchers, psychologists employing functional-behavioral methods of analysis—with ample time for study, can develop approaches to the solution of classes of problems that are not inferior to those inferred from the behavior emitted by students from Psychology 100 when briefly confronted with the task. Perhaps it is idle to inquire, with either multivariate investigations or with process-tracing studies, to what degree the components of "ideal strategies" are exhibited in the behavior of college sophomores or Air Force recruits. When a conception of an "ideal strategy" is available, it often should be possible to develop training procedures that systematically arrange the required skills. If and when a high level of proficiency can be produced, the task will no longer be called a problem, and it may even be said that the task does not require "real thinking" or that it can be performed by "rote." But, then, what is the point of this game anyway?

My conclusion is that under some circumstances description of a complex task in terms of loadings on reference factors might have some value as an adjunct to task analysis. However, from the perspective of the psychologist concerned with training, it is inconceivable that factor descriptions could bear the principal burden of task analysis.

Aptitude Factors and the Effects of Training

This section will examine investigations of the relationships of factor structure and training, which was a popular topic in the 1930's. In recent years there are Fleishman's (e.g., Fleishman and Hempel, 1954; Fleishman, 1957) studies of the changes with practice in the factor structure of complex psychomotor tasks. Stake (1961), Allison (1960), and Duncanson (1964) have recently completed factor-analytic investigations entailing measures of learning on verbal, figural, and concept formation tasks.

Though each has employed factor analysis, there have been distinct differences in methodology among these studies, partly as a function of the particular issue that interested the investigator. In terms of the interests of this paper, Fleishman's method is among the most heuristic. He broke performance up into intervals and as a result was able to study the changing characteristics of performance, interval by interval, as training progressed. Fleishman's work indicates that there are systematic "changes in the patterns of abilities contributing to proficiency on complex tasks as training continues and proficiency increases" (1957, p. 271). In other words, qualitatively different skills, not merely different degrees of the same skill, seem to be involved as proficiency on a task increases. There is a task-specific factor, the importance of which usually increases as training continues. At the same time the amount of variance explained by reference tests usually shows a regular decline as training progresses. Of interest is Fleishman's finding that tests of "higher processes" are important mainly in the early stages of performance. These diminish in importance as training advances.

Humphreys (1960) has convincingly argued that trial-by-trial performance data typically form a simplex. If this is the case, then a factor analysis will reveal a factor with high loadings on the first trials and decreasing loadings thereafter, and a second factor that has loadings increasing from the first to the last trial. Possibly, as Humphreys has suggested, Fleishman gets the results he does because he factors simplexes. The task-specific factor he finds that increases in importance as training continues could be an artifact of the method. Once again, there is much to recommend the procedure of factoring reference tests and then obtaining loadings on the criterion measures by extension, in investigations of the contributions of abilities to performance at stages of learning.

Woodrow completed a number of investigations of the relationship of intelligence test scores to indices of learning. In one of the most thorough of his studies (1938), subjects practiced about ten minutes a day on each of seven tasks for 39 days. Three scores were obtained for each task: initial performance, final performance, and gain, that is, the difference between initial and final performance. The intercorrelations of these scores, scores on two intelligence tests, and scores on several other reference tests were factored using the centroid method. The discussion that follows has reference to the varimax (Kaiser, 1958) rotation of Woodrow's centroid matrix which appears in Table 7. Terminal performance is generally related to both initial performance—that is, entering behavior—and gain or improvement, but initial performance and gain are independent of one another on all but one of these tasks (spot patterns). Notice that terminal performance for any task tends to load on two factors, one of which is saturated with initial performance and the other of which exhibits a high loading on gain or improvement with practice. These latter factors might be called "learning abilities" by anyone who wished to designate them in such a manner. Final performance showed a more pronounced relationship with initial performance in some cases but with gain in others.[2] On the one task that could be said to involve problem solving, the anagrams task, final performance was much more highly related to initial performance than to gain. Speaking generally, one would suppose terminal performance on many tasks employed in laboratory studies of learning would have a relatively slight relation to initial performance; indeed, such tasks are usually selected precisely because they de-emphasize the role of entering behavior. On the other hand, it is to be expected that initial performance will exhibit a hefty association with final performance on many tasks that confront children in school; for culturally relevant tasks, a brief period of training weighs small in proportion to a long history of learning.

On Woodrow's first factor (see Table 7), which can be called g, there is a tendency for final performance on most of the tasks to have

---

[2] Woodrow avoided some of the difficulties that gain scores entail by employing very reliable ($\geq$ .90) initial and final measures. One serious problem was inherent in his procedure. Though he did not present correlations, we can be sure that the correlation between initial scores and gain scores will tend to be spuriously low because of regression effects (Lord, 1963). This fact could have precipitated the factor pattern that has been described.

a smaller loading than initial performance. Though the differences are not impressive, the trend in these loadings is consistent with the view that the skills represented in intelligence tests are less important at the end of training than at the beginning, a result not unlike Fleishman's.

As contrasted with the research of two and three decades ago, the recent investigations of "ability to learn": (a) have been premised on the expectation of relatively weak and specific learning factors instead of a strong general ability to learning; (b) have employed, in any one investigation, a restricted range of tasks upon which subjects received training; and (c) have used rather elaborate procedures to estimate parameters or components of a learning curve, instead of simple gain scores. Nonetheless, the results have not been remarkably different from those obtained by Woodrow and others. What has mainly changed is the interpretation of results. Woodrow, though he obtained weak "learning" factors, preferred to emphasize how slight were the relationships of learning scores to intelligence test scores. Recent investigators (Stake, 1961; Allison, 1960; Duncanson, 1964) have been more sanguine with respect to learning abilities. To be sure, these studies have yielded what may legitimately be called learning factors, and have found relationships between indices of learning and intelligence test scores.

There is reason to be quite perplexed about the answer to this critical question: Is the size of the learned increment independent of the performance base to which it is added? This author is inclined to answer in the affirmative, thus agreeing that the simplex provides a good model for the learning of complex skills, even though this preference seems to fly in the face of the results of the studies mentioned above. Perhaps these results can be reconciled to the model by noting that the learning indices employed in these studies may have confounded the base level of performance and the learned increment.

As a practical matter, aptitude tests can be regarded primarily as measures of entering behavior. In the case of complex behavior and complex training procedures—let us say an auto-instructional program to teach a school subject—it is probably true that relevant, previously learned behavior "enters" at various points during instruction, not just at the beginning.

Gagné (1962; Gagné and Paradise, 1961) has also identified aptitude test scores with entering behavior; however, his analysis suggests that the behavior reflected in basic aptitude tests "enters"—that is to say, is relevant—mainly during the initial stages of instruction, and is decreasingly relevant thereafter. My suspicion is that, even when a com-

TABLE 7
VARIMAX ROTATION OF WOODROW'S CENTROID MATRIX[a]

Test Scores			I	II	III	IV	V	VI	VII	VIII	IX
Horizontal Adding	1	Initial	27	32	09	42	-01	35	30	15	-15
	2	Final	12	22	10	30	06	27	80	16	-11
	3	Gain	-02	08	09	11	12	10	80	08	04
Substitution	4	Initial	06	75	16	-05	08	03	08	12	-08
	5	Final	-06	53	18	-06	24	72	09	19	-04
	6	Gain	-08	05	07	-07	23	70	10	13	06
Patterns	7	Initial	47	35	49	14	-12	04	05	-09	09
	8	Final	20	19	92	04	-12	11	07	-02	05
	9	Gain	-13	05	68	-03	-03	06	10	14	03
Multiple Cancellation	10	Initial	07	72	05	29	21	-04	-13	-05	05
	11	Final	18	48	-04	05	71	26	07	-16	27
	12	Gain	33	07	-04	-12	87	26	15	-08	-08
Length Estimation	13	Initial	14	27	48	17	-02	-52	-01	38	16
	14	Final	09	17	24	03	06	-19	00	12	85
	15	Gain	-06	-05	-21	-10	-08	27	-05	-22	54
Speed, Gates	16	Initial	31	53	-12	13	-08	-05	38	-44	-00
	17	Final	30	69	05	-11	06	10	24	29	15
	18	Gain	-04	05	22	-28	-07	19	-02	73	-04
Anagrams	19	Initial	26	07	07	90	-04	-07	-02	-11	-01
	20	Final	23	08	08	72	-02	-14	30	-21	-03
	21	Gain	-02	01	05	-05	-01	-05	35	-17	-00

Artificial Language (A, before practice)	22	76	16	-03	12	06	-05	02	02	-01
Artificial Language (B, after practice)	23	70	16	27	12	25	01	-01	-07	-17
Form Analogies, A	24	73	08	11	13	09	19	03	21	17
Form Analogies, B	25	63	26	26	-10	06	-03	11	08	26
Verbal Analogies, A	26	86	-00	-05	16	-04	-08	09	-17	-03
Verbal Analogies, B	27	83	08	-09	09	-10	-12	-05	-07	-04
Thorndike CAVD	28	69	-09	05	36	25	09	07	18	23
Average 6 Otis Form A and 6 Otis Form B	29	90	04	13	13	18	06	-04	07	04
Categories	30	79	13	00	-09	14	-20	02	-26	-24
Cancellation, 3-digit	31	12	54	-13	07	56	11	-00	26	-12
Arithmetical Problems	32	28	-10	49	24	23	-11	11	12	-11
Speed, Making Crosses	33	10	66	-01	06	00	11	14	-31	14

[a] Original data from Woodrow (1938). Decimal points have been omitted.

plex skill is analyzed recursively into a hierarchy of subskills using the technique that Gagné has expounded, various previously learned skills will become more or less relevant in a shifting pattern as training progresses. Such shifting patterns were revealed in Fleishman's studies, even though the psychomotor tasks employed in these studies were relatively less complex than the academic tasks that Gagné talks about, and the training procedures used more homogeneous than the instruction required to teach academic skills.

Earlier, it was suggested that there is a naturalistic bias in task analyses in terms of factor loadings. There appears to be another facet to this naturalistic bias. Training, some of the time at least, and perhaps most of the time, has the effect of changing the pattern of factor loadings. The magnitude of the change presumably depends upon the effectiveness and the extent of training and the degree to which previously acquired skills are relevant to the task at hand. Nonetheless, one can speculate that the *direction* of the effects of training is generally toward a shift in factor pattern; in other words, a change in the relevance of previously-learned skills. If this is true, then factor analyses of measures on naive subjects could yield only an imperfect description of the component skills involved in highly proficient performance following a period of training.

We are accustomed to speak of an "increase in proficiency" on a task, but such an expression permits the inference that the same skills comprise novice-level performance and master-level performance, that the two levels and intervening levels differ only in quantitative degree. There are both analytic and empirical grounds for resisting such an inference. It is probable that different levels of proficiency on complex tasks, if not on simple, homogeneous tasks, involve qualitatively different skills. Similarly, even if by some external standard of proficiency, two groups—one with training of a certain sort, the other without—happen to perform at the same level, it cannot be assumed that the same skills are involved. In fact, it is very likely that the skills are different.

To put the whole matter another way, behaviors bearing a certain task or function name can show markedly different topographies. From some frames of reference, these differences in topography are unimportant. When the issue is judging what an organism will be able to do in the future on more complex tasks, based on what it can do now; or planning a training procedure that will most efficiently build upon the organism's current repertoire of behavior; or analyzing a complex skill into simpler, component skills; topography can be very critical indeed.

Interactions of Aptitude Factors and Training Variables

Stolurow (1965) has recently reviewed studies showing interactions between ability and techniques employed in self-instructional programs. The evidence reviewed by Stolurow suggests that programs featuring knowledge of results, overt responding, and immediate feedback make a difference with low-ability students, but that high-ability students do just as well on programs without these features. Other studies seem to indicate that programs allowing "self-direction" are superior to linear programs for bright students while slow students do as well (badly) with either kind. It should be noted that frequently the apparent interactions, usually in the form of correlations of different magnitudes between an ability measure and a criterion performance measure, are discovered in *ex post facto* analyses. Still, considering the fact that most psychologists concerned with learning and training have not been very concerned with individual differences, the facts available suggest that rather often there are interactions between ability and training variables.

Studies involving several training conditions in which scores were obtained on a differentiated battery of aptitude tests are scarce (however, see Dick, 1963). The import of the analysis presented on the preceding pages is to suggest that interactions between aptitude factors and training variables are likely to appear rather often, at least for complex tasks and complex training procedures, such as programs for teaching academic skills.

Of what worth to the training psychologist is it to know that there is an interaction between training conditions and an ability measure? Let it be assumed that the interaction is manifested in differences among training conditions in the degree of correlation between the ability measure and the criterion performance measure. Is a high correlation a favorable sign? According to some educators, the answer is "yes." It is a part of the educational folklore that there is an increase in the variance of the achievement scores of students of the good teacher, since he stimulates bright pupils to forge ahead to a greater degree than does the mediocre teacher. The popular answer of persons in programed instruction is "no"—a high correlation between an ability measure and a performance measure is *not* a favorable sign. The reasoning is that with effective instruction even the dull student will achieve a high level of performance. The fact of the matter is that in and of itself the magnitude of the correlation between a measure of ability and performance is neither favorable nor unfavorable. It depends on the *means*. When the mean level of achievement under a certain training condition is higher than the level under a standard condition, that is good; when the mean of the training condition is lower, that is bad. The difference in the correlation of the ability measure and the achievement measure under the training condition and under the standard condition *and* the difference in mean achievement under the two conditions can, provided several assumptions hold, suggest the *kind* of student who has profited most or least from training. If mean achievement is higher and the correlation between achievement and ability is higher, then probably the dull student did poorly as usual while the bright student did especially well. This is the kind of instance many educators who deal with conventional forms of instruction feel is typical (and perhaps desirable?). If mean achievement is higher but the correlation of achievement and ability is lower under the training condition than under the standard condition, then probably the low-ability student profited especially and the high-ability student did as well as usual. This latter case is often seen in programed instruction studies.

The remarks that have just been set forth apply as well to general ability tests and differentiated aptitude measures. A second aspect of the issue has particular reference to differentiated aptitudes. There are those who say that if, following a certain training regimen, achievement scores show a relatively high correlation with some special ability, this proves that the instruction requires reasoning, creativity, or whatever (see Braund and Heath, 1965). Indeed, such would seem to be the case. Such data prove that the regimen makes salient certain skills. But it does not prove that this training procedure is to be preferred to some other. It is entirely possible that another training procedure that led to *lower correlations* of measures of reasoning or creativity with final performance, would result in *higher levels* of performance on problem-solving tasks involving reasoning or creativity.

Several of the foregoing points are illustrated by the data in Table 8. Thirty first-grade children received training designed to teach them a problem-solving skill, the skill of attaining a concept or solving a problem by varying each factor in succession while holding all other factors constant. The training used the techniques of programed instruction, although it took the form of a script used by a human teacher (with one child at a time) rather than a self-instructional text or teaching-machine program. In the initial phase of training, the program was divided into seven units called "games" that were designed to teach components of the desired terminal behavior. The first three games arranged "conclusion-drawing behavior" and brought this behavior under the appropriate stimulus control. The remaining four

TABLE 8

VARIMAX FACTOR MATRIX FOR THE *CALIFORNIA TEST OF MENTAL MATURITY* WITH A SAMPLE OF FIRST GRADERS

(N = 408)

Test		*I*	*II*	*III*	*IV*	h^2
		\multicolumn{4}{c}{*Factors*}		
Immediate Recall	1	47	00	19	−07	27
Delayed Recall	2	66	−01	−11	01	45
Sensing Right and Left	3	05	−15	60	12	40
Manipulation of Areas	4	−17	62	03	01	41
Opposites	5	02	36	23	−07	20
Similarities	6	07	57	−17	12	37
Analogies	7	25	31	−08	−10	18
Inference	8	25	12	18	−51	37
Number Concepts	9	−12	17	26	57	43
Numerical Quantity	10	−01	07	63	−08	41
Verbal Concepts	11	40	−04	−05	60	52
Variance		25%	25%	25%	25%	

[a] Decimal points in the body of the table omitted. Intercorrelations were factored by the principal components method with the highest correlation of each test as the communality estimate. The four factors that were rotated accounted for 96 per cent of the common variance.

games arranged "instance-selection behavior" and integrated conclusion-drawing with instance-selection. The second phase of training consisted of an abbreviated form of the program with each of five widely different, additional tasks. The purpose of the second phase of instruction was to vanish the control of particular task and problem characteristics and bring the behavior under the control of the relevant abstract or schematic attributes of tasks and problems.

Following training, the training group and a control group that received no treatment of any kind were presented with a series of problems, some from tasks that had been employed during training, in order to assess retention, and some from tasks new to all children, to assess transfer. The problems were exactly like those employed in the Walsh and the Conry studies previously discussed. For each problem, the child began with a stimulus configuration which was, he was told or shown, a positive instance of a concept (e.g., it "shows the secret"). The child was instructed to select or create instances (e.g., "pick cards," "mix chemicals") until he could say the concept. The child was scored as having solved a problem if the instances he selected implied the concept he stated and no other. A further description of the tasks and the method, as well as the main results of the study, can be found elsewhere (Anderson, 1964).

Four hundred and eight first-graders, including the 60 children who were presented the problem-solving tasks, completed the *California Test of Mental Maturity* (Long Form, 1957 Edition). Subtest scores were intercorrelated and factor analyzed by the principal components method. Four factors were extracted and rotated using the varimax (Kaiser, 1958) procedure (see Table 8). Factor scores were computed for the 60 children who received problems. Each task was represented by a composite problem-solving measure, the same measure as was used with the Walsh data previously discussed.[3]

Table 9 contains the correlations of the aptitude factors with the problem-solving measures. It should be noted in passing that the sample was fairly homogeneous with respect to IQ and SES. Perhaps stronger relationships would have been observed with a more heterogeneous sample. Though there is interesting detail in the table, remarks will be limited to two observations. First, the aptitude measures as a whole account for more of the variance of the training group than of the control group. Since the level of performance of the training group was higher than that of the control and since, except for the chemical problems, the reliability of the problem-solving measure was about the same for the two groups, the correlations suggest that this is a case in which training benefited the bright student most. To look at the issue in another way, the entering behaviors or skills represented by the aptitude factors were engaged or made salient by the training procedure. Second, the training seemed to change the pattern of relevant abilities somewhat. Memory was a more prominent factor in the problem solving of those who received training than those who did not. Of particular note are the correlations of memory with performance on the cowboys task and the pegboard task, tasks that were employed during training and upon which most of the children reached a rather stringent criterion of mastery.

Whenever an aptitude measure shows a marked correlation with a terminal performance measure, one type of subject is doing less well than another. This information could be used to improve the training

---

[3] The composite score consisted of the sum of the standardized scores for number of unnecessary trials (reflected) and number of solutions. The measures were standardized separately for the training group and the control group. The median correlation of unnecessary trials and solutions for the various tasks was .58, a coefficient high enough to support the belief that the two scores represented the same thing.

TABLE 9

CORRELATIONS OF PROBLEM-SOLVING PERFORMANCE AND APTITUDE FACTOR SCORES FOR GROUPS OF FIRST GRADERS THAT DID AND DID NOT RECEIVE TRAINING (N = 30 IN EACH GROUP)[a]

Factor Score

Task	I Memory		II Reasoning		III Number/Space		IV Verbal		h^2		Reliability[b]	
	Training	Control	Training	Control	Training	Control	Training	Control	Training	Control	Training	Control
Retention												
°Cowboys	35	-01	04	19	-17	35	34	19	27	19	56	56
°Pegboard	39	03	41	37	42	42	24	38	55	46	64	54
Transfer												
°Screws	14	-04	47	-13	14	-05	22	05	31	02	55	47
°Suburbia	28	-04	08	12	28	00	33	49	27	26	45	62
Pendulum	06	05	22	-07	03	13	00	-06	05	03	—	—
Chemical	08	22	54	-01	37	18	07	24	44	14	68	13
°Pencils	14	12	18	35	12	08	51	16	33	17	55	60
Mean	22	05	29	12	18	17	25	21	33	19	53	50

[a] Decimal points have been omitted. Training group-control group correlation differences ≥ .26 are significant at the .05 level (two-tailed test).

[b] First problem-second problem correlation extended with the Spearman-Brown formula. Only one pendulum problem was presented.

° Task on which the *mean* performance of the training group was significantly higher (P < .01) than the mean performance on the control group.

procedure. One alternative is to develop different training procedures for the different kinds of people. There are a variety of forms that such an approach could take, ranging from wholly discrete programs to a collection of training segments that could be assembled according to a formula based on a vector of scores for each student (see Stolurow and Davis, 1965).

The information that achievement correlates highly with an aptitude measure might be used in a second way. Under some circumstances, it might be possible to modify a training procedure so that those with the low aptitude score have a better chance of succeeding. If one is speaking of differentiated aptitude factors, and this has been the presumption in the foregoing, the aptitude factor itself might suggest the sort of modification that would improve the performance of those with low scores. For instance, if Verbal Comprehension is a factor that is strongly associated with achievement, perhaps a simplified vocabulary is indicated, or perhaps in the sections in which verbal complexity is unavoidable more trials or frames are needed. Ordinarily, aptitude tests are used to diagnose the failings of students. The suggestion is to use aptitude tests to diagnose the failings of training procedures. It is difficult to forecast how useful aptitude tests would prove in the diagnosis of the shortcomings of training procedures. It could be that the information obtained from correlations between aptitude measures and performance measures would turn out to be just an expensive, indirect substitute for information obtainable by more direct means.

In this section, the argument has been that interactions between ability measures and training conditions are probably the rule rather than the exception. But caution is urged in interpreting interactions, especially those that appear in the form of correlation coefficients. Neither the assertion that the correlation between ability measures and terminal performance goes up with effective training, nor the contrary assertion, is universally true. The adequacy of a training procedure must be judged by the level of performance attained. Correlations of achievement with ability measures, particularly differentiated ability measures, can suggest the *kind* of student who profits most or least from a certain training procedure. Based on this information, there are several courses of action that could improve training. When differentiated aptitude measures are employed, the aptitude measure itself might suggest the sort of modification that would improve training, but it remains to be seen whether this suggestion has any actual value.

Summary. From the perspective of the psychologist concerned with developing training procedures to arrange problem-solving skills, a description of tasks in terms of loadings on aptitude reference factors might sometimes prove to be a useful adjunct to other task analysis methods. But there are several reasons why such a technique could not constitute the principal method of task analysis. Studies of the relationship between training and factor structure seem to indicate that aptitude tests are primarily measures of entering behavior, for the most part unrelated to how much improvement will result from training. When the task or the training procedure is at all complex, a shifting pattern of relationships between aptitudes and performance on the training task is likely to appear. The shifting pattern indicates the changing relevance, as training progresses, of the previously-learned skills represented by the aptitude factors. Interactions, more expressly correlations, between aptitude measures and performance after training, contain information that can be employed to improve training by matching the kind of training to the kind of person in one of several possible ways, or by modifying the training procedure so that those with low aptitude scores achieve better. Nonetheless, there is good reason to be suspicious of a judgment about a training procedure when that judgment is based on a correlation coefficient alone.

REFERENCES

Allison, R. B. *Learning parameters and human abilities.* Princeton, N. J.: Educational Testing Service, 1960.

Anderson, R. C. *Shaping logical behavior in six- and seven-year-olds.* Final report, United States Office of Education, Cooperative Research Program, Project No. 1790, 1964.

Anderson, R. C., and Anderson, R. M. Transfer of originality training. *J. educ. Psychol.,* 1963, 54, 300-304.

Braund, R. A., and Heath, R. W. A pilot study of a cognitive restructuring paradigm. Paper read at the Annual Meeting of the American Educational Research Association, Chicago, 1965.

Conry, R. F. *Canonical relationships among measures of concept formation, information processing, and other hypothesized cognitive factors.* Unpublished Master's thesis, University of Wisconsin, 1965.

Dick, W. Retention as a function of paired and individual use of programed instruction. *J. programed Instruction,* 1963, 2, 17-23.

Duncan, C. P. Recent research on human problem solving. *Psychol. Bull.*, 1959, *56*, 397-429.

Duncanson, J. P. *Intelligence and the ability to learn.* Princeton, N. J.: Educational Testing Service, 1964.

Gagné, R. M. The acquisition of knowledge. *Psychol. Rev.*, 1962, *69*, 355-365.

Gagné, R. M., and Paradise, N. E. Abilities and learning sets in knowledge acquisition. *Psychol. Monogr.*, 1961, *75* (14, Whole No. 218).

Fleishman, E. A. A comparative study of aptitude patterns in unskilled and skilled psychomotor performance. *J. appl. Psychol.*, 1957, *41*, 263-272.

Fleishman, E. A., and Hempel, W. E., Jr. Changes in factor structure of a complex psychomotor test as a function of practice. *Psychometrika*, 1954, *18*, 239-252.

Frick, J. W., and Guilford, J. P. An analysis of a form of the water-jar test. *Amer. J. Psychol.*, 1957, *70*, 427-431.

Humphreys, L. G. Investigations of the simplex. *Psychometrika*, 1960, *25*, 313-324.

Kaiser, H. F. The varimax criterion for analytic rotation in factor analysis. *Psychometrika*, 1958, *23*, 187-200.

Lord, F. M. Elementary models for measuring change. In C. W. Harris (ed.), *Problems in measuring change.* Madison: University of Wisconsin Press, 1963.

Maltzman, I., Belloni, M., and Fishbein, M. Experimental studies of associative variables in originality. *Psychol. Monogr.*, 1964, *78* (3, Whole No. 580).

Merrifield, P. R., Guilford, J. P., Christensen, P. R., and Frick, J. W. The role of intellectual factors in problem solving. *Psychol. Monogr.*, 1962, *76* (10, Whole No. 529).

Ray, W. S. Complex tasks for use in human problem-solving research. *Psychol. Bull.*, 1955, *52*, 134-149.

Schulz, R. W. Problem-solving behavior and transfer. *Harvard educ. Rev.*, 1960, *30*, 61-77.

Stake, R. E. Learning parameters, aptitudes, and achievements. *Psychometric Monogr.*, 1961 (Whole No. 9).

Stolurow, L. M. Programed instruction and teaching machines. In P. H. Rossi and B. J. Biddle (eds.), *The impact of new media on education and society.* Chicago: Aldine Publishing Co., 1965.

Stolurow, L. M., and Davis, D. J. Teaching machines and computer-based systems. In R. Glaser (ed.), *Teaching machines and programed learning, II: Data and directions.* Washington, D. C.: National Education Association, 1965, pp. 162-212.

Walsh, N. E. *The relationship between performance on certain long problems and intelligence factors.* Unpublished doctor's thesis, Rutgers University, 1963.

Woodrow, H. The relation between abilities and improvement with practice. *J. educ. Psychol.*, 1938, 29, 215-230.

Woodrow, H. The ability to learn. *Psychol. Rev.*, 1946, 53, 147-158.

APTITUDE, TASK, AND TRAINING VARIABLES IN PROBLEM SOLVING

CARL P. DUNCAN

Northwestern University

Dr. Anderson took the position that an S-R orientation offers the most fruitful approaches to problem solving. I would subscribe to this, but with the caution that the S-R's may range from specific word associations to broad strategies. When the subject must discover the response, often with little or nothing to guide him, as in many problem-solving tasks, it is my guess that S-R's of several levels and complexities enter in, and that this is one reason why we often obtain great individual differences on such tasks. Since we are concerned here with individual differences, it may be noted that on many of the tasks used to study problem solving in the laboratory, the variability among subjects is often very great. For example, in the Maier-type "insight" problem, a few subjects will "see" the solution even before the experimenter finishes giving the instructions, and at the other extreme, there will be some non-solvers. It will take a fairly broad S-R theory to encompass this range of behavior. As another example, I have a problem-solving device involving turning 1-7 switches to activate lights. One of the problems we have used is solved by making six switch turns. Repeatedly, the range of scores is from 8 to over 500 turns.

Much of Dr. Anderson's paper was concerned with aptitude factors. In this connection he mentions briefly Guilford's factor-analytic studies and notes certain of their limitations. I would like to go beyond this and say that I am puzzled as to why these factor-analytic studies have not been followed up in some way. As far as I know, they don't lead to further work, psychometric or experimental. Perhaps Guilford's preference for slicing up the variance into quite a number of small pieces has some inhibiting effect on follow-up. But I can't believe this is the only reason. One approach to individual differences in problem solving would be to measure subjects on certain tests, perhaps derived from Guilford's factors, then attempt to relate these measures to scores on problems such as anagrams. It is quite possible that much research of this kind would turn up only discouragingly low correlations. But we are not going to know if there is anything there until we do the research. In an area where there is large variance, as in problem solving, we can start out by determining whether those above the median on some test perform significantly differently, as a group, from those below the median, when these high and low groups are tested on a problem task. Finding barely significant differences between such groups is all we should hope for at first.

The difficulty that problems we use may not depend on the behavior we assume they do was pointed out by Dr. Anderson, referring particularly to the water-jar problem, and the string and hatrack problems. It is probably true that the water-jar task is not a good psychometric or experimental measure of rigidity or flexibility, whatever they are, but this does not mean that it is not a good instrument for the study of various classes of variables, subject variables (individual differences), task variables, etc., in problem solving, particularly if measures are based on the mean of a series of problems, as is done with anagrams. When used this way, we have found the water-jar task quite useful.

I find it harder to say a good word for the hatrack or two-string problems, particularly the latter, since, as Dr. Anderson notes, these problems have been unusually resistant to training. However, negative results with the two-string problem (e.g., Duncan, 1961; Maltzman, Belloni, and Fishbein, 1964) were obtained chiefly when investigators attempted to produce transfer to the problem from non-specific training procedures, such as listing uses of problem-relevant objects. But when more specific, problem-related training is used, performance on these Maier problems can be influenced. Saugstad (1957) argued that the two-pendulum problem, another problem used by Maier, involved a number of subproblems. In this case, Saugstad made the kind of functional task analysis favored by Dr. Anderson and, as he notes, clearly demonstrated in Gagné's work. Once Saugstad had trained subjects on the subtasks, the final problem was solved more readily.

Joyce Sween, a student of mine, made a direct attack on the two-string problem, pendulum solution. She first explained the problem, and the pendulum solution, to subjects, then gave them a number of objects to rate on the degree to which they would be likely to use each object as a pendulum weight to solve the problem. New groups of subjects were subsequently presented with the problem and provided with either the high-, the median-, or the low-rated object as the only available pendulum weight. Problem performance varied directly with object rating for women. The results were in the same direction for men, but not significant. Thus, I heartily concur with Dr. Anderson's emphasis on functional task analyses, independent of factor analyses. It is possible that subject variables, such as the sex difference found by Sween, will interact with components of a task.

A major section of Dr. Anderson's paper was devoted to the issue of interactions of aptitude factors and training variables. He suggested that such interactions often appear. This may very well be true, but first I want to make some cautionary remarks. My colleague, Ben Underwood, reports that in verbal learning it is uncommon to find interactions between subject variables and task or environmental variables. Also, Underwood does not even find individual differences in retention; in learning, yes, but not in retention. So we should at least be prepared for the possibility of such strange occurrences in problem solving. Common as they are, neither individual differences nor practice effects always occur.

Despite these cautions, it is true that subject variables have been reported to be related to different behaviors in problem solving. I found about 50 studies in problem solving in which such comparisons have been made. Some used an independent measure such as an intelligence test, or some other experimental task, to differentiate subjects. Others divided subjects into good and poor performers, or identified subjects with different strategies on the problem-solving task itself. The fact that all of these studies did get published suggests that many of them found differences in problem behavior that were at least correlationally (not causally) associated with the subject variable.

I am still of the opinion that the real need in the area of human problem solving is a large number of studies manipulating environmental variables and task variables, particularly the latter. If we had a body of systematic information of this kind, I think we would be in a better position to move into the study of subject variables. However, since this conference is devoted to subject variables, perhaps it is worth noting that my preference, among individual differences studies, is for those investigations that differentiated subject groups on performance on one form of the experimental problem itself, rather than with a separate test. Usually the groups so differentiated are identified merely as good and poor problem solvers, although occasionally other group characteristics can be specified. These studies must be on guard against regression errors, but I think they can provide valuable information. For example, Fattu, Mech, and Kapos (1954) differentiated good and poor solvers on pretest problems on their gear train device. Then they gave both groups just two training lectures, following each lecture with a test on additional problems. There were a number of findings that I think are important for individual differences. I will mention just these: the good group remained better solvers to the end; some of the poor group showed considerable improvement, but some did not. So, at the end of the study, Fattu *et al.* had differentiated, by a combination of brief testing and training procedures, at least three subgroups of subjects. These subgroups differed in a number of ways, and one would guess that they should be treated differently in, e.g., a more extensive training program. Thus, I think that one good way to study individual differences is to combine the study of task and training variables with the subject variable consisting of good and poor solvers, identified on a pretest version of the final problem. Then we should find out if interactions, predicted by Dr. Anderson, between subject and other variables do in fact occur.

REFERENCES

Duncan, C. P. Attempts to influence performance on an insight problem. *Psychol. Rep.*, 1961, 9, 35-42.

Fattu, N. A., Mech, E. V., and Kapos, E. Some statistical relationships between selected response dimensions and problem-solving proficiency. *Psychol. Monogr.*, 1954, 68 (Whole No. 377).

Maltzman, I., Belloni, M., and Fishbein, M. Experimental studies of associative variables in originality. *Psychol. Monogr.*, 1964, 78 (Whole No. 580).

Saugstad, P. An analysis of Maier's pendulum problem. *J. exp. Psychol.*, 1957, 54, 168-179.

5

INDIVIDUAL DIFFERENCES IN "ATTENTION": THE ORIENTING REFLEX [1]

IRVING MALTZMAN

University of California, Los Angeles

Early Views of Attention

"Attention" was the cornerstone of consciousness-centered psychologies at the turn of the century (Pillsbury, 1908; Titchener, 1908; Wundt, 1897). It was the glue for bonding the basic elements of consciousness, sensations and feelings. Laws of association used for this purpose by the British Associationists were replaced by what Wundt considered to be the more dynamic process of attention. Concluding his book on feeling and attention, an optimistic Titchener wrote: "There is not the slightest doubt that the patient application of the experimental method will presently solve the problems of feeling and attention" (Titchener, 1908, p. 317).

Problems of attention obviously have not been solved, and the experimental method as Titchener knew it is no longer in general use. The two failures are not unrelated. Persistent failure to solve problems contributed to the demise of consciousness-centered psychology. Nev-

[1] Research reported in this paper was supported by Public Health Service Research Grant MH-04684 from the Institute of Mental Health and a grant from the Carnegie Corporation of New York. I am greatly indebted to the assistants who made this research possible, U. Ekele, J. Gould, Ola Johnson, G. Padilla, M. Smith, R. Wellman, C. Wolff, and, particularly, Dr. David C. Raskin.

ertheless, research using the "expressive method" resulted in what we can now evaluate as important findings relating physiological changes to verbal reports defining attention. These findings were not explored further for several reasons. Behaviorism became the dominant systematic approach in experimental psychology, and it was primarily concerned with problems of learning and motivation. Early behaviorists also tended to ignore mentalistic concepts rather than considering whether or not an important problem existed—objectively defining the concept and then exploring its implications within a theoretical framework.

Another reason for the absence of continued development of research and theory was that "attention" as studied by consciousness-centered psychology was not part of a viable general theory and body of experimental principles. No such deficiencies were present in Pavlovian psychology, and problems of attention under its own terms and in terms of the orienting reflex have been studied for many years in the Soviet Union (Simon, 1957).

Writing as a Functionalist, Pillsbury (1908) presented many propositions that are pertinent today. There was agreement that an initial condition for attention is stimulus change. Among the motor manifestations following stimulus change are physiological responses, such as constriction of the peripheral blood vessels and dilation of the cephalic vessels. Pillsbury (1908) cites reports of observations of the cerebrum of a subject with a portion of his skull removed. When "paying attention," the capillaries in the cortex changed color. There was an increase in cerebral temperature and an increase in blood volume. Surveying the relevant studies, Pillsbury concluded that attention *per se* is pleasant and that slight contractions of muscles increase the adequacy of attention. Additional motor manifestations of attention were said to include movements of the sense organs which facilitate stimulus reception.

Contemporary Treatment of Attention and the Orienting Reflex

These observations by Pillsbury and other early investigators of attention (Bonser, 1903; Stevens, 1905) were relatively unnoticed for many years. Gradually, however, there has been a renewal of interest in the problem of attention by S-R psychologists, particularly Berlyne (1960), and a growing demand for more complex S-R analyses of stimulus reception. Such interpretations usually involve mediated response chains (Guttman, 1963; Osgood, 1957; Schoenfeld and Cumming, 1963). A serious shortcoming in these approaches, and even more so in cognitive formulations, is that there are no independent measures of the assumed mediating responses or processes. A major step toward the solution of this problem has been made by Soviet investigators. Contributing importantly to the possible solution of problems of perception and attention is the concept of the orienting reflex (OR) and related principles and theory (Anokhin, 1961; Luria and Vinogradova, 1959; Sokolov, 1960, 1963).

For our purposes the OR is a defined concept with observable antecedent and consequent conditions. Interpreted in this fashion, there are striking similarities between the initial conditions and consequent physiological changes accompanying "attention" as described by Pillsbury and some of his colleagues, and the contemporary formulation of the concept of the OR in Soviet research.

According to Sokolov (1960, 1963), a leading authority on the orienting reflex, an initial condition for elicitation of an OR is stimulus change. Any increase, decrease, qualitative or quantitative change in stimulation may evoke an OR. Consequent response changes defining an OR include cephalic vasodilation and peripheral constriction, the GSR, alpha desynchronization, and pupillary dilation. While any change in stereotyped stimulation may be followed by these physiological responses, repeated occurrence of stimuli in a uniform manner results in habituation of the OR. In addition to the above vegetative components of the OR there may be overt responses, such as turning of the head and eye movements, which also have the effect of facilitating stimulus reception. The latter instrumental responses have been more commonly considered in this country under the heading of observing responses or receptor-adjustor acts (Spence, 1960). Pillsbury also notes "voluntary" motor manifestations of attention which correspond to instrumental observing responses. Our concern here, however, is solely with the vegetative or respondent measures of the OR.

Soviet investigators suggest that the OR has two important effects. First, evocation of an OR under certain conditions may increase sensitivity. For example, following establishment of a visual threshold, presentation of an extraneous sound which evokes an OR may result in a lowered threshold as determined by verbal report and by physiological measures. A dim light previously unseen is reported as seen if the test stimulus is preceded by an extraneous sound. Repeated presentations of the sound and the consequent habituation of its OR is followed by a return of the visual threshold to its previous level (Sokolov, 1963).

A second important effect of the OR is upon learning. Elaboration of conditioned reflexes is facilitated by the prior occurrence of an OR. Establishment of a conditioned reflex under uniform experimental conditions is accompanied by eventual habituation of the OR. Preliminary habituation of the OR to the CS retards subsequent conditioning, thus demonstrating the importance of the OR in the elaboration of temporary connections, the acquisition of learning.

A variable such as the OR which is asserted to facilitate the reception of stimuli and the elaboration of learning must be of fundamental importance, since its effects would pervade behavior in a great variety of situations. Individual differences in this variable must also be of great significance. If individual differences in the OR are stable across different situations, the result would be stable differences in many learning and perceptual tasks. If the OR corresponds to what is commonly thought of as attention, then such pervasive effects are to be expected, provided that individual differences of this kind are not entirely specific to the stimulus conditions operating at the moment.

Another effect of the OR, one which is particularly important for personality theory, stems from the relationship between the orienting and defensive reflexes. An antecedent condition for the elicitation of the defensive reflex (DR) is intense stimulation. Its distinctive response measure is vasoconstriction, cephalic as well as peripheral. Related to elicitation of the DR is increased responsivity to noxious stimuli and reduced responsivity to innocuous stimuli (Sokolov, 1963). Elicitation of one reflex inhibits the other. Individual differences in the strength of one or the other reflex would result in a great many different effects in normal and pathological behavior (Maltzman and Raskin, 1965). The present discussion, however, will be limited to the effects on learning of individual differences in the orienting reflex. Semantic conditioning and generalization is one type of experimental situation in which we have studied the effects of individual differences in the OR.

Recent Experiments

In a typical experiment, subjects were instructed that we were studying the physiological correlates of relaxation. They were told that they would hear occasional words and noises over earphones and that they were simply to sit quietly and listen. After several minutes of silence the subjects heard a list of prerecorded words via earphones. An initial list of words was presented in order to produce generalized habituation of the OR to words (Luria and Vinogradova, 1959). Since the first word in the habituation list followed a period of at least three minutes of silence and background noise, it constituted a radical change in stimulation, the initial condition for an OR. The first word is characteristically followed by peripheral vasoconstriction and cephalic dilation, and a GSR. On the basis of the distribution of GSR's to this word, subjects are classified as either high or low orienters. Subjects scoring above the median magnitude are classified as high while those scoring below the median are classified as low orienters.

Figure 2 shows the GSR trends for high and low orienters during habituation, semantic conditioning, generalization, and extinction.[2] Starting from the response to the first word in the habituation list, the high and low OR groups usually converge after approximately 25 words, presented on the average of every 12 seconds. The present list was not quite long enough to eliminate the difference in OR level. The OR, and individual differences in its magnitude, is a process rather than a state variable, since high and low OR subjects differ only when the initial conditions for an OR are present, and for a relatively short time thereafter. These initial conditions involve stimulus change. What constitutes a change in stimulation is a problem at times and often must be decided empirically. Each word in the habituation list is a different stimulus, but habituation occurs, presumably due to generalization of habituation to words. We do not know the limits of generalization of habituation among words at present, although we have conducted some research on this problem.

Conditioning in this experiment was accomplished by interspersing a particular word nine times among a list of different unrelated words. Each presentation of the CS word was followed by a 100 db burst of white noise. Semantic generalization was studied by presenting a word which was associated with the CS word according to the Minnesota revision of the Kent-Rosanoff list. Extinction was introduced by interspersing the CS word five times among filler words while omitting the US.

In this kind of experiment, it is worth noting the subject makes no overt response and cannot verbally describe the responses that are recorded. Social acceptability or similar factors, therefore, are un-

---

[2] A number of experimental conditions were present in this experiment, including different CS-US intervals ranging from .5″ to 20.5″, and two kinds of instructions. Since OR was a significant main effect, these experimental conditions have been collapsed in the figure shown here. N = 200 in the habituation, generalization, and extinction phases of the experiment. N = 160 in the conditioning phase, because anticipatory conditioned responses could not be obtained for the .5″ interval group during conditioning.

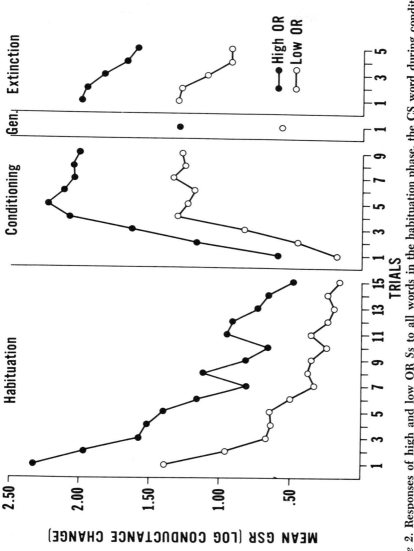

Figure 2. Responses of high and low OR Ss to all words in the habituation phase, the CS word during conditioning, the associated test word in the generalization test, and the CS word during extinction.

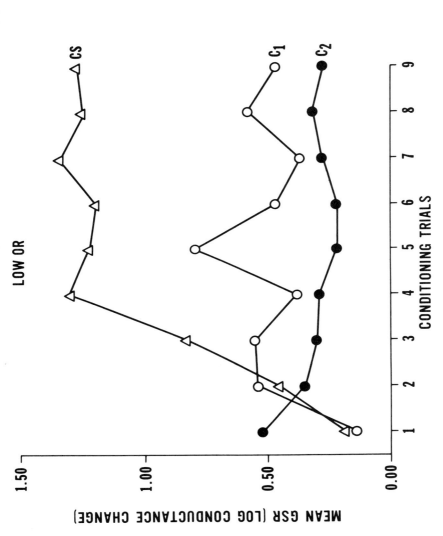

Figure 3. Responses during conditioning of low OR Ss to the conditioned stimulus word (CS) and the neutral words preceding (C_1) and following (C_2) the CS word on each trial.

likely influences contributing to the experimental results and their individual differences.

It is apparent from Figure 2 that the initial difference in the GSR to the first word, which formed the basis for classifying the groups as high and low orienters, is maintained throughout all phases of the experiment. Differences between high and low orienters are even more pervasive than indicated by the conventional measures of conditioned and generalized responses shown in Figure 1. We typically score the responses to the different filler words immediately preceding the CS word, and the word immediately following the US. Results of some analyses of this kind are shown in Figures 3 and 4. It is evident in these figures that high and low OR subjects differ in the magnitude of their response to the filler words as well as the CS word. However, we usually obtain a reliable OR $\times$ Word interaction, as was the case in the present study. The difference between the CS and control words is greater for the high OR group than the low OR group.

Classically, two views were espoused concerning the effects of attention (Pillsbury, 1908). Mach contended that the sensation attended to is directly and immediately increased in intensity. Wundt believed that there was a relative increase in the intensity of the sensation, because the remaining contents of consciousness have their intensity decreased by the attending process. In S-R terms the question becomes one of whether responsivity to a given stimulus shows an absolute increase in magnitude or there is a relative increase in responsivity to a given stimulus because responsivity to other stimuli is inhibited. Figure 3 indicates that the response to the critical word is enhanced in absolute magnitude in the high OR group with no suppression of response to filler stimuli. It could be argued, however, that the filler stimuli are not irrelevant, in that sequential presentation of the words in a restricted random order evokes orientation to each of the words. Such responsivity is necessary if the subject is to orient differentially to the critical word. To put it differently, the OR evoked by the CS word generalizes to similar stimuli, other words.

In different experimental situations we have obtained augmentation of the OR to the critical stimulus accompanied by some inhibition of responses to non-critical stimuli, or no apparent effect in response to non-critical stimuli. Variations of this kind are a function of the task at hand and the instructions administered to the subjects. Both Mach and Wundt were partially correct.

Figure 5 shows the unconditioned responses to the US by the high and low OR groups. Consistently larger responses are again obtained by high as compared to the low OR group. The first UR to the US also

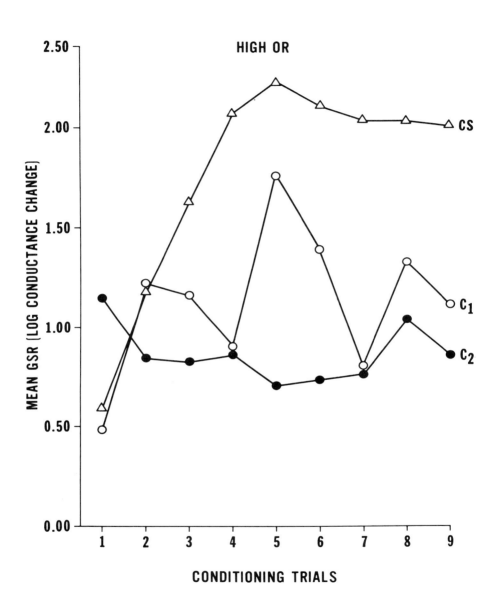

Figure 4. Responses during conditioning of high OR Ss to the conditioned stimulus word (CS) and the neutral words preceding (C_1) and the folowing (C_2) the CS word on each trial.

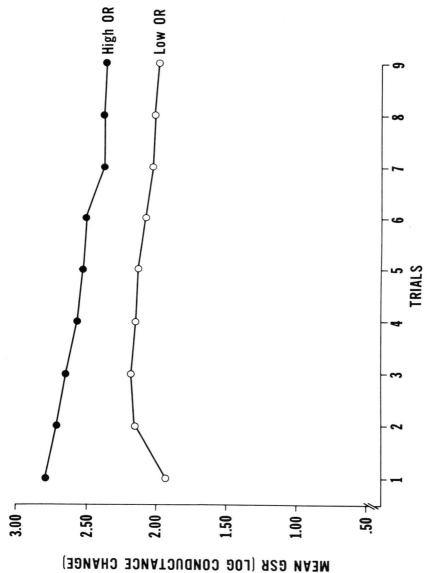

Figure 5. Unconditioned responses of the high and low OR Ss to the US during conditioning.

qualifies as measure of the OR, since the US is a new stimulus which is introduced following a series of words. Measures of the OR obtained from the first word and the first US correlate approximately .80. Classifying the subjects on the basis of the magnitude of response to the first US yields the same results as the classification based upon the first word in the habituation list.

Generality of the OR Concept

Results described thus far raise two problems. First, what generality do the OR and individual differences in the OR possess? Differences in magnitude of the GSR, determined at the start of an experiment, that persist throughout the experiment and are manifested in different measures of the same response, are of limited interest. If individual differences in the OR are to be of general significance, they must relate to different kinds of performance measures. A second problem is to determine the most appropriate theoretical interpretation of the obtained individual differences in the GSR. Is it necessary to introduce the concept of an OR? All of the results mentioned, particularly the difference in magnitude of the GSR to the noxious US, sound like the operation of a drive concept: emotionality, anxiety, arousal, startle, etc.

In connection with the first question, the relation of the OR to other performance measures, there are several kinds of evidence showing a reliable relationship between measures of the OR and performance. A relationship that we have obtained between measures of the OR and verbal reports is one kind of evidence showing that the OR has some generality. This kind of evidence is also difficult to interpret in terms of drive theory. We have found that measures of the OR differentiate between subjects who can and those who cannot verbalize the contingency between the CS word and the semantically-related generalization test words. Individual differences in so-called awareness are related to differences in measures of the OR (Maltzman and Raskin, 1965). These results are in accord with the hypothesis that the OR facilitates discrimination, and are what one would expect in terms of the ordinary usage of "attention." The relationship between the OR and verbal reports is obtained in the following manner.

At the conclusion of our experiments on semantic conditioning and generalization, subjects were interviewed and given a semantic differential on which they rated some of the filler words and the conditioning and generalization test words. For each of the words, the subjects were also asked if they had expected it to be followed by the US.

Semantic differential ratings were immediately examined, and if any word was rated as unpleasant by the subject he was asked his reason for the rating. Since the words employed in the experiment are approximately neutral in their semantic differential ratings, an extreme rating presumably is due either to an idiosyncratic response or an effect of the experimental treatment.

Semantic differential ratings characteristically showed evidence of conditioning and semantic generalization. Almost all subjects reported that they expected the US to follow the CS word and that they rated it as unpleasant on the semantic differential because it was followed by the noise. Fewer subjects showed evidence of semantic generalization. Most of these subjects verbalized that they expected the US to follow the generalization word, and they rated the word unpleasant because when they heard the word it made them think of the CS. Subjects who verbalized the relationship between conditioning and test words in this manner had reliably larger measures of the OR than non-verbalizers.

The precise conditions under which individual differences in the OR and verbalizations occur cannot be stated at present. Undoubtedly the relationship is complex and determined by many different variables. Recognizing these limitations, the fact that a relationship can be obtained under any circumstances and can be replicated, which we have been able to do, indicates that the measures defining the OR do have some generality. Finding an inter-relationship between individual differences in measures of the OR, conditioning, and the ability to verbalize, also suggests that "awareness" is not the simple determiner of conditioning or generalization that is implied by some investigators.

The OR and Drive

Another kind of experiment was designed to establish some additional measure of generality for the OR and to answer in part the second question; the relationship between OR and drive (Belloni, 1964; Nies, 1964).

Standish and Champion (1960) have shown that subjects with high Taylor manifest anxiety scores (MAS), as compared to low scorers, are reliably superior on an easy paired-associate list, but inferior on a difficult list. The familiar D × H interaction was obtained. If the OR is a form of emotionally-based drive, then an interaction between level of OR and task difficulty should be obtained in the same manner as MAS and task difficulty.

Standish and Champion used two paired-associates lists. An initial list consisted of highly associated word pairs taken from the Kent-Rosanoff list. Paired-associates such as needle-thread and table-chair were used in this easy list. A second list consisted of word pairs that were not strongly associated, such as needle-street and table-quiet. Such a list introduces a relatively great amount of interference and would be difficult to learn as compared to the preceding list. In accord with drive theory, Standish and Champion found that high-MAS subjects showed a higher speed of association on the first list than low-MAS subjects. But on the second, relatively difficult, list the low-MAS subjects were faster. If the OR as measured by the GSR under the prescribed conditions contributes to drive state, then the same effects should be forthcoming when high- and low-OR subjects are compared on these lists. However, if differences in attention or the ability to discriminate among stimuli is the critical variable, then high-OR subjects should be superior on the easy list and, particularly, on the difficult list.

Results obtained by Belloni (1964) support the OR interpretation rather than a drive conception, at least for males. High-OR men were faster than low-OR men on the easy and the difficult lists. High- and low-OR females did not differ reliably on either list. Her subjects were also classified on the basis of high and low anxiety scores, but the results failed to replicate those of Standish and Champion. A reliable interaction between MAS and task difficulty was not obtained. Belloni used GSR measures of the OR in response to a tone, word, and noise. These measures were obtained approximately one week before the paired-associate task for most subjects. For men, none of these correlated reliably with manifest anxiety scores. For women, one correlation of borderline significance was obtained, in the direction opposite to that predicted by a drive interpretation. Magnitude of the GSR was negatively correlated with MAS. Significant correlations for men were obtained between measures of the OR and linear slope scores for speed of association on the easy list, and especially on the difficult list. Significant positive correlations for men were also obtained between measures of the OR and maximum speed of association obtained at the criterion of learning and the number of trials to reach criterion. Women displayed no significant correlations between measures of the OR and learning.

While the positive relationship between magnitude of the GSR and performance on the difficult list for men supports an OR rather than a drive interpretation, the sex difference is inexplicable at present. We have often obtained sex differences in conditioning. Factorial experiments are needed with a number of male and female exprimenters as well as male and female subjects in order to determine whether the sex difference is a main effect, an interaction with the experimenter, or both.

Nies (1964) also conducted an experiment which employed the Standish and Champion easy and difficult paired-associate lists. He used three experimental groups of men who learned while exerting different degrees of pressure on a dynamometer, 0, $\frac{1}{10}$, or $\frac{1}{5}$ of their maximum pressure. Under each dynamometer pressure high-OR subjects were superior to low-OR subjects on the easy and the difficult list.

The experiments by Belloni (1964) and by Nies (1964) provide information pertinent to the questions previously raised. They indicate that measures of the OR may be related to quite different performance measures, in this case to paired-associate learning. These two experiments also provide evidence that the measures of the OR are not related to paired-associate learning in the manner implied by the assumption that the OR is a form of drive, at least according to the Hull-Spence drive theory.

An experiment by Raskin (1963) provides further evidence that individual differences in the OR do not function in the same manner as emotionally-based drive. Employing a semantic conditioning experiment, he instructed one group of subjects to sit quietly and listen, and they would hear words and occasional noises via their earphones. A second group was instructed that the noises followed certain words. The latter, partially-informed group showed reliably better conditioning than the uninformed group. In each of these groups the high-OR subjects were superior to the low-OR subjects. When the subjects were classified on the basis of their anxiety scores, a different relationship was obtained. Low anxiety was superior to high anxiety in the uninformed group, while high anxiety was superior to low anxiety under the partially-informed condition. A significant interaction between anxiety level and instructions was obtained. In contrast, OR level was a significant main effect. Raskin also found that the MAS and the GSR measure of the OR were not reliably correlated. The OR in this experiment was defined in terms of the response to the first unconditioned stimulus, a 110 db burst of white noise, following the habituation list of words.

The OR and Other Arousal Measures

While the OR does not seem to correspond to manifest anxiety, it might still be argued that its measures are simply those of a startle response. Equating the OR with startle, however, has little justification.

For one thing, the notion of a startle response is quite ambiguous. In terms of the startle pattern of Landis and Hunt (1939), the two are obviously not equivalent. The startle pattern is relatively specific to the initial condition of intense, sudden stimulation such as a gunshot (Landis & Hunt, 1939). The OR, in contrast, can be obtained by the omission of a stimulus (Unger, 1964) or by a change or discrepancy in the pattern of stimulation. Intensity is not a prerequisite. If anything, intense stimuli are more likely to evoke a defensive reflex (DR). Startle, interpreted as an emotional response contributing to drive (Brown, 1960), does not correspond to the OR because, as already indicated, the OR is not related to performance in the manner implied by drive theory. Finally, neurophysiological evidence indicates that what may be called a startle response is different from the OR in terms of central nervous system measures (Grastyan, 1961).

The relationship between arousal and the OR is complex and rather ambiguous. Various authors, including Hebb (1955), Malmo (1959), and Schlosberg (1954), have considered arousal to be a drive concept, and have identified such measures as alpha blocking and conductance level as measures of arousal-drive produced by the non-specific ascending reticular activating system (ARAS). However, there is growing neurophysiological evidence demonstrating that the ARAS has relatively specific effects (Anokhin, 1960; Magoun, 1963), contrary to the kind of drive theory with which it has been coordinated. It could be argued, of course, that drive, likewise, does not have non-specific energizing effects as originally formulated by Hull (1943). Evidence from our laboratory, however, has failed to support the hypothesis that conductance level functions as a measure of drive in either a specific or non-specific sense.

Belloni (1964) found a reliable positive correlation between conductance level and association speed on the difficult paired-associates list. If conductance level as a measure of arousal is to function as drive, high-conductance-level subjects should do poorer than the low-conductance-level subjects on the difficult paired-associates list during the early stages of learning. The positive relationship between conductance level and performance on the difficult paired-associates list is, however, in keeping with the Soviet interpretation of conductance level as representing a tonic-orienting reflex (Sokolov, 1963). Since conductance level and the GSR were correlated, Belloni (1964) ran partial correlations between the measures of associates learning and physiological responses. She found that when the GSR was held constant the correlation between conductance level and learning was not significant. A significant correlation between paired-associate learning and the GSR measure of the OR remained when conductance level was held constant.

We have examined the effects of high and low conductance levels in semantic conditioning, generalization, and extinction, in a manner similar to the analyses using levels of magnitude of the GSR. High- and low-conductance-level groups were formed on the basis of conductance level measured at the time the first word in the habituation list was presented. Magnitude of the GSR in all phases of the experiment was reliably greater in the high- as compared to the low-conductance-level group. Conductance level was a reliable main effect during conditioning, generalization, and extinction. However, the effects of levels of GSR and conductance can be differentiated when within-subject comparisons are made. As previously indicated, the difference between the responses to filler words and the CS word is greater in the high-OR than in the low-OR group. There is a significant OR × Words interaction as well as a main effect of OR on words. We have not obtained a comparable reliable interaction between conductance level and words. High-OR subjects as compared to low show differential responsivity to critical stimuli. Groups differentiated on the basis of conductance do not show a comparable degree of differential responsivity. The phasic OR is relatively selective; the tonic OR is not.

Absence of a reliable interaction between conductance level and words is contrary to the cluster of hypotheses that assumes that conductance level is a measure of arousal which corresponds to drive in behavior theory. The hypothesis that drive multiplies habit implies such an interaction. Our evidence indicates that conductance level is a measure of arousal, but arousal is not drive, at least in its role as a multiplier of habit.

The OR and Observing Responses

The OR defined in terms of the physiological responses previously mentioned and the antecedent condition of change in stimulation, is a relatively non-specific response. Regardless of the kind of stimulus change, essentially the same pattern of physiological responses occur. A complete account of the conditions of the organism influencing reception and discrimination of stimuli requires a consideration of instrumental as well as vegetative components of the OR. Contributions of one or the other component vary depending upon the initial experimental conditions. Situations we have employed such as classical conditioning with auditory stimuli tend to minimize the role of instrumental observing responses. In other kinds of situations observing responses and their individual differences assume considerable importance. Many visual discrimination situations demand appropriate eye movements as observing responses in order to assure reception of the relevant stimuli.

A study by Mackworth, Kaplan, and Metlay (1964) illustrates the obvious role of observing responses, and their individual differences, in tasks requiring the discrimination and detection of stimulus change. They studied eye movements during a vigilance task in which the subjects had to report the pauses in the movements of a pointer on a dial, and in another condition, pauses in the movement of pointers on two different dials. It was found that in the one-dial condition every missed signal had been fixated by the subject. We would assume that the vegetative components of the OR were not elicited under these conditions of missed signals despite appropriate observing responses. In contrast, in the two-dial situation the largest proportion of missed signals were not fixated. Under conditions where reception of stimuli depends upon motor adjustments of the receptors, observing as well as orienting responses are necessary conditions for optimal detection of stimuli. A considerable range of individual differences in the frequency of shifts in eye movements was found under conditions of the two-dial situation. Frequency of shifts were related to frequency of detected signals on the two dials.

Concurrent measurement of the two components of the OR, in conjunction with measures of performance and principles of conditioning and physiology, may yet provide solutions to the problem of "attention," a solution which eluded Titchener and his contemporaries.

The experiments cited here are only a meager beginning in the study of individual differences in "attention." Studies of "attention," defined objectively, have much to recommend them, but much remains to be done. In this connection, there is much that we may learn from Soviet studies of individual differences in higher nervous activity, including "attention."

REFERENCES

Anokhin, P. K. On the specific action of the reticular formation on the cerebral cortex. In H. H. Jasper and G. D. Smirnov (eds.), *The Moscow colloquium on electroencephalography of higher nervous activity*. Montreal: The EEG Journal, 1960, pp. 257-270.

Anokhin, P. K. Features of the afferent apparatus of the conditioned reflex and their importance for psychology. In N. O'Connor (ed.), *Recent Soviet psychology.* New York: Liveright Publishing Corp., 1961, pp. 75-103.

Belloni, Marigold L. The relationship of the orienting reaction and manifest anxiety to paired-associates learning. Unpublished doctoral dissertation, University of California, Los Angeles, 1964.

Berlyne, D. E. *Conflict, arousal and curiosity.* New York: McGraw-Hill, 1960.

Bonser, F. G. A study of the relations between mental activity and the circulation of the blood. *Psychol. Rev.,* 1903, *10,* 120-138.

Brown, J. S. *The motivation of behavior.* New York: McGraw-Hill Book Company, 1960.

Grastyan, E. The significance of the earliest manifestations of conditioning in the mechanisms of learning. In J. F. Delafresnay (ed.), *Brain mechanisms and learning.* Oxford: Blackwell, 1961, pp. 243-263.

Guttman, N. Laws of behavior and facts of perception. In S. Koch (ed.), *Psychology: A study of a science.* Vol. 5. New York: McGraw-Hill Book Company, 1963, pp. 114-178.

Hebb, D. P. Drives and the c.n.s. (conceptual nervous system). *Psychol. Rev.,* 1955, *62,* 243-254.

Hull, C. L. *Principles of behavior.* New York: Appleton-Century, 1943.

Landis, C., and Hunt, W. A. *The startle pattern.* New York: Farrar & Rinehart, 1939.

Luria, A. R., and Vinogradova, Olga S. An objective investigation of the dynamics of semantic systems. *Brit. J. Psychol.,* 1959, *50,* 89-105.

Mackworth, N. H., Kaplan, I. T., and Metlay, W. Eye movements during vigilance. *Percept. mot. Skills,* 1964, *18,* 397-402.

Magoun, H. W. *The waking brain.* (2d ed.). Springfield, Ill.: Charles C Thomas, 1963.

Malmo, R. B. Activation: A neurophysiological dimension. *Psychol. Rev.,* 1959, *66,* 367-386.

Maltzman, I., and Raskin, D. C. Effects of individual differences in the orienting reflex on conditioning and complex processes. *J. exp. res. Personal.,* 1965, *1,* 1-16.

Nies, R. The orienting reflex as conceptually distinct from drive. Unpublished doctoral dissertation, University of California, Los Angeles, 1964.

Osgood, C. E. A behavioristic analysis of perception and language as cognitive phenomena. In Bruner, J., *et al.*, *Contemporary approaches to cognition*. Cambridge, Mass.: Harvard University Press, 1957, pp. 75-118.

Pillsbury, W. B. *Attention*. New York: The Macmillan Company, 1908.

Raskin, D. C. Some factors influencing semantic conditioning and generalization of autonomic responses. Unpublished doctoral dissertation, University of California, Los Angeles, 1963.

Schlosberg, H. Three dimensions of emotion. *Psychol. Rev.*, 1954, *61*, 81-88.

Schoenfeld, W. N., and Cumming, W. W. Behavior and perception. In S. Koch (ed.), *Psychology: A study of a science*. Vol. 5. New York: McGraw-Hill Book Company, 1963, pp. 213-252.

Simon, B. (ed.). *Psychology in the Soviet Union*. London: Routledge & Kegan Paul, 1957.

Sokolov, E. N. Neuronal models and the orienting reflex. In Mary A. B. Brazier (ed.), *The central nervous system and behavior*. New York: Josiah Macy, Jr. Foundation, 1960, pp. 187-276.

Sokolov, E. N. *Perception and the conditioned reflex*. New York: The Macmillan Company, 1963.

Spence, K. W. *Behavior theory and learning*. New York: Prentice-Hall, Inc., 1960.

Standish, R. R., and Champion, R. A. Task difficulty and drive in verbal learning. *J. exp. Psychol.*, 1960, 59, 361-365.

Stevens, H. C. A plethysmographic study of attention. *Amer. J. Psychol.*, 1905, *16*, 410-483.

Titchener, E. B. *Lectures on the elementary psychology of feeling and attention*. New York: The Macmillan Company, 1908.

Unger, S. M. Habituation of the vasoconstrictive orienting reaction. *J. exp. Psychol.*, 1964, *67*, 11-18.

Wundt, W. *Outlines of psychology*. Leipzig: Engelmann, 1897.

THE ORIENTING REFLEX AND ATTENTION

DELOS D. WICKENS
Ohio State University

My discussion will touch upon two aspects of the orienting reflex which are raised in Professor Maltzman's paper. One of these is concerned essentially with the nature of the construct of the orienting response and its utility as a term in behavior theory; the other is concerned with his own research studies in the use of the orienting response to predict behavior. I will begin with a brief consideration of the experiments, which impress me as being very fresh and very exciting in their demonstration of the effectiveness of this variable for predicting individual differences in certain activities.

The strategy of his research is to obtain a measure of the OR by presenting a controlled sequence of identical events followed by a single event of a different nature. The magnitude of response to this aberrant event characterizes the OR for the individual. Thus, to compare individuals in OR magnitude, each one must be subjected to the identical procedure, and the OR measure must be taken to the first stimulus which departs from the pre-established norm. These restrictions are introduced because, as Professor Maltzman states and the Russians have also shown, the orienting reflex varies as a function of a process variable rather than a state variable. For the most part the measure he used is a single one, the log conductance change in GSR. He has then demonstrated that groups who differ in this measure of the OR behave differently in their performance on subsequent tasks. I gain the impression that we are dealing very clearly with work in progress, and that the trend of the results are not simple. In general, they suggest that the high-OR subjects are more sensitive to their environment than are the low-OR subjects, but the conclusion is complicated, for positive trends are obtained for the male subjects but not for the females. The studies are interesting and are obviously an appropriate way of evaluating the significance of the OR concept. It also seems to me that Professor Maltzman is worrying about some of the proper problems of interpretation, such as whether or not the results could be handled by the concept of general arousal or by drive of the Hullian type, rather than a more selective perceptual process. At the same time he seems to be concerned with the relationship between base level and conductance score. Well he might be, because base level has traditionally been assumed to measure arousal or drive, but change is used to measure the OR and the two measures are usually correlated, hence they must each be examined. In the first experiment the same response, the GSR, is used as a measure of OR and as an index of the subjects' learning. While this is not completely objectionable, I prefer the latter experiments wherein a different behavior is used as the predictor and predicted as, for example, when GSR is used to measure the OR, and paired associated learning serves as the dependent variable. I doubt that there is much I'm going to suggest about the experimentation that Professor Maltzman has not already thought of and plans to do, so I will turn to the more general topic of the OR as a theory for behavior prediction.

What began to puzzle me as I read the literature on the OR in preparation for this paper is the extent to which the OR is a dependent variable of certain operations performed in the laboratory—that is, an established procedure and departure from it—and to what extent it is an independent variable of which the overt behavior in which we are interested is a function.

Very clearly Sokolov views it as an independent variable of considerable importance, for he states at one point in his paper *Neuronal Models and the Orienting Reflex* that "The orienting reflex includes some vegetative, somatic, electroencephalographic and sensory components; is a unitary system; and the role of these components is to increase the discriminatory powers of the analyzers" (1960, p. 191).

This statement certainly implies that the OR is a sort of intervening variable or hypothetical construct which includes a variety of measurable responses, but that it is not simply one or another of these responses. Our knowledge of the relationship between these kinds of responses tells us also that they are far from perfectly correlated. Finally, it is assumed that the occurrence of the OR serves the function of increasing our capacity to interpret our environment. Conceived of in this latter capacity, there is no doubt that the OR serves a role in behavior theory such as that which is played by the concepts of attention or stimulus selection; at the same time it would seem to have the advantage over attention of being objectively and independently measurable in physiological terms.

There are, however, some problems which arise in its use in theory as an intervening variable. Since the various measures of the OR are far from perfectly correlated, which measure should be used to predict its occurrence? Further, some of the responses used in measuring it—as the GSR or blood changes—are usually of longer latency than the response whose proficiency is determined by the OR. At one point Sokolov states that every stimulus has two different properties—an orienting reflex property and one related to the sensory system to which it belongs—and that the OR has a "causal" connection in improving the process of sensing. It is somewhat embarrassing to note that the responses defining the OR occur subsequent to the facilitated response. The embarrassment would vanish if the OR were considered as an intervening variable, but then it would lose some of its apparent objectivity.

Another characteristic of the OR is puzzling; it drops out as conditioning occurs and is reported to be incompatible with defensive reflexes. One might expect that attention, or one's degree of sensitivity to the environment, should be high in situations which provoke defensive reactions, although this point might be argued. It is not clear why the OR should drop out as proficiency (as estimated from degree of training) increases. If OR is an initial behavior step in data handling and filtering, one might expect it to be maintained at a fairly high level during task performance. In defense of this characteristic of the OR, I should point out that this decline is found in simple conditioning and the response re-occurs in discriminatory conditioning.

From a utilitarian, a Darwinian, point of view it does make sense that the simple environment with a single re-occurring stimulus demands little in the way of information processing; whereas a more complex environment does. The OR fits these expectations.

In conclusion, I do not feel that as of now the OR is a completely satisfactory substitute for a concept such as attention, which is clearly coming back into vogue in America. I think it is a promising concept but I do believe it needs to be scrutinized not only by empirical research, but also for its validity as a concept useful for prediction of behavior. When this has been done it seems possible that, as Professor Maltzman has said, a new concept rooted in the present OR approach may emerge and serve the functional purposes of the older concept of attention. Since the OR presupposes a capacity to be measured independently of its effect upon efficiency of behavior, and the concept of attention seems not to be, the OR—or its derivitive—would promise to be a superior concept. To return, however, to the topic of individual differences and the OR, Professor Maltzman's work has demonstrated the value of this concept as measured operationally as a means of predicting differences on various tasks; so regardless of the philosophical status of the concept as it now stands, it certainly has a large heuristic value.

REFERENCES

Sokolov, E. N. Neuronal models and the orienting reflex. In Mary A. B. Brazier (ed.), *The central nervous system and behavior*. New York: Josiah Macy, Jr. Foundation, 1960, pp. 187-276.

6

VARIETIES OF INDIVIDUAL DIFFERENCES IN LEARNING

ARTHUR R. JENSEN

University of California

Individual Differences and Learning Research

One thing we can all be quite certain of: Wherever in the vast realm of human learning we wish to look for individual differences, we surely will find them.

What we do about this fact will depend upon several things. First, it will depend upon the strength of our faith that some kind of order and structure do in fact exist in individual differences (ID's) in learning. If we have this faith, it is then up to our fortitude and ingenuity to discover this structure. What we do will depend also upon whether or not we believe that a science of learning can be developed independently of the problem of ID's. If we think it can, we might prefer to ignore ID's, except to the extent that anyone planning an experiment must take some account of their nuisance value as "error variance."

Since both these points are still regarded by some psychologists as open questions, I shall begin by stating my own biases. On the first issue, I will only say that I do have faith that we can eventually make sense out of this realm, which at first glance admittedly looks pretty

117

chaotic. I have made the plunge, and while my groping is still quite untidy, I am not yet discouraged.

On the second issue, I believe that most of what experimental psychologists really want to find out about the nature of learning actually requires an individual differences approach. Often the questions we ask cannot be answered adequately by making statistical comparisons between group means, yet this is the traditional method of assessing the effects and the importance of independent variables on learning. If an independent variable makes for a clear and unanimous difference between experimental and control groups, well and good. But if the group mean difference is meagre, we must ask if the effects of our independent variable have been buried in the error term. The error term contains the Subjects × Independent Variable interaction, whether or not our design has provided for testing its significance. Only if it has been demonstrated that the Subjects × Independent Variable interaction is negligible can we be very sanguine about the psychological importance of a particular independent variable, when our conclusions are based on group mean differences. It is preferable to know what happens to *individuals* under the effect of the independent variable. Experimental psychologists are not interested fundamentally in *group* effects. Our aim essentially is to devise experiments that will yield information capable of narrowing the range of alternative models of the mind. As far as I know, no one ever really thinks of his model or theory as pertaining only to the averaged characteristics of a group of subjects. Yet without adequate recognition of the problem of ID's, psychological theory risks being shaped by the averaged characteristics of the group, which may or may not represent the state of affairs that exists within individuals. Imagine an independent variable, say some drug, which markedly speeds up learning in some individuals and slows it down in others. Averaging the individual performance scores could result in the false conclusion that the drug has no significant effect on learning. The means and standard deviations of the Drug and No Drug groups could conceivably be identical. Or, in the same type of experiment, a greater proportion of one type of individual might be sampled than of the other type. But what would it mean? Obviously, a different sort of experimental design is required in order to deal properly with this type of problem. It is a rather sobering exercise to keep this analogy in mind while reading much of the experimental literature on learning. The effect of distribution of practice on rote learning may serve as one classic example. Hovland (1939) carried out an experiment which showed an insignificant mean difference between massed and distributed practice in paired-associate learning. He then proceeded to note that some 44 percent of the subjects in his experiment learned more rapidly under distributed practice, while some 38 percent learned more rapidly under massed practice; about 18 percent showed no effect of the independent variable one way or the other. Hovland found similar results in serial learning. Distribution of practice has since become a heavily researched topic; yet, by and large, the mainstream of this research has proceeded without any regard for the S's × Independent Variable interaction noted by Hovland. We do not know if this interaction was significant in Hovland's experiment. But would anyone argue that the S's × Independent Variable interaction is not the proper place to look if we want to assess the potency of our experimental variable? Underwood (1964, p. 149) has referred to this ID source of variance as producing "pesky statistical problems resulting from the wide range of scores," even among a supposed homogeneous population of college students. Instead of viewing ID's as merely a pesky statistical problem, I believe the experimental psychology of learning is coming to recognize ID's as the very heart of its subject matter. By making ID's the center of focus, we of course face problems that are staggering as compared with the kinds of statistical problems referred to by Underwood, which can usually be solved simply by increasing our N.

Even for those with no stomach for so messy a subject as ID's in learning and who would want nothing to do with the problem for its own sake, I think it will become apparent that ID's can be *used* in the design of experiments. Individual differences can serve as one additional means of narrowing the range of competing models of the learning process. Any new source of facts is a potential challenge to all existing theories. Some theories fall in the face of the facts and some remain standing, usually with certain modifications. We then search for new facts to challenge these theories, and so on. The process can proceed until, as happened in color theory, two or three competing models stand up equally well to all the facts we are capable of producing in the psychological laboratory. Then it becomes necessary to pit the models against facts derived from another realm, which in the case of color theory was retinal neurophysiology, in order to find a basis of choice between our alternative theories. I propose that individual differences might be used in this fashion, as a further source of information for the development and testing of psychological models. Consider, for example, a theory which postulates a single process of interference or response competition to explain both pro-active and retroactive inhibition. If measures of individual differences in PI and RI were then found to be only slightly correlated, even after correction for attenuation, we might have grounds for doubting the validity of a uniprocess theory of RI and PI. In this fashion individual differences may be put to work in helping to solve some of the major theoretical issues of general experimental psychology.

Classification of Individual Differences

Coming back to the title of this paper, to speak of *varieties* of individual differences in learning implies some scheme of classification. Hints for such a scheme may be gleaned from the traditional categories of learning, such as conditioning, discrimination learning, rote learning, perceptual-motor learning, concept attainment, and so forth. Another possible source of suggestions is to look at the labels given to some of the factors derived from factor-analytic studies of ID's in learning. These unfortunately turn out to look exceedingly like the traditional categories of the variables which originally entered into the factor analyses. Thus we again find factors labeled as motor learning, rote learning, conceptual learning, and so on through the list. Now and then we find that some of the factor labels more nearly resemble the titles of psychometric tests, such as the *Primary Mental Abilities*, and we have factors such as verbal conceptual learning, spatial conceptual learning, and so on. All these labels, incidentally, are taken from published factor analyses. The forty or more factor-analytic studies of ID's in learning fall quite short of providing even the rough outlines for a comprehensive taxonomy of ID's. Perusal of this material might even cause us to give up in despair or to conclude, as some investigators have done, that ID's in learning are specific to each and every learning task under each and every condition of learning. Then all we could hope to do successfully would be to measure the final products of learning by means of psychometric tests. The attempt to understand ID's in the learning process itself would be rendered futile by the curse of task-specific variance.

Gaining some perspective on the taxonomy of this problem will help to suggest why the examination of past studies can result in such a gloomy picture. It might also indicate how we can view the total situation in a more hopeful light.

Intrinsic and Extrinsic Individual Differences

The first broad distinction that should be made in order to avoid future confusion, and the lack of which has caused trouble in the past, is the difference between what I call intrinsic and extrinsic individual differences. The essence of the difference is exemplified by the two statements: (*a*) individual differences *in* learning, and (*b*) the effects of individual differences *on* learning.

Extrinsic ID's are those subject variables which operationally bear no resemblance to the learning process as we generally conceive of it. Yet these ID's may influence the individual's performance in a learning situation. Certain attitudes and personality traits are probably legitimately regarded as belonging in this category. We should be explicitly aware of this category, since it is not uncommon for psychologists to identify the whole field of individual differences in learning with this particular category. It is a category I would regard as of relatively minor importance. Yet there is a widespread tendency to think of all individual differences as being phenomena outside the realm of learning, something quite independent, which may at times exert some influence on the subject's performance in a learning task. According to this view, if we could eliminate these kinds of individual differences subjects would all perform alike in laboratory learning tasks. Much of the talk about controlling for individual differences in laboratory experimentation is based on this conception of extrinsic ID's. Chronological age, mental age, IQ, sex, and other personal characteristics are included. We have the picture of the individual as a bundle of traits and mental abilities, as these are assessed by psychometric techniques, and these traits and abilities are seen as acting upon the functioning of the more basic processes of perception and learning, to produce the intersubject variance in performance we see in the laboratory and in the classroom. This view has been a hindrance to the proper appreciation of individual differences in learning. It creates the impression that ID's are really not the learning researcher's business, but someone else's—the differential psychologist's, perhaps, or the personality theorist's. These extrinsic factors are regarded merely as bothersome intruders in the learning domain. The strict control of these extrinsic sources of ID's, however, usually results in disappointingly little reduction in the intersubject variance in our experiments. Psychometric ability measures may at times account for a fair share of the variance in learning, but mental abilities of this type are not properly classed as extrinsic ID's. They fit into another niche in my scheme, and I will save them for a later point in the discussion.

By the term *intrinsic* individual differences I refer to those individual differences which are inherent in learning and which do not exist independently of learning phenomena. In other words, intrinsic individual differences consist of intersubject variability in the learning process itself.

A moment ago I included personality traits in the class of extrinsic ID's. In some cases, however, a personality trait must be regarded on theoretical grounds as belonging to the intrinsic type of ID's, when the development of the personality trait itself is based on some essential variable in the learning domain. A case in point is Eysenck's conception of extraversion, which is hypothesized to develop as a consequence of ID's in the rate of build-up and dissipation of cortical inhibition. Where such forms of inhibition play a role in learning, we should expect to find correlations with the trait of extraversion. In other words, the personality trait and the learning performance both would have some ID "genotype" in common. On a more superficial level the trait of extraversion might also have extrinsic effects on the subject's performance in a learning situation, and this would occur even when the learning task does not involve any inhibitory factor. It would result from generalized tendencies associated with the extraverted syndrome, such as not taking the experiment seriously, not being conscientious, and wishing to get the whole thing over with as quickly and easily as possible. Separation of the extrinsic and intrinsic aspects of this type of personality trait could presumably be achieved by means of experiments which manipulate the conditions hypothesized to afford an opportunity for the intrinsic or genotypic aspect of the personality trait—in the present case, cortical inhibition—to manifest itself in learning. In the case of extraversion we would select and manipulate tasks in which varying degrees of inhibition were inferred to operate. As another example, the trait of neuroticism or anxiety would be expected to show itself in the learning realm through variations in task complexity, along with the manipulation of instructional variables intended to arouse varying amounts of stress or ego involvement.

A more detailed look at this domain of intrinsic individual differences in learning can be facilitated if we hold in mind the following picture: Imagine a very large cube made up of many small cubes—the sort of diagram you have seen in many of Guilford's recent publications. This 3-dimensional figure can be used to represent three major classes of variables and the enclosed 3-dimensional space in which almost any particular learning task may be located. We begin with the horizontal dimension, which is labeled "Content Variables." This refers to the stimulus classes of the materials to be learned. The columns of this dimension bear labels such as "verbal," "spatial," "numerical," "perceptual-motor," etc. To avoid adding a fourth dimension to this cube I will also include sensory modality of the learning materials on this horizontal dimension, with the labels "visual," "auditory," "haptic," etc.

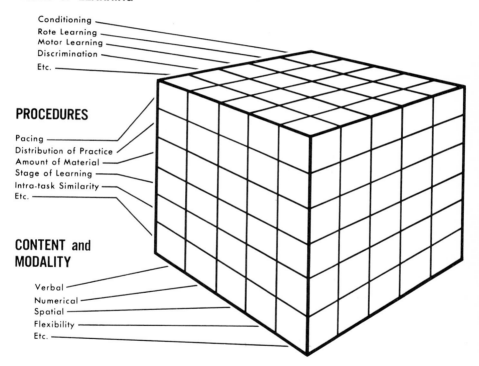

TYPES OF LEARNING

Conditioning
Rote Learning
Motor Learning
Discrimination
Etc.

PROCEDURES

Pacing
Distribution of Practice
Amount of Material
Stage of Learning
Intra-task Similarity
Etc.

CONTENT and MODALITY

Verbal
Numerical
Spatial
Flexibility
Etc.

Figure 6. A representation of the classes of variables in learning tasks.

Along the perpendicular axis, going from front to back, we can represent types of learning—the traditional categories such as classical and operant conditioning, rote learning, selective trial-and-error learning, concept learning, and so on. On each of the axes I shall leave some columns blank so that anyone can fill in anything else he thinks belongs in this scheme.

Along the vertical axis we have what I will call the procedural variables, such as stimulus duration, CS-UCS interval, task pacing, distribution of practice, degree of intra-task similarity with its associated generalization effects along both primary and semantic generalization gradients, and also the corresponding intra- and inter-task interference effects. Also on this axis we would have variables such as association value or meaningfulness, task complexity, length of task or amount of material to be learned, the stage of practice on a given task or a particular class of tasks, original learning and relearning after some interpolated activity. Instructional variables, such as differentially motivating sets, also may be included on this axis. While each of these variables is allotted a single row, we should think of each one as representing a continuum of values, such as various pacing rates, various degrees of distribution of practice, different degrees of task complexity, and so forth.

Now, in looking at this 3-dimensional structure, we may be tempted to conclude that *n* more dimensions are needed to represent adequately all the types of phenotypic variations among all the kinds of learning tasks we can think of. I would not argue about this. I only claim that this simple picture will serve my immediate didactic purpose. After I have made my point with it, it can be discarded altogether. So I shall not bother about its flaws, such as the fact that many of the cells will have to remain empty because certain variables on one axis have no relevance to a particular category on one of the other axes. Also it would be more accurate, but much more confusing, to try to represent all the procedural variables as being completely orthogonal to one another. Obviously, any given learning task can be located in more than one of the rows simultaneously, taking some particular value on each of the procedural variables.

As we contemplate this whole structure, we have to face the awful possibility that each row or column on each of the dimensions could yield significant Subjects × Variables interactions. That is, if we run a group of subjects through all the tasks and conditions represented in this cube, there is the possibility that as we go from cell to cell the rank order of the subjects' learning performance will continually be changing. I am assuming that this change is not due to experimental error in the strict sense and that the different rank orders of subjects are reliable. At present we have no idea just how much shifting of rank order to expect in this situation. Nor do we know which variables will have the greatest interactions with subjects.

This, then, is the task for research on ID's in learning—to delineate the basic dimensions or genotypes of all of the between-subjects variation associated with all of the phenotypes of learning depicted in this 3-dimensional scheme. And then some!

I find it useful to keep this scheme in mind while perusing the factor-analytic studies reported in this field. Many such studies have involved a number of learning tasks sampled more or less arbitrarily from here and there in this taxonomic cube. That is to say, one finds batteries of learning tasks which have few if any of their rows or columns in common. Not surprisingly, the correlations between tasks selected under these conditions turn out to be generally meagre. No semblance of a general factor can possibly emerge, and the communalities of the learning measures are nearly always very small. The few factors that emerge are hard to interpret and usually are given uninteresting labels which merely duplicate the names of the learning tasks that entered into the analysis. We thus gain the impression that true genotypes have not been discovered and that at best the factor analysis has only classified the learning tasks along the same obvious phenotypic lines we had previously arrived at by mere inspection of task characteristics. When we sample too widely and too sparsely from the whole learning domain, this is what tends to come of our factor analysis. The analysis indeed reveals hardly more than what we already knew we were putting into it.

It is common practice to "overdetermine" factors by including several tests for each hypothesized factor. These hypothesized factors have nearly always been named and looked for in terms of the variables listed under content or under the type of learning task. Variance arising from the procedural variables is generally overlooked. For example, even if we had several rote learning tasks, we might not find much factorial communality among them if they all differed from one another on these procedural dimensions. It is primarily to this source of variance that I attribute the meagre communalities that are found in most factorial studies of learning.

What happens when we include psychometric reference tests, such as the *Primary Mental Abilities*, among a battery of learning tasks more or less haphazardly sampled from this cube? We find that the reference tests do absorb some of the variance—usually not very much—and we find that the variance they account for corresponds primarily to the *content* of the learning material. In the factor analysis, therefore, learning tasks tend to line up with reference tests on factors such as verbal rote learning, spatial learning, and so on. Many learning tasks, however, seem to share almost none of this variance.

Thus, the total variance in the learning tasks accounted for by the reference tests is generally very small. And how can we expect it to be otherwise? Psychometric tests obviously have little resemblance to most of the procedural variables that are necessarily involved in learning tasks. My hunch is that the largest source of ID variance in learning is connected with these procedural variables. By systematically including variance from this source in our factor analyses, we are apt to discover some of the most basic and pervasive genotypes of individual differences.

At this stage it might be profitable for someone to search the experimental literature on learning with an eye out for Subjects × Independent Variable interactions in the analyses of variance, in order to get some preliminary ideas of the kinds of variables most likely to be important sources of ID's. As we begin to look into this matter, we hopefully may find that some of the variables indicated on the three axes of our cube do not interact with subjects, that is, they might not constitute independent sources of ID variance. Every such variable that we can discover is a blessing, for there will still be plenty of subject interaction variables to keep us all busy for a long time.

In some of my own work, for example, I was happy to find that the sensory modality of the learning task turned out to be unimportant on the genotypic level, at least among normal subjects. I was measuring individual differences in a variety of memory span tasks under variations in the procedural variables, and found that the same genotypes were tapped whether the experiments were conducted in the visual or the auditory modality. Absolute values of certain parameters often differ significantly from one modality to another, but sensory modality in these experiments did not interact with subjects.

Coming back to this taxonomic cube for the last time, its implications for systematic research seem quite plain. The key idea is to focus on only one or two of the cells in this system in any one study or series of studies. By keeping constant as many sources of variance as we can while manipulating one narrow class of variables at a time, we will be more apt to obtain sets of intercorrelations that have sufficiently substantial structure to reveal the underlying genotypes.

The question immediately arises concerning the role of psychological theory in this search, as contrasted with mere systematic exploration of all possible variables. There is so much work to be done here that in order not to be completely arbitrary in our procedures, I think we will have to plan our experiments around theoretical hunches concerning the nature of the genotypes underlying ID's associated with particular classes of experimental variables. An atheoretical, systematic exploration of Subjects × Independent Variable interactions and the intercorrelations among these interactions is not to be despised, however. For there are probably surprises in store for us in this realm which lie beyond almost anyone's theoretical imagination. Then, too, I would warn of the danger of proliferating ad hoc theoretical explanations for ID's in any given learning situation. The basic genotypes we are in search of are probably relatively few in number and enter into phenotypically wide varieties of learning. And the structure or dimensionality of the basic genotypes might well look very different from the structure of the phenotypes we have outlined in terms of task characteristics.

Phenotypes and Genotypes

Phenotypes are described in terms of task characteristics, that is, the location of a learning task in our 3-dimensional scheme. The genotypes are the underlying factors or basic processes which cause the patterns of intercorrelations among the phenotypes. The primary task of research on ID's consists of discovering these genotypes. Hopefully, the number of these genotypes will be quite limited as compared with phenotypic variations. I am not at all sure what these genotypes will look like once they have been isolated. There are those who might imagine them to look something like the constructs of Hullian theory, with genotypes for habit strength, reactive and conditioned inhibition, drive, oscillation, the threshold of reaction evocation, and so on. Zeaman and Kaufman (1955), using a motor learning task, carried out a now classic study of ID's along Hullian lines. It is one of the few studies of ID's which focused attention on what I have called the procedural variables.

But other genotypes may bear little resemblance in their isolated state to anything we would be inclined to identify as learning. As an example, from some recent research of my own (Jensen, 1965), there appears to be some common genotype or set of genotypes underlying memory span, serial rote learning, and performance on the Stroop color-word test, particularly the speed factor in the Stroop, which is measured by having subjects read the names of colors as fast as they can. It would be interesting to speculate upon why this particular ability to read color names rapidly should be substantially correlated both with memory span for digits and with the speed of serial learning of verbal materials. On the other hand, two types of learning which phenotypically appear very much alike—serial learning and paired-

associate learning—have been found not to be significantly intercorrelated in the college population, even when the stimulus materials
are identical in both tasks. Furthermore, there seems to be little if
any transfer from the paired-associate to the serial list, even when the
S-R connections are common to both lists and subjects overlearn
the S-R connections in the first task (Jensen, 1963). Such are the
kinds of surprises that turn up when we begin looking for the genotypes that underlie phenotypes.

Serial learning has been found to have a great deal in common
genotypically with memory span. The two types of tasks, when their
intercorrelations are analyzed, have approximately equal loadings—
in the range of .60 to .70—on the general factor or first principal component. But it would be a mistake to regard even memory span as a
unitary ability determined by a single genotype. By putting 14 variations of memory span tasks into one factor analysis, along with an
equal number of serial learning tasks, there emerge at least three
factors needed to account for the intercorrelations among the various
memory span tasks. The nature of these factors can provide clues for
the formulation of a psychological model of memory span. Forward
span and backward span come out on different factors. And memory
span, when measured on series which do not appreciably exceed the
subject's span, is factorially different from memory span measured in
lists that considerably exceed the subject's span; that is, where more
items are presented than the subject can possibly recall, but the subject is required to recall as much as he can. This latter procedure increases variance on what I have hypothesized as a factor of susceptibility to interference. This factor is itself far from simple. Individual
differences in retroactive inhibition in short-term memory tasks, for
example, seem to have a different genotype than retroactive inhibition
in a task like serial learning, where more of the original learning gets
consolidated before the interfering task is interpolated. Thus we can
speak of retroactive interference with the process of consolidation in
short-term memory, and interference with the sequential retrieval of
a learned series of responses which involves some consolidated or relatively permanent acquisition.

In my factor analysis of the memory span tasks, one of the most striking findings arises from a comparison of the proactive and retroactive
inhibition paradigms. We present series A, followed after a brief pause
by series B, and then ask the subject to recall series A; and, of course,
we get retroactive inhibition as measured against the appropriate control condition. (Each subject is his own control.) If, after the same
sequence, we ask the subject to recall series B, we get proactive inhibi-

tion. It so happens that the proactive and retroactive inhibition measures come out on different dimensions in the factor analysis. Phenotypically, the RI and PI paradigms look much alike, and the over-all magnitude of the inhibition is similar for both. Yet the factor analysis suggests quite different underlying processes in these two types of interference.

One of the most interesting findings is the genotypic change in ID's in serial learning when we go from the original learning of a list to relearning the list after the retention of the original learning has been completely retroactively inhibited by an interpolated interfering task. Though the relearning takes as long or longer than the original learning, and everything looks as though the subject is learning the list for the first time, individual differences in relearning are only barely correlated with individual differences in original learning. Consequently, of course, OL and RL come out on different factors.

I mention these examples without going into further detail only to indicate the kinds of things that turn up when we work within a rather narrow slice of the learning domain and examine one or two tasks under a number of different procedural variations. Investigation of the dimensionality of individual differences just in memory span and serial learning is itself a huge undertaking. My initial investigations in this area have so far just scratched the surface. But certain basic methodological problems have been solved and hypotheses have been generated which will now carry this work forward at a much faster rate.

A word about methodology is in order at this point. First, a great deal more attention has to be paid to the reliability of our measurements in this kind of work than has ever been thought necessary in general experimental work. Another surprise is in store for us if we expect that most of our laboratory phenomena will yield individually reliable measures comparable to those of psychometric tests. A good part of a year was spent on my own project on ID's just trying to solve some of these reliability problems. Correcting correlations for attenuation is one solution, but one likes to know he is correcting intercorrelations with reliabilities that are at least significantly greater than zero. In fact, it has been possible to obtain very satisfactory reliabilities, so that no corrections of the correlation matrix are called for. We have achieved this by eliminating types of learning tasks which tend to elicit strategy types of behavior in subjects, by perfecting our preliminary instructions to subjects, by running subjects through brief pretests consisting of shortened and simplified versions of the experimental tasks in order to make sure that they are behaving in a standard way, and by the use of repeated measurements, made possible by running subjects on a number of parallel forms of every task. We have found, incidentally, that whatever the subject does in his first experience in the laboratory, regardless of the task, correlates with little else he ever does for us in later sessions. Initial performance usually sticks out in a factor analysis and has difficulty fitting anywhere into the factor structure, even though there may be a dozen other similar tests in the battery, all highly intercorrelated. Subjects apparently need some time to simmer down in the laboratory; the between-subjects variance we find in the first half-hour of a learning task reflects little of the learning genotypes manifested in subsequent laboratory performance. It is an interesting thought that so much of the experimental literature on learning is based on subjects' first hour in the laboratory. Subjects do change after this first experience, often quite dramatically. Almost nothing is known concerning the extent to which such changes in subjects affect the interactions among experimental variables. Someone had better look into this matter before long.

Another methodological or analytical risk consists of thinking one has found a source of ID's when in fact none exists. In the simplest case, ID's are thought to be detected when we find a significant Subjects × Independent Variable interaction in our analysis of variance, or when we find a significantly less than perfect correlation between two sets of learning scores (assuming a proper correction for attenuation). Interactions should be examined to determine if they can be removed by some transformation of the scale of measurement. As a simple example, say that subjects' learning scores suffer some decrement under an increase in the rate of stimulus presentation. If the amount of decrement is some constant proportion of the subject's original score or is some exponential function of the original score, analysis of variance or Pearson's r based on the original measures will give the appearance of ID's in the amount of decrement, due to an increase in stimulus pacing. The results would falsely imply that a different genotype is involved in the decrement than that which underlies the original score, while actually there is only one source of variance for both measures. The decrement scores in this case are completely predictable from the original scores, given the proper transformation of the scale. Thus, one should keep an eye out for spurious genotypes of this kind.

My final point on methodology is to recommend sticking with traditional laboratory learning procedures, at least for the time being. We have a considerable advantage if we begin already knowing a good deal about the characteristics of the learning tasks and materials we use in our studies of ID's.

The ultimate genotypes of individual differences will probably have to be described in physiological or biochemical terms. But before we reach that point, let me indulge in some rather unrestrained speculation and suggest some of the kinds of genotypes on the psychological level that we might be apt to find by means of the type of analysis I have indicated. These are some of the kinds of processes underlying individual differences that I imagine we might fathom through the welter of phenotypic variation: (*a*) the rate of decay of stimulus or associative traces in the absence of rehearsal; (*b*) the rate of consolidation of stimulus traces; (*c*) the initial strength of reception of stimuli; (*d*) proneness to interference with trace consolidation or external inhibition of the trace; (*e*) the degree of susceptibility of consolidated associations to interference through associative competition; (*f*) reactive inhibition and stimulus satiation; (*g*) the degree of spread of primary and semantic stimulus generalization gradients—and individual differences in this might not be general across all sensory modalities; (*h*) a complex of factors under the heading of drive, arousal, and attention; (*i*) something which for lack of a better term I will call "personal tempo"—the sort of variance found in tapping tests and the like—but this could be only a derivative of other processes such as drive and inhibition; (*j*) oscillation tendency, that is, the tendency for response strength to fluctuate up and down over the course of practice, though again this may be a derivative from more basic processes, probably of the interference type. Even a list as short as this may be further reduced conceptually. ID's in susceptibility to associative competition, for example, might well be based on differences in primary or semantic generalization gradients.

This list suggests that the basic processes from which all phenotypic ID's are generated may be quite few. The big question, of course, is whether this is a false hope or, even if it were theoretically plausible, whether it will ever be at all empirically feasible to penetrate to such a level of elemental basic processes. At the moment, from a purely scientific standpoint, it seems to me a desirable goal.

Primary Mental Abilities

One of the major tasks of differential and experimental psychology is the theoretical integration of ID's in learning and the structure of mental abilities as represented by tests like the *Primary Mental Abilities.* I see mental abilities measured on this level as less basic and more derivative than the dimensions of individual differences in learning which I have suggested. Therefore, I would not expect to understand individual differences in learning, in any fundamental sense, in terms of psychometric reference tests. What such tests measure is best conceived of as points on the learning curves of various kinds of behavior. The predictive power of psychometric tests is due to the fact that they sample learned behavior and therefore reflect something about the rate of learning in the natural environment. Also, they index the degree of acquisition of certain broad verbal or symbolic mediational systems—systems which are learned in the verbal-symbolic environment and which play an important generalized transfer function in complex learning and problem solving. Furthermore, most psychometric tests are phenotypically closer to the products of learning which we are often interested in predicting, such as ability in school subjects, than are the kinds of variables we generally deal with in the learning laboratory.

But one of the questions that needs to be answered in terms of learning processes is why mental abilities are found to have the particular structure or dimensionality which is more or less consistently revealed by factor analysis. Do the *Primary Mental Abilities*, for example, reflect anything about the structure or functioning of the brain, or are they more properly regarded as a product of a complex interaction among certain classes of stimulus input from the natural and social environment and innate ID's in the basic learning processes?

Among the possible means of working toward a theoretical unification of learning abilities and mental abilities is the developmental study of the dimensionality of these two realms. Further insights might be gained from studies of how various types of aphasia and other disabilities arising from brain damage are manifested in these two spheres of ability measurement. Still another approach is through the experimental study of behaviors which are highly correlated with psychometrically measured abilities and which, at the same time, have some of the phenotypic characteristics of learning tasks. Memory span is a good example of this. It is, of course, a subtest of the Stanford-Binet and the Wechsler intelligence tests and shares at least half its variance in common with the general intellectual abilities measured by these tests. At the same time, various aspects of the memory span test can be manipulated experimentally along many of the procedural variables common to a variety of learning tasks. Discovery of the dimensionality of ID's in memory span in terms of processes common to the learning domain thus affords some link between learning abilities and mental abilities.

Transfer and Individual Differences

An inevitable and complicating fact we must contend with is that learning abilities also grow out of learning itself. This fact is perhaps best conceptualized in terms of a complex hierarchy of transfer functions. In theory, basic learning abilities, on the one hand, and abilities attributable to transfer from earlier learning, on the other, must constitute a true dichotomy, since something has to be learned initially and some primitive, basic abilities must be present to accomplish this. Beyond a very early stage of life, however, we are forced to think of these basic learning abilities as an idealized point at one end of a continuum of types of learning in which transfer, learning sets, mediational systems, and the like, play an increasingly important role as we move along the continuum. For practical purposes, such as the understanding of ID's in school learning, in problem solving, and in the acquisition of complex skills, the study of transfer hierarchies will be of paramount importance. Basic learning abilities will, of course, be manifested in the sense that they will underlie the rate of acquisition of learning sets, mediational systems, and the like. At the same time, the development of these systems will also facilitate the acquisition of other systems in the hierarchy. The more elemental learning processes and abilities may become thoroughly camouflaged under the elaborate overlay of transfer functions. But if we are interested in the description of ID's in complex learning situations, we would perhaps do best to measure ID's directly in the network of already-learned subabilities which form the basis for the acquisition of more complex behaviors higher up in the transfer hierarchy.

The effects of early environment on readiness for school learning, and the complex chain of prerequisite learnings throughout the entire educational process are most readily thought of in terms of transfer. The broadest bases of transfer are probably to be found in attentional and discrimination hierarchies and in the processes of verbal mediation. The experimental paradigms that lend themselves to the analysis of individual differences in these processes constitute an immense topic in themselves, which I have elaborated upon elsewhere (Jensen, in press). In brief, individual differences in this area can be studied by assessing the properties of the verbal associative network as they are revealed through phenomena such as chained word associations, the degree of subjective organization and associative clustering in the free recall of verbal materials, the differential effects of varying degrees of meaningfulness or association value on the rate of acquisition in verbal learning tasks, and the differential rates of learning in tasks which differ in the amounts and kinds of verbal or symbolic mediation that they involve. Serial and paired-associate learning, for example, apparently stand at different points on this continuum involving degrees of verbal mediation. This fact could partly account for the low correlation between ID's in these two forms of learning (Jensen and Rohwer, 1963; Jensen and Rohwer, 1965; Jensen, 1965).

These, then, are a few of the possible approaches to gaining some theoretical mastery over the multifarious phenomena we find in human learning and the ID's associated with them. Let me conclude by pointing out that in this attempt to offer some description of the domain of ID's in learning at our present state of knowledge, or at least my own state of knowledge, I feel very much like one of the legendary blind men who tried to describe an elephant. At this stage more than one approach is obviously warranted.

REFERENCES

Hovland, C. I. Experimental studies in rote-learning theory. V. Comparison of distribution of practice in serial and paired-associate learning. *J. exp. Psychol.*, 1939, *25*, 622-633.

Jensen, A. R. Transfer between paired-associate and serial learning. *J. verb. Learn. verb. Behav.*, 1963, *1*, 269-280.

Jensen, A. R. *Individual differences in learning: Interference factor.* Final report, Cooperative Research Project No. 1867, U. S. Office of Education, 1965.

Jensen, A. R. Social class and verbal learning. In Deutsch, M., Jensen, A. R., and Katz, I. (eds.), *Race, social-class and psychological development.* New York: Holt, Rinehart & Winston Inc., in press.

Jensen, A. R. Rote learning in retarded adults and normal children. *Amer. J. ment. Defic.*, 1965, *69*, 828-834.

Jensen, A. R. and Rohwer, W. D., Jr. Verbal mediation in paired-associate and serial learning. *J. verb. Learn. verb. Behav.*, 1963, *1*, 346-352.

Jensen, A. R. and Rohwer, W. D., Jr. Syntactical mediation of serial and paired-associate learning as a function of age. *Child Developm.*, 1965, *36*, 601-608.

Underwood, B. J. Laboratory studies of verbal learning. In E. R. Hilgard (ed.), *Theories of learning and instruction.* Chicago: National Society for the Study of Education, 1964.

Zeaman, D., and Kaufman, H. Individual differences and theory in a motor learning task. *Psychol. Monogr.*, 1955, 69, No. 6 (Whole No. 391).

THE SPECIFICITY OF INDIVIDUAL DIFFERENCES IN LEARNING

CHARLES N. COFER
Pennsylvania State University

In discussing Professor Jensen's paper, I suffer from two disadvantages. One is that the study of individual differences has not been a major facet of my work. The other is that I have always worked in the areas of verbal learning and verbal behavior. Individual differences (ID's) outside these realms are *terra incognita* for me indeed.

Let me applaud Dr. Jensen's emphasis on those ID's which are intrinsic to learning. In a general sort of way, it seems very plausible to me that attempts to understand such ID's may lead to significant advances in theoretical understanding of the tasks we use to study learning and of the processes involved in learning. However, I am not as optimistic as is Professor Jensen that there are but a few genotypes underlying the varied tasks, procedures, and situations which characterize the things people learn. Let me speak briefly of two kinds of studies of ID's in which we have been (half-heartedly) engaged this year, one of which was by design, the other by accident. Then I shall conclude with more general remarks concerning the theme of Professor Jensen's paper.

---

[1] The work reported here was carried out in conjunction with Contract Nonr 656(30) between the Office of Naval Research and the Pennsylvania State University. I am indebted to Miss Nancy Bennie, who carried out the first of the experiments described, and to Mr. Richard Olsen, who performed the other experiments discussed. These studies have been described in detail in Technical Reports No. 6 and No. 8 under the contract indicated.

Some Studies of Paired-Associate Learning

There is a good deal of interest in how meaningfulness, or *m*, achieves its great effects in verbal learning. The study I shall describe had its inception in considerations of this problem, but so far as it has gone, does not bear on its solution.

One can argue that, in verbal learning, the more one can eliminate interfering or competing responses, or, alternatively, the more that one can arrange that appropriate responses will occur in the situation from the start, the faster the learning should be. Thinking about the effects of *m* in this way reminded me of studies in problem solving, which might be interpreted in a similar way and which involved individual differences. Olga McNemar (1955) was able to differentiate good and poor performers on certain of Guilford's (Guilford, *et al.*, 1950) reasoning tests by means of tests of verbal fluency which measure fluency under response restrictions. Specifically, she found that good scores on the reasoning tests were given by subjects who were fluent when asked to give as many words as possible (1) that started with the letter P; (2) that started with the letter S and ended with L; or (3) that were similar in meaning to the stimulus words. Battig (1957) has also found that certain verbal skills are related to performance on other tasks. He observed, for a word-guessing task, that the best performances were achieved by those subjects who guessed letters in accordance with their actual frequency of occurrence in the English language, and he presented evidence that knowledge of actual letter frequency is related to performance on the word-guessing task (p. 103, fn. 4). Battig's (1958) subjects improved their performances when they had a list of letters ordered according to frequency of usage.

We decided to examine the relation of McNemar's tests to performance on two paired-associate problems, one consisting of nonsense-syllable pairs, the other of word pairs. Data were collected from subjects for unrestricted free association and for McNemar's three restricted association tasks. All subjects learned both paired-associate tasks. Subjects ($N = 41$) scoring in the mid-range of the unrestricted association tasks were divided into subgroups on the basis of their scores on the restricted association tasks, and their learning scores were compared.

Although the results are suggestive, they are not entirely consistent and, of course, require replication to be convincing. There was a generally positive relation between learning scores (number of correct responses) and number of P-word responses (in unit time) for both the syllable and the word paired-associate learning tasks, and the extreme P-word groups in both cases differed at about the 5 percent level. There was little relation between learning scores on either task and scores on the S-L association test, but performance on the similar words association test did correspond generally and significantly with learning scores on the paired-associate CVC task, but not significantly on the paired-associate word task. These results suggest that an ability to be fluent under some conditions restrictive of response freedom may be related to success in verbal learning. But the predictors here, if indeed they are valid, seem specific and closely related to processes found only in verbal problems.

The other situation in which ID's have become involved in my recent research was not anticipated. In the last year, we have performed three experiments in which the chief interest has involved the comparison of the anticipation and recall methods of paired-associate learning. In the first experiment, word-two digit number pairs were employed, and the recall groups showed faster learning than the anticipation groups at each of the three exposure intervals employed. Further, there were no significant sex differences or significant interactions of other variables with sex.

In the next experiments nonsense-syllable pairs were employed. In the first of these, the methods were still significantly different, with recall superior, but less so than with the word-number pairs. Intrapair similarity, i.e., similarity between the S and R terms of a pair, was studied in this experiment. Sex differences were not significant as such, but the Sex × Methods interaction was significant. In the last experiment, inter-stimulus and inter-response similarity were varied. Here, sex differences became highly significant, the Methods difference was not, but there was no significant Sex × Methods interaction.

I am very uncertain about the interpretation of this set of experiments, and I should not wish to conclude much of anything from them. A suggestion, however, might be that where response integration is a minor factor, as it is, presumably, in the word-number pair experiment, the recall method leads to faster learning than the anticipation method, i.e., facilitates the association stage. We had no sex differences here. The sex differences arose in the experiments employing nonsense syllables, which presumably must be integrated; and, in general, the girls did better than the boys. Is there something about girls which provides some integration of nonsense syllables at the beginning of the experiment or permits their rapid integration which is not present in boys? The answer, of course, is that we do not know, but it is possible that girls have knowledge of letter frequencies or of letter combinations that boys do not have, or that the girls have stronger letter associations than boys, which foster response integration.

Implications

I have had two purposes in describing these studies. One is to underscore a dilemma in which many experimentalists find themselves. It is whether to go on with these individual difference problems or not. The problems of experimental design concerning ID's are new ones for most of us. Professor Jensen's point that performance in the first hour in the laboratory is not predictive of later sessions is relevant here. This is a further caveat about the results I have been discussing, tentative as I have made them out to be, and it would augment the reluctance of the experimentalist to become involved in ID's.

The other purpose is to display the specific and fine-grained character of factors that may be involved in individual differences as they arise in verbal learning. Let us assume that we know that verbal fluency under response restrictive conditions, that effective knowledge of letter frequencies and letter combinations, and that letter associations are importantly involved in varying rates of response integration when nonsense syllables are the response terms in paired-associate learning. Can their analogues be found with respect to other tasks? May other tasks be described in terms of a two-stage conception corresponding to that given for verbal learning (cf. Underwood & Schulz, 1960)?

I find it difficult to answer either of these questions affirmatively. My hesitation in the second case, which may be reformulated in the question, "Are there general 'traits' of learning tasks?", arises from a lack of knowledge about the properties of tasks. In the first case, I find it difficult to conceive of a subject trait, related to letter frequencies, letter combinations, and word or letter associations, which would be related to coordinate factors outside the verbal sphere. Perhaps I expect more simplicity than he intends from Professor Jensen's belief that the basic processes or genotypes are few and enter into ID's over wide varieties of learning; and, of course, the phrase "a few" is capable of widely varying quantitative interpretations. Nevertheless, I remain to be convinced, or perhaps better, remain to be instructed, that there are but a few basic processes underlying ID's in learning, and that the interactions of specific task characteristics with highly specific individual propensities and abilities are not the basis of the enormous ID's which everyone finds in most learning tasks.

REFERENCES

Battig, W. F. Some factors affecting performance on a word-formation problem. *J. exp. Psychol.*, 1957, *54*, 96-104.

Battig, W. F. Effects of previous experience and information on performance on a word-formation problem. *J. exp. Psychol.*, 1958, *56*, 282-287.

Guilford, J. P., Comrey, A. L., Green, R. F., and Christensen, P. R. A factor analytic study of reasoning abilities: I. Hypotheses and description of tests. *Psychology Laboratory Reports, University of Southern California*, Report No. 1, 1950, 1-23.

McNemar, O. W. An attempt to differentiate between individuals with high and low reasoning ability. *Amer. J. Psychol.*, 1955, *68*, 20-36.

Underwood, B. J., and Schulz, R. W. *Meaningfulness and verbal learning.* Chicago: J. B. Lippincott Co., 1960.

7

INDIVIDUAL PERFORMANCE, R-R THEORY AND PERCEPTION

MURRAY GLANZER
New York University

The study of individual differences, although it initially had close ties with experimental psychology, as in the early work of James McKeen Cattell, quickly became an applied psychometric problem, divorced from experimental work and outside the concern of theorists dealing with experimental data. Recent developments are ending this separation, however. Individual performance has become of both theoretical and experimental concern. It may be noted that I have already shifted from the term "individual differences" to the term "individual performance." This predicts a shift in point of view that I will discuss later.

There have been good reasons, of course, why psychologists with an experimental orientation did not, in the past, focus on the performance of the individual subject. In areas of human performance such as learning and perception, the first job was to rough in the general outlines of theory. In order to set out the general outlines of theory for an area, crude or average theories suffice. Theorists concerned with experimental data have therefore postponed consideration of the individual subject. There have been, of course, gestures towards incorporating individual differences in theory. For example, both Tolman and Hull indicated a place for such a variable in their theories. However, these indications were little more than gestures.

The area of perception has shown a variety of reactions to the problem of individual performance. In what might be called the classical areas of perception, for example, the study of the constancies, there is recognition of the importance of individual differences but little attempt to cope with these differences. There is one area in perception that has devoted thorough analysis to the problem of individual differences, namely, the area of social perception. In this work, the individual judges' standpoint is specified in the analysis of sets of judgments. The work stems from the insight of Coombs (1952) that phenotypically different orderings of objects by judges may conceal an underlying genotypic identity. The apparent difference in the ordering stems from a difference in the point from which the judge makes his judgments.

Another area of perception, in which systematic attempts have been made to handle individual performance, is concerned with the relation of personality to perception. There have been perennial attempts to demonstrate a relation between personality characteristics and performance on perceptual tasks. These attempts, starting from the work of the Jaensches, have the general form which postulates two main types. In Jaensch's typology (1930), one of the types was responsive to the environment and flexible; the other was not responsive in this way, and was rigid. Later day variants have altered the constellation of characteristics somewhat. For Frenkel-Brunswick and her associates (1945, 1947), the polar types are opposed on such characteristics as authoritarian beliefs, rigidity, and intolerance of ambiguity. For Witkin and his associates (1954), the polar types are opposed on the basis of such characteristics as field-dependency. Much of this work involves correlations between perceptual measures and verbal measures obtained either in the context of projective tests or objective inventories.

Recent Developments

At the present time, there is a greater readiness by both experimental and applied psychologists to view individual performance closely and directly. The crude average theories, having served their function, now free the experimental psychologist to build more complete and more complex theories. The applied psychologist, I believe, is interested in a more detailed study of individual performance because the further attempts to use individual differences in the applied situation have ground to a halt. It is necessary for the investigator to go beyond the predictors currently available. These predictors have been empirically rather than rationally defined. Just as the experimental psychologist was concerned with those variables which gave him some degree of over-all control, the applied psychologist has been concerned with those measures which give him gross prediction. Both groups now appear to be ready to move towards more powerful and sensitive systems.

There are two developments that have taken place in theoretical and experimental psychology that are important in making for the merging of interest. The first is the growth of skills in coping with complex intervening mechanisms. The second is the concern with the individual case. The problem of individual performance is intimately tied with this notion of intervening mechanisms. Without such mechanisms, there is no room for theoretical analysis of the performance. It is one of the paradoxes of the history of psychology that a psychologist who played a critical role in the study of individual differences, E. L. Thorndike, was also one whose aversion to intervening mechanisms ruled out any theoretical handling of these differences. During the '40's and the '50's, it became clear that even relatively simple performance, by relatively simple organisms such as rats, required the specification of intervening processes. I have in mind here, in particular, the work of Lawrence (1949, 1950) on acquired distinctiveness of cues and the work of several investigators on the observing response (Wyckoff, 1952; Atkinson, 1958). Several other instances come readily to mind, e.g., Amsel and his associates' (1952, 1954) work on frustration, Mowrer's (1947, 1960), and Miller's (1948) work on fear. In the case of human subjects, the instances range in complexity from Kendler and D'Amato's (1955) two-stage process, postulated to account for data on discrimination reversal, to Bruner, Goodnow, and Austin's (1956) strategies.

The second development is the growing commitment to the explanation of the individual case. Psychologists have always been committed in principle to the study of the individual's performance. Under urging by Skinner and his associates (e.g., Sidman, 1960), they have become committed in fact. This commitment is not restricted to the type of investigation sponsored by Skinner. Even when the data dealt with are group data, there is greater concern with the underlying individual performance. The rational, mathematical theories developed recently have started from a concern with the process within the individual subject.

Restatement of the Problem of Individual Performance

I would first like to set the problem of individual differences in a general theoretical framework, rather than viewing it in its usual special form. The particular interest in the special form is in part due to historical accident. Focusing solely on the special form has the possible disadvantage of making work in the area awkward or impossible. By placing the problem of individual performance in its general context, it becomes possible to analyze the difficulties in the area, to see possible solutions for these difficulties, and to keep open various approaches to the problems in the area.

The study of individual differences is a special case of a general and important approach in psychology—the study of R-R relations. It also reflects some problems related to the study of the individual case.

What I will do below is expand on the matter of R-R relations and the study of the individual case by considering four topics.

1. The structure of R-R data.
2. The requirements of R-R theory.
3. The special problems posed by the study of the individual case.
4. Some work in the field of perception with reference to both R-R relations and the study of the individual case.

The Structure of R-R Data

The special characteristics of R-R data become apparent upon some study of the basic data involved. In all cases there are at least two data matrices (see Table 10). The large S's refer to the subjects. The small s's refer to stimuli or test items. The small r's refer to responses. Thus r_{23} is the response of the second subject to the third stimulus. In any study that involves analyses of individual differences, the same subjects appear in the two data matrices. The relation that is most frequently studied is that between the row sums of two or more such data matrices. This is clearly, however, not the only and not the most interesting relation that can be studied. Consideration of the basic data matrices indicates that there are a variety of other relations that can and should be studied.

Reference to the basic data matrices clarifies the interrelations of several different types of R-R studies. If the same stimuli are repre-

TABLE 10
BASIC DATA MATRICES

	s_1	s_2	s_3	•	s_n		s_1	s_2	s_3	•	s_n
S_1	r_{11}	r_{12}	r_{13}	•	r_{1n}	S_1	r_{11}	r_{12}	r_{13}	•	r_{1n}
S_2	r_{21}	r_{22}	r_{23}	•	r_{2n}	S_2	r_{21}	r_{22}	r_{23}	•	r_{2n}
S_3	r_{31}	r_{32}	r_{33}	•	r_{3n}	S_3	r_{31}	r_{32}	r_{33}	•	r_{3n}
•	•	•	•	•	•	•	•	•	•	•	•
S_n	r_{n1}	r_{n2}	r_{n3}	•	r_{nn}	S_n	r_{n1}	r_{n2}	r_{n3}	•	r_{nn}

sented in the two data matrices and the same aspects of the same responses are being measured at different times, simple response reliability is being studied by the test-retest method. By relating the row sums, the reliability of gross or average individual differences can be evaluated. By relating the column sums for the two matrices, the reliability of gross stimulus differences can be evaluated.

If the same stimuli are presented in both data matrices while different aspects of the same response are being measured, then the relation between these response aspects can be determined using either the stimuli or the subjects as units. Thus, for example, the relation between latency and amplitude of response can be evaluated, pairing these measures on the basis of subjects or pairing them on the basis of stimuli.

Instead of two different aspects of the same response appearing in the cells of the matrices, there may be measures taken from two different responses which occur at the same time to the stimuli. For example, the responses may be accuracy of verbal responses to the stimuli for one matrix and amplitude of GSR for the other, as in some studies of perceptual defense (McGinnies, 1949), or a stage of problem solving and an EEG measure, as in some studies of electrophysiological correlates of performance (Glanzer, Chapman, Clark and Bragdon, 1964).

There may be measures taken from two different responses which occur at different times to the same stimuli. I have been engaged in studying such a case for some time. My concern stemmed from an interest in the particular stimuli involved. I therefore worked with column sums rather than row sums.

A frequent case is one in which different stimuli are represented in the two matrices and different responses are measured. Since there is no way to pair the columns, the relation evaluated is, of necessity, a gross one, i.e., the relation between row sums. This type of relation is studied when, for example, the total score on an embedded figures test is correlated with the total number of faces recalled on a memory test (Messick and Damarin, 1964).

In moving from the study of individual differences to the closely related study of personality, the combination of response scores becomes peculiarly complex. For example, with projective tests there is a complex weighting of the stimulus or test items in combining them for purposes of prediction.

Requirements of R-R Theory

There is one characteristic of the relation between data matrices that is of major importance. When the responses in the data matrices are different, i.e., when they no longer represent a simple reliability case, there is a need for a theoretical structure to relate the two data matrices. I would like to make explicit the characteristics that have to be present in order for this theoretical relation to be satisfactory.

The reasons for dealing with two data matrices vary. In some cases the investigator has one matrix which displays a sizable amount of uncontrolled or unexplained variance. The investigator therefore postulates an additional variable, some characteristic of the individual's response system, and develops a set of new response measures to test this conception. These new response measures are related by means of a theory to the original set of response measures. In some cases, the investigator starts with a theory or general picture of the organization of the subject's response system. Two or more sets of measures are then taken. The purpose of these multiple measures is, in part, to define the conception. In part, it is to validate the relevance of the measures. For example, a relation is obtained between the embedded figure test and the rod-and-frame test (Witkin, *et al.*, 1954). This relation is used both to define the conception of field-dependence and to validate the two measures. In both cases, the one in which the theory precedes the measures and the one in which it is generated by the measures, a theory is involved. The theory is an R-R theory.

Spence (1944), in an early paper on theory construction, made the distinction between S-R theories, in which the subject's response is a function of some stimuli or conditions imposed by the experimenter, and R-R theories, in which the subject's response is a function of some other response by the subject. For Spence, the R-variables include a wide range of measures—"attributes of simple response patterns (actones), complex achievements (actions), and generalized response char-

acteristics (traits, abilities, etc.)" (p. 48). Spence acknowledges the
contributions made by R-R theory in certain instances, citing particularly Köhler's handling of the perception of reversible figures. He
points out that this type of theory does not give the control that S-R
theory gives. He then turns to the developments of the role of intervening variables in S-R theory.

Since its initial consideration by Spence, R-R theory has been relatively neglected. Attention has centered on S-R theorizing, and on
situations that permit experimental control. It is becoming more apparent now, however, that simple S-R theories are not adequate for
certain purposes. The variety of mediational processes proposed has
been indicated above. These may be viewed as a merging of S-R and
R-R theories. For the handling of perception within a behavioristic
framework it is necessary to use a combined theory—S-R-R, as Schoenfeld and Cumming (1963) phrase it. For the handling of any complex
performance by the adult subject, it is necessary to take account of
very different training that each subject may have had before reaching
the experimental situation. The effects of such training are incorporated in the analysis of the performance by postulating a mediator or
R-R relation.

The neglect of R-R theory is seen in the absence of a set of requirements on this type of theory. I will suggest here a set of three specific
requirements which will serve to make this type of approach viable.
The general requirement is that attention be focused on relatively
simple tasks and that in these tasks the individual's performance should
be described and analyzed. The three specific requirements are as
follows:

Requirement One. A psychological theory, whether R-R or S-R,
should be a specification of a process. By that I mean that a theory or
explanation details a series of successive events that carry the organism from one state to another. The intervening events may or may not
be directly related to observations made of the performance. In the
case of learning, the process is one that carries the organism from one
state in trial N to another state in trial N + 1. In Estes' (1950) stimulus
sampling model, the intervening events are the sampling and conditioning of a set of stimuli. In Restle's (1955) adaptation model for discrimination learning, the intervening events are both the conditioning
and adaptation of cues with some internal mechanism that decides
which one is going to happen. In the case of perception, the process
is one that carries the subject from one perceptual state to another,
following presentation of a stimulus. In Sperling's (1960) analysis of

perceptual recall, the intervening events are traces that decline as a function of time.

Requirement Two. A psychological theory should be a specification of a process within the individual. This assumption implies that an adequate theory is one that can be used for the individual case. It does not mean group data cannot be handled. It does mean that the theory, when applied to group data, must take account of the characteristics of the hypothesized individual functions. Thus, if the theory states that the individual learning curve is a growth curve, then the relation of the averaged group curve to the individual curve must be specified. In the case of certain functions, e.g., the growth function, the job of relating parameters obtained from averaged data to parameters obtained from individual data becomes quite complicated. This point concerning the relation between individual and group or averaged functions has been developed fully by Sidman (1952) and Estes (1956).

Requirement Three. The intra-individual process should be available to experimental manipulation. This means that the theory has to specify in detail the moves necessary to change performance within the individual. It also means that the overt responses involved should be well specified and clearly related to the hypothesized process. This requirement leads to the relating of R-R and S-R approaches.

I believe that aiming to meet requirements such as these puts an R-R theory on a serious basis. I believe it will also furnish the basis for an effective system. When the requirements are not met, R-R data are not found acceptable. It is because Requirement One is not met that correlations between I.Q. and other performances are not interesting. Again, when Requirement One is not met, correlations relating personality to performance are not satisfactory.

Most work on individual differences has a futile air about it. A set of measurements shows that one individual is worse than another on some measure. In some cases these measurements might help predict performance on a criterion task. The measurements could therefore be used for purposes of selection. They do not, however, give a basis for doing anything about the performance. They do not tell how the subject should be trained to improve his performance. They do not tell how the situation should be changed to make the criterion performance easier. Since they do not give a basis for doing anything about the performance, they do not give a basis for the understanding or analysis of the performance.

It is true that a set of measurements of the type described above could be factor-analyzed and the factor analysis used to categorize the test performance. The factor analysis would not, however, meet Requirement One. It does not specify a process, a sequence of events. It gives, at best, a static summary of the components of performance. Consider, for example, attempting to discover the workings of a computer by factor-analyzing its output. There have been, of course, attempts to get around the static character of factor analysis. Here, I have in mind the work of Fleishman (1965) on changes in the factorial composition of tasks at different stages of training.

The approach that I am proposing furnishes a basis for the analysis of abilities that leads to statements concerning both training and structuring of the situation. Since the performance is viewed as being mediated by a series of specific successive events, the level of subjects' over-all performance may be traced to the level of performance on any one of several of these component events. Let me first give you an example out of the area of perception.

There have been a number of theoretical structures set up in the area of perception that involve R-R relations. One perceptual model has been set up by Bruner (1951) to account for differences in thresholds for tachistoscopically exposed words. In this model, it is assumed that each individual has a set of responses or hypotheses ranked in order of strength. An input either confirms or infirms the predominant hypothesis. If the input confirms the hypothesis, then the subject makes one response. If it does not confirm the hypothesis, then a checking procedure is carried out to determine which hypothesis will be accepted. This, then, presumably leads to some final response. Bruner is quite specific about the variables which affect hypothesis strength; they include the frequency of past confirmation, the number of alternative hypotheses, and its cognitive, motivational, and social consequences.

There is less detail presented on the decision-making mechanism referred to above. In order to meet the requirements I have outlined, there should be specification of the procedure used by the subject in deciding whether the input confirms or infirms his strongest hypothesis. There should also be specification of the procedure carried out by the subject when the input does not confirm the strongest hypothesis.

The general approach outlined by Bruner has generated a large number of studies. One was a study carried out by Postman, Bruner, and McGinnies (1948). Another study was one by Vanderplas and Blake (1949). In both studies, the investigators reported a positive relation between an individual's hierarchy of personal values and the ease with which he recognized words related to these different values. These studies were straightforward R-R studies. The investigators worked with the relation between individual rows of the data matrices.

They also made use of the relation between the two rows of column sums.

The underlying relation between the data matrices is given in enough detail for Bruner to have a basis for recommendations concerning the training to be given to an individual to change his performance. Thus, each of the variables that affect hypothesis strength may be used to alter performance. With some further specification of the confirming-infirming process, another independent set of variables could be obtained that affect performance. Subsequent work has led to a reinterpretation of these R-R relations to one in terms of word frequency (Solomon and Howes, 1951; Goldiamond and Hawkins, 1958). These changes in interpretation would, of course, alter the type of recommendations that would be made for training and structuring of the situation.

Special Problems of the Individual Case

Requirement Two is that a psychological theory should be a specification of a process within an individual. This leads to a concern with the individual case. In attempting to handle the individual case, the first problem inevitably is the problem of reliability. The way to insure reliability, of course, is to increase the number of measures. When interest centers on the individual subject, it is no longer possible to obtain multiple measures by increasing the number of subjects. The multiple measures have to be obtained within each subject. However, if repeated measures change the pattern of subjects' responses to a set of stimuli, then there is an interaction of trials or measurements with the stimuli. This makes it difficult to assert any over-all relation between the set of R's and any other set of measures. However, if this interaction exists it cannot be avoided by returning to groups of subjects. There is no guarantee that subjects are at the same level of training or experience when they enter an experiment. If they are at different levels, then the same interaction would appear confounded with the interaction of individuals with the stimuli.

Study of Form Perception

I have recently been engaged in a series of studies concerned with the perception of form or organization. The work involves R-R relations. The studies started with the general question "What makes one stimulus well organized or easy to handle, while another is poorly organized or difficult to handle?" The answers that have been suggested in the past to this question were given either in terms of Gestalt theory or information theory. These attempts have not, however, met with much success. The Gestalt attempt did not give a satisfactory theory because its concepts did not lend themselves to measurement, were not well organized theoretically, and could not be applied systematically to complex stimuli. Information theory, which was designed to replace Gestalt concepts with a better defined and better ordered set of concepts, when applied to the perception of individual stimuli, presents certain logical difficulties. These difficulties have been discussed by Garner (1962) and others (Glanzer and Clark, 1963a).

Part of the difficulty in making use of Gestalt theory is that it often has been used as an R-R theory with the superficial appearance of an S-R application. For example, prägnanz is basically an R-variable. It requires definition in terms of some independent response measures. Information theory has had related difficulties in its application to perceptual phenomena. For example, to apply the measure to the individual stimulus requires some definition of the units within the stimulus. These units cannot be defined, however, by the experimenter. They require some kind of response measurement. By a less obvious route we end up with an R-R system again. I am tempted toward the generalization that any adequate handling of perception involves R-R relations. I mentioned above Schoenfeld's and Cumming's S-R-R formulation. There is certainly no harm in dealing with such relations. The harm comes from dealing with them without recognizing their special character.

The occasion for the question asked above, "What makes one stimulus well organized or easy to handle?" was the observation of pronounced differences in the difficulty of reproducing members of a set of patterns. These differences in difficulty corresponded to intuitive notions of goodness of organization of figures. Attempts to use either Gestalt theory or information theory to explain these differences proved to be awkward and inadequate. In the attempt to handle these differences more effectively, a new hypothesis was generated. This hypothesis outlines the perceptual process as follows. In a perceptual reproduction task the subject receives an input of information. This input of information is encoded in the subject's language and held in this verbal form until the subject makes his final response; here, the reproduction of the figure. This hypothesis was labeled the verbal loop hypothesis and was schematized as in Figure 7. From the hypothesis, the following implication was drawn—that under short exposure, those stimuli that generate a long translation or code will be less likely to be completely encoded. They are, therefore, less likely to be reproduced accurately. The main aim in setting up the verbal loop hypothesis was to handle differences in perceptual organization. A model of this general type has been arrived at independently by other investigators concerned with a variety of problems in visual perception and memory: Conrad (1962), in attempting to explain confusions in the recall of visually presented letters, and Sperling (1963), in attempting to handle long-term retention of visually presented material. Conrad found that he could account for errors in the recall of sequences of visually presented letters on the basis of auditory confusions between the letters when presented with white masking noise. Sperling also bases his proposal on evidence concerning auditory confusions in recall.

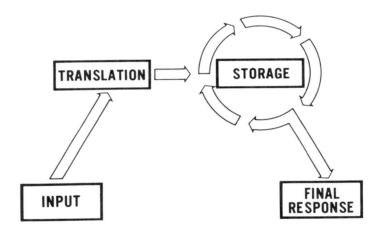

Figure 7. Schematic outline of the verbal loop hypothesis.

Under the verbal loop hypothesis, the covert code length of each stimulus is important. It is necessary, however, to obtain a measure of this covert code length. On the basis of the hypothesis, it was decided to use the lengths of subjects' descriptions of figures as estimators of the covert code lengths of the figures. A series of experiments was carried out in which the accuracy of reproduction of stimuli under brief exposure was measured for sets of figures. Using different groups of subjects, who viewed the figures for relatively long periods of time (30 sec.) and described the figures in words, mean verbalization lengths for each stimulus were obtained. The relations found between verbalization length and accuracy of reproduction support the verbal loop hypothesis. For three classes of stimuli—complex patterns of black and white objects (Glanzer and Clark, 1963a), binary numbers (Glanzer and Clark, 1963b), and conventional line drawings (Glanzer and Clark, 1964)—the correlation between verbalization length and accuracy of reproduction is approximately −.80. It was further demonstrated that when the physical form of the stimuli was changed—e.g., changed from 8-place binary numbers (that go from 00000000 to 11111111) to variable place binary numbers (that go from 0 to 11111111)—the accuracy of reproduction of particular stimuli changed and the verbalizations changed in a corresponding way. The final result was that the relation between the verbalization length and accuracy of reproduction was maintained. It was also demonstrated that the verbalization length was an efficient predictor of judged complexity of stimuli. More recently, it was demonstrated that the hypothesis affords a basis for systematic variation of the perceptual serial-position effect (Glanzer, 1966). I will not go into any detail on this study because we were still in an R-R case. We used stimuli that differed in their average verbalization length to change the form of the perceptual serial position effect.

We are clearly dealing with R-R relations in all of these studies. Let us see how well the three requirements that I have mentioned are met.

Requirement One is that the theory specify a process. This has been done. The specification is set forth in Figure 7.

Requirement Two is that it specify a process within the individual. This is asserted in the formulation of the hypothesis.

Requirement Three is that the process be available to experimental manipulation. A recent study is relevant to this requirement.

Experimental Work on Process Availability

A study, carried out with Joseph Fleischman, was set up to determine whether Requirement Three could be met. The main purpose of the study was to determine the effect of encoding training on the accuracy of reproduction of stimuli. In other words, can an experimental manipulation be set up to change the first member of the R-R pair so that a change is induced in the second member? The stimuli were 512 nine-place binary numbers from 000000000 to 111111111. A group of eleven subjects was first shown the 512 stimuli in a different random order each day for five days. The exposure time was ½ sec. As each binary number was shown, the subjects attempted to record it in answer booklets. After the five days of preliminary accuracy testing, the subjects were divided into three groups—control group, English group, and octal group. The three groups differed in the type of encoding they practiced during the training period that followed. This training period was approximately two weeks in length.

The control subjects were required to report orally each of the numbers they saw. They were not required to use any special form of reporting. Both the number of words they used in reporting each stimulus and their accuracy was recorded. The English group was trained to give a response in the following form—a one, a zero, a one; two zeroes, a one; a one, two zeroes; that is, they reported groups of three digits each. (This was for the binary number 101001100.) The octal group was trained to report the number as three octal digits. Thus they reported the same binary number given above as 5, 1, 4. All groups went through an initial phase of training with three-digit binary numbers before starting on the nine-digit binary numbers. Throughout the training—both on three-digit and nine-digit numbers —the subject was informed as to whether his response was correct or not. This is in distinction to the testing phases that preceded and followed. During both the pre- and post-training periods, no feedback was given to the subjects.

After the two weeks of training the subjects were switched back to direct testing. The stimuli were again presented 512 per session, and the subjects required to record their responses in their test booklets. No overt verbalization was required during this phase.

The results from the three groups are summarized in Figure 8. During the initial phase the three groups show the same course of learning. This is to be expected since the subjects were sorted into groups on the basis of their over-all performance during the pre-training period.

After the initial phases of the training period with three-digit numbers, the subjects were again presented the 512 nine-digit stimuli. The second section of the curve shows the performance of the subjects with these 512 nine-place binary numbers during the training phase. A marked divergence between the three groups may be observed. This divergence cannot be interpreted simply, however, since there are different overt responses given by the three groups—the control, English, and octal. The control group gave its ad lib form. The experimental groups gave their various prescribed forms. It is possible, however, to determine the effects of the training by looking at the performance of the three groups when they are returned to the simple testing procedure. Now, the same overt response is required of all subjects—recording the number. As can be seen by examining Fig-

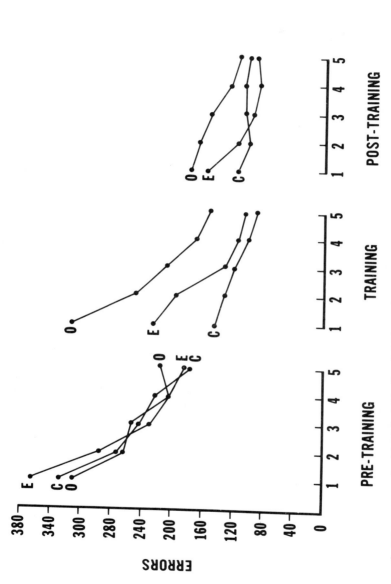

Figure 8. Mean errors for English (E), Octal (O), and Control (C) Groups before, during, and after encoding training.

ure 8, the English group catches up with the control group by the third session of testing and shows somewhat better performance on that day and on subsequent days. The octal group shows the same disadvantage that it suffered during the training session. This disadvantage persists over the five post-training sessions.

We were able to demonstrate an effect of encoding training on performance on the perceptual task. This effect was marked and persistent. The effect was not quite in line with our theoretical expectations. We had expected that the octal, which gave a short code for each stimulus, would be somewhat better than the control and the English somewhat poorer than the control. The reasons for the difficulties that subjects have with the octal probably lie in the specific training procedures. We had, however, been able to change performance in the perceptual task by means of our experimental intervention. In doing this we had made the first step beyond the relation between the column sums for the two underlying data matrices. A number of additional steps are necessary to explore the relation between the two sets of response measures fully. The standard relation—that between the row sums of the two matrices—has not been examined. The effect of encoding training on specific items within the set of stimuli needs to be determined. The reasons for the adverse effect of octal encoding training require further consideration. However, the direction of the work and its theoretical setting are clear.

Summary. In summary, I have considered a general problem that includes individual differences as a special case. The general problem is that of R-R relations. I have outlined some of the requirements of an R-R theory. I have also examined some R-R studies in the area of perception and considered the degree to which these studies met the requirements. I believe that this type of theory is going to play a considerably larger role in psychology than it has in the recent past. I believe that informed and systematic use of this type of theory will permit the handling of complex processes in learning, particularly in perception and cognition.

REFERENCES

Amsel, A., and Roussel, J. Motivational properties of frustration: I. Effect on a running response of the addition of frustration to the motivational complex. *J. exp. Psychol.*, 1952, *43*, 363-368.

Amsel, A., and Ward, J. S. Motivational properties of frustration: II. Frustration drive stimulus and frustration reduction in selective learning. *J. exp. Psychol.*, 1954, *48*, 37-47.

Atkinson, R. C. A Markov model for discrimination learning. *Psychometrika*, 1958, *23*, 308-322.

Bruner, J. S. Personality dynamics and the process of perceiving. In Blake, R. D., and Ramsey, G. V. (eds.), *Perception—An approach to personality*. New York: The Ronald Press Company, 1951, pp. 121-147.

Bruner, J. S., Goodnow, J. J., and Austin, G. A. *A study of thinking*. New York: John Wiley & Sons, Inc., 1956.

Conrad, R. An association between memory errors and errors due to acoustic masking of speech. *Nature*, 1962, *193*, 1314-1315.

Coombs, C. H. *A theory of psychological scaling*. Ann Arbor: University of Michigan Press, 1952. (Engineering Research Institute Bulletin No. 34.)

Estes, W. K. Toward a statistical theory of learning. *Psychol. Rev.*, 1950, *57*, 94-107.

Estes, W. K. The problem of inference from curves based on group data. *Psychol. Bull.*, 1956, *53*, 134-140.

Fleishman, E. A. The description and prediction of perceptual-motor skill learning. In R. Glaser (ed.), *Training research and education*. New York: John Wiley & Sons, Inc., 1965.

Frenkel-Brunswick, E., Levinson, D. J., and Sanford, R. N. The anti-democratic personality. In T. M. Newcomb, and E. L. Hartley (eds.), *Readings in social psychology*. New York: Holt, Rinehart & Winston, Inc., 1947.

Frenkel-Brunswick, E., and Sanford, R. N. Some personality correlates of anti-Semitism. *J. Psychol.*, 1945, *20*, 271-291.

Garner, W. R. *Uncertainty and structure as psychological concepts*. New York: John Wiley & Sons, Inc., 1962.

Glanzer, M. Encoding in the perceptual (visual) serial position effect. *J. verb. Learn. verb. Behav.*, 1966, *5*, 92-97.

Glanzer, M., Chapman, R. M., Clark, W. H., and Bragdon, H. R. Changes in two EEG rhythms during mental activity. *J. exp. Psychol.*, 1964, *68*, 273-282.

Glanzer, M., and Clark, W. H. Accuracy of perceptual recall: An analysis of organization. *J. verb. Learn. verb. Behav.*, 1963a, *1*, 289-299.

Glanzer, M., and Clark, W. H. The verbal loop hypothesis: Binary numbers. *J. verb. Learn. verb. Behav.*, 1963b, *2*, 301-309.

Glanzer, M., and Clark, W. H. The verbal loop hypothesis: Conventional figures. *Amer. J. Psychol.*, 1964, *77*, 621-626.

Goldiamond, I., and Hawkins, W. F. The log relationship between word-frequency and recognition obtained in the absence of stimulus words. *J. exp. Psychol.*, 1958, *56*, 457-463.

Jaensch, E. R. *Eidetic imagery*. New York: Harcourt, Brace & World, Inc., 1930.

Kendler, H. H., and D'Amato, M. F. A comparison of reversal and non-reversal shifts in human concept formation behavior. *J. exp. Psychol.*, 1955, *49*, 165-174.

Lawrence, D. H. Acquired distinctiveness of cues: I. Transfer between discriminations on the basis of familiarity with the stimulus. *J. exp. Psychol.*, 1949, *39*, 770-784.

Lawrence, D. H. Acquired distinctiveness of cues: II. Selective association in a constant stimulus situation. *J. exp. Psychol.*, 1950, *40*, 175-188.

McGinnies, E. Emotionality and perceptual defense. *Psychol. Rev.*, 1949, *56*, 244-251.

Messick, S., and Damarin, F. Cognitive styles and memory for faces. *J. abnorm. soc. Psychol.*, 1964, *69*, 313-319.

Miller, N. E. Studies of fear as an acquirable drive: I. Fear as motivation and fear reduction as reinforcement in the learning of new responses. *J. exp. Psychol.*, 1948, *38*, 89-101.

Mowrer, O. H. On the dual nature of learning: A reinterpretation of "conditioning" and "problem-solving." *Harv. educ. Rev.*, 1947, *17*, 102-148.

Mowrer, O. H. *Learning theory and behavior*. New York: John Wiley & Sons, Inc., 1960.

Postman, L., Bruner, J. S., and McGinnies, E. Personal values as selective factors in perception. *J. abnorm. soc. Psychol.*, 1948, *43*, 142-154.

Restle, F. A theory of discrimination learning. *Psychol. Rev.*, 1955, *62*, 11-19.

Schoenfeld, W. N., and Cumming, W. W. Behavior and perception. In Koch, Sigmund (ed.), *Psychology: A study of a science*. Vol. 5. New York: McGraw Hill Book Company, 1963, pp. 213-252.

Sidman, M. A note on functional relations obtained from group data. *Psychol. Bull.*, 1952, *49*, 263-269.

Sidman, M. *Tactics of scientific research.* New York: Basic Books, Inc., Publishers, 1960.

Solomon, R. L., and Howes, D. S. Word frequency, personal values and visual duration thresholds. *Psychol. Rev.*, 1951, *58*, 256-270.

Spence, K. W. The nature of theory construction in contemporary psychology. *Psychol. Rev.*, 1944, *51*, 47-68.

Sperling, G. The information available in brief visual presentations. *Psychol. Monogr.*, 1960, *74* (Whole No. 498).

Sperling, G. A model for visual memory tasks. *Human factors*, 1963, *5*, 19-31.

Vanderplas, J. M., and Blake, R. R. Selective sensitization in auditory perception. *J. Pers.*, 1949, *18*, 252-266.

Witkin, H. A., Lewis, H. B., Hertzman, M., Machover, K., Meissner, P. B., and Wapner, S. *Personality through perception.* New York: Harper & Row, Publishers, 1954.

Wyckoff, L. B., Jr. The role of observing responses in discrimination behavior. *Psychol. Rev.*, 1952, *59*, 431-442.

PERCEPTUAL EXPERIMENTS AND PROCESS THEORY

PAUL M. FITTS
University of Michigan

Dr. Glanzer's paper is one of several offered at this conference which approach the topic from the viewpoint of process theory, using experimental data and method. Thus, I feel at home in discussing it.

Perhaps the broadest implication of the paper is that process or R-R theory should point the way to productive experimentation on training and individual differences. I believe it does. In fact it should indicate where and even to what extent training can modify these processes, and perhaps where individual differences should be most prominent.

I shall begin with some comments on the experiment which Dr. Glanzer reports. This experiment illustrates not only the opportunities for studying some of the relations between training, individual differences, and perception, but some of the difficulties.

Glanzer's Experiment in Relation to Process Theory

Let me begin by examining the experiment in the light of Dr. Glanzer's requirements that "a psychological theory . . . should be a specification of a process," as illustrated schematically in Figure 7. I want now to engage in a detailed consideration of what this notion implies for the particular experiment which he reports. I believe Glanzer would agree that the task which he required of subjects, that of perceiving and reporting a nine-unit binary number, is properly described as a *perceptual-plus-memory* process. Recent experimental work on short-term memory clearly emphasizes the difficulty or impossibility of separating perceptual and memory processes. Consider, for example, the relative improvement in memory for selected items that is found when the experimenter uses a post-stimulus cueing technique. This provides clear evidence that subjects often perceive and store temporarily more information than they ever report in a conventional memory-span or span-of-perception experiment which uses the method of complete stimulus reproduction as employed by Glanzer. *If* it is granted that we are dealing in part here with a memory process, and it is hypothesized, as Glanzer does, that binary numbers may be remembered better if they are transformed into some other form of verbal code before they are put into short-term memory, *then* the experimental method used in testing the hypothesis should be examined in terms of what is known about short-term memory processes as well as in terms of the hypothesized coding processes. I refer especially to the short time ($\frac{1}{2}$ sec.) during which the nine-unit stimulus was available for direct visual inspection by Glanzer's subjects. I assume that $\frac{1}{2}$ second is not sufficient time for the stimulus coding process and thus that we are dealing with a supra-span task. Recent work by Yntema (1964), for example, indicates clearly that when stimuli are presented successively at high rates, such as ten per second, short-term memory is much worse than it is for slower rates of stimulus presentation. This leads to the hypothesis that a comparison of different verbal recoding procedures should be very sensitive to or interact with stimulus exposure duration. Furthermore, the recoding procedure required by a set of binary symbols may require more time than many other recoding processes. Generalizing from choice reaction time data, for example, I estimate that it should require more than a second to translate a nine-unit binary into a three-unit octal number; thus, whether or not this recoding process can be accomplished at all may depend on whether the proximal stimulus remains available (visible) for a second or more. In summary, it seems to me that the series of binary symbols used here places a special burden on *memory process* as contrasted with the load placed on the initial sensory and perceptual process.

My second comment on the experiment has to do with another aspect of its relevance to Glanzer's general emphasis on S-R-R processes. I have a strong belief in the importance of manipulating experimentally not only the properties of the proximal stimulus but also of the overt responses in studies of perceptual processes. Perhaps I am old-fashioned in this respect. However, I agree with many of the old "motor theories" of perception, such as those expressed by Margaret

Floy Washburn in her book on "Movement and Mental Imagery" (1916), and in early distinctions, such as those of McComas (1911), between types of perceivers in terms of their use of *visual, auditory,* or *proprioceptive* encoding of memory images. I agree especially with the emphasis which early introspective psychology placed on feedback processes (or "backlash" as it was often called) as a factor in perceptual and memory processes. Further I assume that the perception of the stimulus depends in part on what responses are to be made to the stimulus information. Therefore, I would like to complicate Glanzer's model of a perceptual process by introducing at least one additional feedback loop, that from the response to the translation and storage process, and I would suggest that experimental tests of the theory should include variations in the response code used by subjects, along with the variations in stimulus codes and in the kinds of training in verbal recoding which were used in the present experiment. Let me offer two examples as illustrations. I would predict, on several grounds, that perception of a nine-unit binary visual stimulus, such as that used here, might be greatly facilitated by use of a 3 × 3 matrix (such as has recently been studied by Garner and Lee, 1962), for example,

$$1 \ 0 \ 0$$
$$0 \ 1 \ 0$$
$$1 \ 0 \ 1$$

One rationale is that the internal structure of such a pattern (presumably) can more readily be perceived and recoded into groups for short-term memory than is the case when a horizontal array of nine symbols is presented. In a like vein, I would predict that the performance of subjects should change significantly as different response modes are used, such as vocal responses which are "matched" to the verbal recoding process. For example, octal encoding for short-term memory should result in enhanced performance when subjects are permitted to respond in octal code rather than having to translate back into decimal code.

Both of the preceding comments illustrate, I believe, how process theory can influence the planning and interpretation of studies of perception, such as training in stimulus recoding. They also emphasize the importance of the old habits of perceiving and coding which subjects bring to the experiment.

One other aspect of the method used in the experiment strikes me as very relevant to the general theory. It is the use of five uniform "pretraining" sessions for all subjects followed by the use of three special and different training procedures. First, the control group may have simply continued to use the same recoding processes during the training session that they were using during pre-training. This may account for their superiority over the subjects who "transferred" to new methods. Second, it might be more directly relevant to the study of individual differences in perception to attempt to find out how individual subjects prefer to code stimuli and then to reinforce or reverse some of these "natural" modes of perceiving and remembering rather than assigning new training methods arbitrarily. I am not sure how this could have been done, but perhaps the data from Glanzer's verbal descriptions could have been used to infer how subjects were encoding the stimuli.

Some General Implications for Theory

Turning to some more general comments on the paper, I believe it should be clear to the audience that I like the theory, but feel that the specific experiment used to illustrate its implications raises more questions than it answers. So, in closing, let me offer some supporting comments about the first part of the paper.

I heartily agree that experimental psychology must eventually deal with the behavior of individuals, and not be satisfied with the prediction of average performance differences among groups. It is encouraging that several new methods for such individual analyses are becoming available. In some of my own work on choice reaction time, for example, I often record up to 1000 responses per hour for a single subject and I routinely analyze behavior in separate blocks of 100 responses, thus obtaining 10 semi-independent data matrices per subject per hour, for several sessions. Work in the area of signal detection theory, such as that conducted by Tanner (1964), makes similar use of intensive studies of individual subjects. So does the work of Melton (1963) on short-term memory, especially studies of recognition memory, and studies of the build-up of interference effects during repeated cycles using similar stimulus materials. In other words, we now have many of the tools needed for the microscopic analysis of psychological processes in individuals, and we are in a position to exploit Glanzer's approach.

I also agree with, and would give even greater emphasis to, Glanzer's point that R-R theory must deal with sequential psychological processes, and I was pleased to see decision models included in the list of examples of promising models of sequential processes. I have personally become very interested of late in such ideas as sequential stimulus sampling, iterative processing of sensory data, successive revision of opinions regarding the state of the world, optional termination of perceptual processes, and other versions of decision-type information processing activities of the individual. Thus, it appears that we now possess not only new methods, but some new theories for undertaking the study of dynamic, sequential psychological processes in individual subjects.

REFERENCES

Garner, W. R., and Lee, W. An analysis of redundancy in perceptual discrimination. *Percept. mot. Skills*, 1962, *15*, 367-388.

McComas, H. C. Some types of attention. *Psychol. Monogr.*, 1911, *13*, No. 55.

Melton, A. W. Implications of short-term memory for a general theory of memory. *J. verb. Learn. verb. Behav.*, 1963, *2*, 1-21.

Tanner, W. P., Jr. Theory of recognition. In J. A. Swets (ed.), *Signal detection and recognition by human observers*. New York: John Wiley & Sons, Inc., 1964.

Washburn, M. F. *Movement and mental imagery*. Boston: Houghton Mifflin Company, 1916.

Yntema, D. B., Wozencraft, F. T., and Klem, L. Immediate serial recall of digits presented at very high rates. Paper read at Annual Meeting, Psychonomics Society, Niagara Falls, Ont., October, 1964.

8

INDIVIDUAL DIFFERENCES AND MOTOR LEARNING

EDWIN A. FLEISHMAN

American Institutes for Research
Washington, D.C.

The purpose of this paper is to review some recent research relating individual differences variables to the learning of motor skills. Specifically, I wish to consider (a) the kinds of individual differences variables which have been investigated in work undertaken by me and several colleagues, (b) some conceptual issues involved in linking individual difference and learning variables together, (c) a methodology which has been developed to study the relationships among these variables, and (d) some findings about motor learning which have emerged from the study of individual differences.

Some Conceptual Issues

Central to our work relating individual differences to learning has been the concept of "abilities." This is the class of individual difference variables around which most of our research has centered. The more traditional approach to the study of learning has been in stimulus-response terms and has focused on the input and output aspects of the learner's behavior. There is, however, an increasing interest in the "mediators" which intervene between stimuli and response (e.g., Osgood, 1953). Our use of the term ability is consistent with what is typically meant by a "mediating process." Psychology is becoming increasingly concerned with such mediating processes of behavior and, in fact, the distinction between stimulus and response is less clear than it formerly was. Certainly, there is a transformation that goes on within the organism which results in similar responses to "different" stimuli, and vice versa. While this has always been difficult to deny, the means by which it could be inferred both logically and explicitly has previously presented difficulties.

Abilities are defined by score consistencies among separate performances. In this definition one is not dealing with R-R relationships in Spence's terms (1944), but rather in score consistencies which might be derived from very different R's. We have also been interested in the subsets of stimuli which lead to these relative consistencies between scores. The fact that individuals who do well in Task A also do well in Tasks B and C but not in Tasks D, E, and F indicates, inferentially, a common process involved in performing the first three tasks distinct from the processes involved in the performance on the latter three. To "account for" the observed consistencies, an ability is postulated. Once this has been achieved, further experimental-correlational studies are conducted to sharpen and define the limits and definition of this particular ability.

The ability-skill distinction. To clarify our definition of the term, *ability* refers to a more general trait of the individual which has been inferred from certain response consistencies (e.g., correlations) on certain kinds of tasks. These are fairly enduring traits, which in the adult are relatively difficult to change. Many of these abilities are, of course, themselves a product of learning, and develop at different rates, mainly during childhood and adolescence. Some abilities (e.g., color vision) depend more upon genetic than on learning factors, but most abilities depend on both to some degree. In any case, at a given stage of life, they represent traits or organismic factors which the individual brings with him when he begins to learn a new task. These abilities are related to performances in a variety of human tasks. For example, the fact that spatial-visualization has been found related to performance on such diverse tasks as aerial navigation, blueprint reading, and dentistry, makes this ability somehow more basic.

The term *skill* refers to the level of proficiency on a specific task or limited group of tasks. As the term skill has been used in our work, it is task oriented. When we talk about proficiency in flying an airplane, in operating a turret lathe, or in playing basketball, we are talking about a specific skill. Thus, when we speak of acquiring the skill of operating a turret lathe, we mean that this person has acquired the sequence of responses required by this specific task. The assumption is that the skills involved in complex activities can be described in terms of the more basic abilities. For example, the level of performance a man can attain on a turret lathe may depend on his basic abilities of manual dexterity and motor coordination. However, these same basic abilities may be important to proficiency in other skills as well. Thus, manual dexterity is needed in assembling electrical components and motor coordination is needed to fly an airplane. There are, of course, certain characteristics of skill on which we could elaborate. Thus, most skills involve some (a) spatial-temporal patterning, (b) interaction of responses with input and feedback processes, and (c) learning.

Abilities and skill learning. Implicit in the previous analysis is the important relation between abilities and learning. Thus, individuals with high manual dexterity may more readily learn the specific skill of lathe operation. The mechanism of transfer of training probably operates here. Some abilities may transfer to the learning of a greater variety of specific tasks than others. In our culture, *verbal* abilities are more important in a greater variety of tasks than are some other types of abilities. The individual who has a great many highly developed basic abilities can become proficient at a great variety of specific tasks. The concept of intelligence really refers to a combination of certain basic abilities which contribute to achievement in a wide range of different activities.

In other publications (Fleishman, 1964; Gagné and Fleishman, 1959), I have elaborated an analysis of the development of basic abilities. This included a discussion of their physiological bases, the role of learning, environmental and cultural factors, and evidence on the rate of ability development during the life span. Particularly critical is the notion that basic abilities are relatively enduring traits of the individual. Unless he is subjected to marked environmental changes, a man's basic abilities are not likely to change much once he reaches adulthood. Thus, such abilities are fairly stable attributes of behavior over lengthy periods of time. This probably results from the fact that they have been learned, relearned, and practiced so many times during the individual's lifetime. The mechanism here is probably what we typically call overlearning. Thus, individuals may show no impairment of performance even after lengthy periods of time without practice. Probably, man's abilities are stable because certain kinds of human performances have been practiced in varying degrees throughout an individual's lifetime and have become "overlearned."

Evidence for the stability of these traits comes mainly from cross-sectional studies. It is true that these have limitations, but on the whole their findings are consistent with the notion of stable abilities.

Cross-sectional ability comparisons for ages 17-60 have previously been described (Gagné and Fleishman, 1959). Typically, these curves indicate that no improvement and very little fluctuation in the levels of abilities occur during much of the adult life span. Some decline with age often occurs, but this is true only of some abilities, not all. And the age at which decline begins and the rate of decline varies with the ability. Thus, verbal ability shows virtually no decline, numerical ability declines after age 50, but spatial ability and memory span decline after age 40, the spatial curve dropping more steeply.

Human adults, of course, show marked learning over time in practically any type of specific *skill*. However, according to our conceptualization, the rate of learning and the final level achieved by particular individuals in certain skills are both limited by the basic abilities of these individuals. The fact that these basic abilities are themselves fairly stable permits the making of useful predictions about subsequent performance in specific tasks. For example, knowledge about a person's numerical ability helps one to predict his probable success later on in engineering training. Knowledge about the relevant physical fitness components should help predict performance in complex athletic skills. It is very clear that knowledge about basic abilities makes possible the prediction of subsequent more complex performances. It is also evident that some abilities may be more important late in the course of skills learning, while other abilities are critical early in learning. The idea that basic abilities place limits on later skill proficiency emphasizes the need to develop these abilities in pre-adult life.

The central role of learning in the development of general abilities has been suggested by Ferguson (1954, 1956). Ferguson views abilities as developing through processes of differential transfer and exerting their effects differentially in subsequent learning situations. The stability of abilities in the adult are attributed, in Ferguson's theory, to overlearning. To Ferguson, an ability is analogous to Hull's habit strength. However, in Hull's use of the term (1951), habit strength has reference to changes precisely defined by stimulus-response situations. Ferguson's use of the term *ability* as an intervening variable differs in that it is conceptualized as (a) a limit reached over a large number of trials, and (b) more generally, an intervening variable in a great variety of stimulus-response situations. In this sense, the concept of ability is not unrelated to Harlow's learning sets (1949). Ferguson's important theory is entirely consistent with the notions developed here and, indeed, our work has been influenced by his earlier papers.

Abilities as learning parameters. It is important to note that abilities are defined in terms of what people can do in a broad set of tasks; they can be described operationally in terms of specifiable behavioral measures. Of relevance here is the fact that abilities may be legitimately considered as descriptive parameters in the learning process. This is true since it can be shown that these are characteristics which are associated with skill changes resulting from practice. This point may be illustrated with Figures 9A and 9B taken from Fleishman and Hempel (1955). In Figure 9A are acquisition curves for performance on the Discrimination Reaction Time task where the group has been stratified on the basis of a test of verbal ability. This ability clearly differentiates our two groups early in learning. Figure 9B shows curves for the same group when stratified on an independent measure of their reaction time obtained previously. Here it is clear that larger differences occur later in learning as a function of this ability variable. The discovery of the importance of these two ability variables was originally accomplished by a factor analysis of the correlations among ability measures and practice-task measures (Fleishman and Hempel,

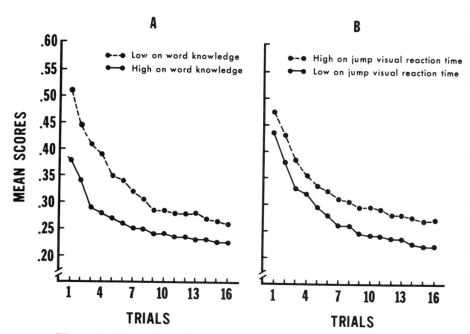

Figure 9. Comparison of Discrimination Reaction Time acquisition curves for groups stratified on different ability test variables. Data from Fleishman and Hempel (1955).

1955). The factor loadings of the practice-task measures on the verbal and reaction-time factors revealed the importance of individual differences in "verbal ability" early and "reaction time" late in the degree of improvement on the Discrimination Reaction Time task. This, in turn, suggested what would happen if the group were to be stratified on representative measures of these abilities.

Abilities and an information-processing model of human learning. The ability-skill paradigm and the experimental results based on it is consistent with an information-processing model of human learning. Abilities can be thought of as "capacities for utilizing different kinds of information." Thus, individuals who are especially good at using certain types of spatial information, make rapid progress in the early stages of learning certain kinds of motor tasks (see, e.g., Fleishman and Hempel, 1954, 1956), while individuals sensitive to proprioceptive cues do better in tasks requiring precise motor control (Fleishman and Rich, 1963).

Abilities as constructs. Abilities, as we refer to them, have the status of constructs. It is assumed that traits exist in people, and that it is these one must attempt to understand. The ability construct represents the psychologist's synthesis of the available facts, and his current best understanding of them. Loevinger (1957) has recently clarified many of these distinctions and has extended the earlier thinking of McCorquodale and Meehl (1948) and Cronbach and Meehl (1955).

Abilities and faculties. The criticism is sometimes made that ability factors are like the faculties of the old faculty psychology. In some sense this is true, but with important differences. Factors are not products of armchair thinking. They are rigorously defined; they are empirically determined; and they are subject to verification in repeated studies. Factors cannot be identified unless there are concomitant variations in people which point to common processes. Furthermore, there appear to be many more ability factors than the faculty psychologists were willing to postulate.

Abilities and transfer. In 1901, Thorndike and Woodworth presented evidence against the then traditional doctrine of formal discipline. The general emphasis thereafter was on the learning of specific stimulus-response bonds. Subsequent work on transfer effects indicate this to be much too specific a view. The search for such "identical elements" has not resulted in evidence of much help in predicting transfer.

Retreat from an extreme specifistic view of transfer has been made possible by the concepts of stimulus and response generalization. As a result, the term "similarity" has replaced the term "identity"; however, the dimensions of similarity still remain largely unspecified. In other contexts, it is recognized that similarity applies to such things as sets, methods, meanings, organizations, and principles. Nevertheless, in learning research it is usually restricted to similarity as represented by some physical scale such as size, shape, brightness, etc. The pendulum seems to be swinging back to a general theory of transfer in a modified formal discipline form.

Guilford (1958) has pointed out that the lack of transfer demonstrated between memory tasks may be "explained" by the fact that memory is not a unitary ability. Many transfer studies are carried out with tasks requiring an unspecified set of abilities. It is possible to conceive of "identical elements" as including the common abilities required by the learner to perform the tasks in question.

The requirement of stability and generality. It is important to emphasize that the demonstration of individual differences along a particular variable in a particular experiment is not sufficient. Individual differences variables refer to traits within the individual which have some *stability* and *generality*. Thus, it is meaningless to say that "susceptibility to associative interference" is an individual difference variable, just because one can show differences among subjects in such a measure in a single experiment. One would still need to show that it is the same individuals who show such effects with a variety of different tasks. Lewis and his associates (1953) have tried in vain in many ingenious ways to identify such a trait. It may be that the same individuals show these effects in a given range of tasks, but not in others. This is nothing new to the differential psychologist, and represents the factor-analytic approach when properly applied. Such findings make it possible to better define the limits and generality of the individual difference variable, whose interaction with treatment effects are to be investigated. In the case of "associative interference," we have only recently been able to show that these effects can be explained in terms of ability-task interactions (Fleishman and Ellison, unpublished).

It should also be pointed out that while "ability variables" as defined above are important in our work, there are other kinds of individual difference variables (e.g., motivational, personality) which have been investigated, some of which will be described later.

Tasks, tests, and measures. There is an emotional block which sometimes occurs when the experimental psychologist is confronted with the word "test." Tests are perceived as psychometric devices useful mainly to the applied psychologist. Certain kinds of tests can be thought of as highly standardized stimulus materials, about which much is known regarding reliability, difficulty, practice effects, variability, and factor loading. How many experimental psychologists know so much about their experimental materials? The critical point, of course, is the manner in which such materials are used, the constructs they are developed to represent, and the experimental contexts in which they are employed.

What is learned through the arrangements of the experimental conditions and through the response measures obtained from subjects is something about a set of functional relationships, making possible an inference about the human processes involved. This is no less true in the study of human abilities in other areas.

Developing a Taxonomy of Human Motor Abilities

Our studies of individual differences in abilities and learning has proceeded on several fronts. First, it appeared necessary to develop a taxonomy, a classification system for describing human motor abilities. The extent to which research results can be generalized may, in some measure, depend on the development of an adequate taxonomy. This is also needed to assist in the standardization of experimental tasks. The second line of research we undertook attempted to relate the ability variables thus defined to performance at different stages of learning more complex tasks and to variations in the conditions of learning.

Perhaps a not too extreme statement is that most of the categorization of human skills which is empirically based, comes from correlational and factor-analysis studies. Many of these studies in the literature are ill-designed or not designed at all. This does not rule out the fact that properly designed, systematic programmatic correlational research can yield highly useful data about general skill dimensions. Such categories can be thought of as representing empirically derived patterns of *response consistencies* to task requirements varied in systematic ways. In a sense this approach describes tasks in terms of the common abilities required to perform them.

An example is provided by the term "tracking," a frequent behavioral category employed by laboratory and systems psychologists alike. There is a wide variety of different tasks in which some kinds of tracking are involved. Can one assume that the behavioral category of tracking is useful in making it possible to generalize results from one such situation to another? Is there a general tracking ability? Are individuals who are good at compensatory tracking also the ones who are good at pursuit tracking? Do people who are good at positional tracking also do well with velocity or acceleration controls? What happens to the correlations between performances as a function of such variations? It is to these kinds of questions that our program of research has been directed.

In subsequent years, my colleagues and I have conducted a whole series of interlocking experimental-factor-analytic studies, attempting to isolate and identify the common variance in a wide range of psychomotor performances. Essentially this is laboratory research in which tasks are specifically designed or selected to test certain hypotheses about the organization of abilities in a certain range of tasks. Other studies have introduced task variations aimed at sharpening or limiting our ability factor definitions. The purpose has been to define the fewest independent ability categories which might be most useful and meaningful in describing performance in the widest variety of tasks.

Our first study (Fleishman, 1953b) reviewed previous factor analyses of motor skills and described the methodological issues. Our second study (Fleishman, 1954) was a large-scale attempt to put into a single study representative measures of factors previously identified. The purpose of this study, which involved more than 40 carefully designed psychomotor tests, was to (a) better define previously identified factors, (b) test the usefulness of certain printed measures of psychomotor abilities, and (c) to attempt to account for variance in tests used to select pilots in the Air Force program. In short, the study confirmed most of the hypothesized factors and resulted in better definitions of these factors. But there were some exceptions and new discoveries. We also showed that printed tests are not too successful in reproducing variance in apparatus tasks, and we failed to identify the variance in the complex Air Force tests. For this latter source of individual variation, we had to look elsewhere.

Our later studies have included analyses of fine manipulative performances (e.g., finger and manual dexterity, etc.), (Fleishman and Hempel, 1954a and Fleishman and Ellison, 1962) and gross physical proficiency (e.g., pushups, chins, etc.), (Hempel and Fleishman, 1955; Nicks and Fleishman, 1960; Fleishman, Kremer, and Shoup, 1961; Fleishman, Thomas, and Munroe, 1961; and Fleishman, 1964). One study focused on positioning movements (reaching, moving controls to specified positions, etc.) and "static reactions" (e.g., hand steadiness), (Fleishman, 1958a). The former concerns movements in which the terminal accuracy of the response is critical, and the latter involves, primarily, maintenance of limb positions (see Brown and Jenkins, 1947). An important series of studies (Fleishman, 1956; Fleishman, 1958b; and Parker and Fleishman, 1960) concerns "movement reactions," where the performance involves coordinated responses, or smooth responses, or precisely controlled movements, or continuously adjustive reactions.

Thus far, we have investigated more than 200 different tasks administered to thousands of subjects in a series of interlocking studies. From the patterns of correlations obtained, we have been able to account for performance on this wide range of tasks in terms of a relatively small number of abilities. In subsequent investigations, our definitions of these abilities and their distinctions from one another have become more clearly delineated. Furthermore, it is now possible to specify the tasks which should provide the best measure of each of the abilities identified.

Some of the important individual differences variables that have been revealed in this series of investigations to be of possible usefulness in analytic studies of learning are listed as follows. For details on their definition and the devices which best measure them, the reader is referred to other publications (Fleishman, 1958b, 1962, 1964).

Control precision. This factor is common to tasks which require fine, highly controlled, but not overcontrolled, muscular adjustments, primarily where larger muscle groups are involved (Fleishman, 1958b; Fleishman and Hempel, 1956; Parker and Fleishman, 1960). This ability extends to arm-hand as well as to leg movements. It is most critical where such adjustments must be rapid, but precise.

Multilimb coordination. This is the ability to coordinate the movements of a number of limbs simultaneously, and is best measured by devices involving multiple controls (Fleishman, 1958b; Fleishman and Hempel, 1956; Parker and Fleishman, 1960). The factor has been found general to tasks requiring coordination of the two feet (e.g., the Rudder Control Test), two hands (e.g., the Two Hand Pursuit and Two Hand Coordination Tests), and hands and feet (e.g., the Plane Control and Complex Coordination Tests).

Response orientation. This ability factor has been found general to visual discrimination reaction psychomotor tasks involving rapid directional discrimination and orientation of movement patterns (Fleishman, 1957a, 1957b, 1958b; Fleishman and Hempel, 1956; Parker and Fleishman, 1960). It appears to involve the ability to *select* the correct movement in relation to the correct stimulus, especially under highly speeded conditions.

Reaction time. This represents simply the speed with which the individual is able to respond to a stimulus when it appears (Fleishman, 1954, 1958b; Fleishman and Hempel, 1955; Parker and Fleishman, 1960). There are consistent indications that individual differences in this ability are independent of whether the stimulus is auditory or visual and are also independent of the type of response which is required. However, once the stimulus situation or the response situation is complicated by involving alternate choices, reaction time is not the primary factor that is measured.

Speed of arm movement. This represents simply the speed with which an individual can make a gross, discrete arm movement where accuracy is not the requirement (Fleishman, 1958b; Fleishman and Hempel, 1954b, 1955; Parker and Fleishman, 1960). There is ample evidence that this factor is independent of the reaction-time factor.

Rate control. This ability involves the making of continuous anticipatory motor adjustments relative to changes in speed and direction of a continuously moving target or object (Fleishman, 1958b; Fleishman and Hempel, 1955, 1956). This factor is general to tasks involving compensatory as well as following pursuit, and extends to tasks involving responses to changes in rate. Our research has shown that adequate measurement of this ability requires an actual response in relation to the changing direction and speed of the stimulus object, and not simply a judgment of the rate of stimulus movement alone.

Manual dexterity. This ability involves skillful, well directed arm-hand movements in manipulating fairly large objects under speeded conditions (Fleishman, 1953b, 1954; Fleishman and Hempel, 1954b; Fleishman and Ellison, 1962; Parker and Fleishman, 1960; Hempel and Fleishman, 1955).

Finger dexterity. This is the ability to make skill-controlled manipulations of tiny objects involving, primarily, the fingers (Fleishman, 1953b, 1954; Fleishman and Hempel, 1954a; Parker and Fleishman, 1960; Hempel and Fleishman, 1955; Fleishman and Ellison, 1962).

Arm-hand steadiness. This is the ability to make precise arm-hand positioning movements where strength and speed are minimized; the critical feature, as the name implies, is the steadiness with which such movements can be made (Fleishman, 1953b, 1954, 1958a, 1958b; Fleishman and Hempel, 1955; Hempel and Fleishman, 1955; Parker and Fleishman, 1960).

Wrist, finger speed. This ability has been called "tapping" in many previous studies through the years (Greene, 1943; Fleishman, 1953b). It has been used in a variety of different studies, primarily because these are in the form of printed tests which are quick and easy to administer. However, our research shows that this factor is highly restricted in scope and does not extend to many tasks in which apparatus is used (Fleishman, 1954; Fleishman and Ellison, 1962; Fleishman and Hempel, 1954a). It has been found that the factor is best measured by printed tests requiring rapid tapping of the pencil in relatively large areas.

Aiming. This ability appears to be measured by printed tests which provide the subject with very small circles to be dotted in where there are a large number of circles when the test is highly speeded (Fleishman, 1953b, 1954; Fleishman and Ellison, 1962; Hempel and Fleishman, 1955). The subject typically goes from circle to circle placing one dot in each circle as rapidly as possible. This factor has not been found to extend to apparatus tests; hence, the naming of this factor as "aiming" or as other investigators have called it, "eye-hand coordination," seems much too broad.

Before closing our discussion of the classification of motor abilities, we should refer to the area of motor performance often called *physical proficiency*. Our experimental-factor analytical work indicates the following factors account for performance in more than sixty different physical fitness tests. (For details, see Fleishman, 1964; this reference also indicates the tests most diagnostic of each factor.)

Extent flexibility. Ability to flex or stretch the trunk and back muscles *as far as possible* in either a forward, lateral, or backward direction.

Dynamic flexibility. The ability to make repeated, *rapid* flexing movements in which the resiliency of the muscles in *recovery* from strain or distortion is critical.

Static strength. The maximum *force* which a subject can exert, for a brief period, where the force is exerted continuously up to this maximum. In contrast to other strength factors, this is the force which can be exerted against external objects (e.g., lifting heavy weights, pulling against a dynamometer), rather than in supporting or propelling the body's own weight.

Dynamic strength. The ability to exert muscular force repeatedly or continuously over time. It represents muscular endurance and emphasizes the resistance of the muscles to fatigue. The common emphasis of tests measuring this factor is on the power of the muscles to propel, support, or move the body repeatedly or to support it for prolonged periods.

Trunk strength. This is a second, more limited, dynamic strength factor specific to the trunk muscles, particularly the abdominal muscles.

Gross body coordination. Ability to coordinate the simultaneous actions of different parts of the body while making gross body movements.

Gross body equilibrium. The ability of an individual to maintain his equilibrium, despite forces pulling him off balance, where he has to depend mainly on non-visual (e.g., vestibular and kinesthetic) cues. Although also measured by balance tests where the eyes are kept open, it is best measured by balance tests conducted with the eyes closed.

Stamina. The capacity to continue maximum effort, requiring prolonged exertion over time. This factor has the alternate name of "cardiovascular endurance."

The specification of an individual difference variable is an arduous and exacting task. The definition of the rate control factor may provide an example. In early studies it was found that this factor was common to compensatory as well as to following pursuit tasks. To test its generality, tasks were developed to emphasize rate control, which were not conventional tracking tasks (e.g., controlling a ball rolling through a series of alleyways). The factor was found to extend to such tasks. Later studies attempted to discover if the primary emphasis in this ability is in judging the rate of the stimulus as distinguished from ability to respond at the appropriate rate. A task was developed involving only a button-pressing response, based upon judgments of moving stimuli. Performance on this task did not correlate with other rate control tasks. Finally, several motion-picture tasks were adapted in which the subject was required to extrapolate the course of a plane moving across a screen. The only response required was marking an IBM answer sheet. These tasks did not relate to the core of tasks previously found to measure "rate control." Accordingly, our definition of this ability was expanded to include measures beyond pursuit tasks, but restricted to tasks requiring a muscular adjustment to the stimulus change.

A similar history can be sketched for each ability variable identified. Thus, we know that the subject must have a feedback indicator of how well he is coordinating before the multilimb coordination factor is measured; we know that in complicating a simple reaction time apparatus by providing additional choice reactions, we measure a separate factor (Response Orientation), but that varying the stimulus modality in a simple reaction-time device does not result in measurement of a separate factor.

The development of stable and reliable measures of individual difference variables will continue to be an arduous task requiring much additional systematic work. The factors described here do not represent any kind of final list of individual psychomotor ability variables. But they do provide our current best evidence on recurrent ability factors, and it is notable that we have not been able to add to this list in our later studies of task intercorrelations. In other words, these factors continue to account for individual differences in a wide range of tasks. It may be mentioned that these categories have also proven useful in accounting for the interrelations among component proficiencies in such practical skills as piloting fixed-wing aircraft (Fleishman and Ornstein, 1960), and piloting helicopters (Locke, Zavala, and Fleishman, 1965), as well as among driving proficiencies (Herbert, 1963).

A legitimate question here concerns the proportion of common variance that can be accounted for in terms of the relatively small number of abilities identified. It does appear that in the perceptual-motor domain a relatively few abilities are very useful in organizing quite meaningfully a wide variety of performances. This does not mean that there are no more factors to discover. And it does not mean the factors identified account for a large proportion of the variance in every psychomotor task—far from it, as will be seen later. There is much specificity; but the pursuit of the common variance is one of the primary tasks of the psychologist.

Relating Abilities to Skill Acquisition

I turn now to those studies which have related individual differences in abilities to performance at different stages of learning complex skills.

Special interest in these studies has been in predicting eventual high proficiency levels in such skills. These studies have utilized (but have not been confined to) combinations of experimental and factor-analysis designs. As the confidence in our concepts and variables has increased, we have relied more on multiple regression and a variety of experimental approaches. First, let me acknowledge a debt to the earlier study by Adams (1953), and before that, one by Reynolds (1952). Related earlier work by Perl, by Woodrow, and by Edgerton and Valentine has been mentioned in other chapters of this volume. Many of these earlier studies used fairly brief practice periods, paper and pencil tests, and relatively unsophisticated reference measures. Except for Woodrow's, they were not programmatic efforts. We have been fortunate in being able to pursue the general problem in a fairly persistent fashion over the past dozen years.

One of our early studies was confined to the analyses of inter-trial correlations of two similar tasks practiced in different orders (Fleishman, 1953a), but subsequent studies have always included "reference measures," external to the practice task. In a typical study, 200-300 subjects received a battery of reference tests known to sample certain abilities and then received practice on a criterion practice task. Through the use of factor-analysis techniques of the correlation patterns obtained, we could examine the loadings of successive trial scores on the criterion task in the factors defined by the reference tasks.

In general, these studies, using a great variety of practice tasks, show that (a) the particular combinations of abilities contributing to performance changes as practice continues, (b) these changes are progressive and systematic and eventually become stabilized, (c) the contribution of "non-motor" abilities (e.g., verbal, spatial), which may play a role early in learning, decreases systematically with practice, relative to "motor abilities," and (d) there is also an increase in a factor specific to the task itself. Figure 10 illustrates a typical result obtained using a visual discrimination-reaction task.

Although our earlier studies factor-analyzed matrices containing both reference and learning-trial variables, a variety of different approaches have since been used, all confirming these basic findings. Additional designs have used separate cross-sectional analyses of skilled and unskilled psychomotor performances (Fleishman, 1957a), regression techniques in predicting practice trial loadings or reference factors (Parker and Fleishman, 1960; Fleishman and Fruchter, 1960), analyses of interrelations among component and total-task measures at different practice stages (Fleishman, 1965; Fleishman and Fruchter,

1965); and still later work uses straight experimental procedures, as we gain confidence in our individual difference variables (Fleishman and Rich, 1963). It is possible, of course, to represent some of the results shown in Figure 10 in more traditional terms, as has been done earlier in Figure 9.

The repeated finding of an increase in specificity of the tasks learned indicates that performance in perceptual-motor tasks becomes in-

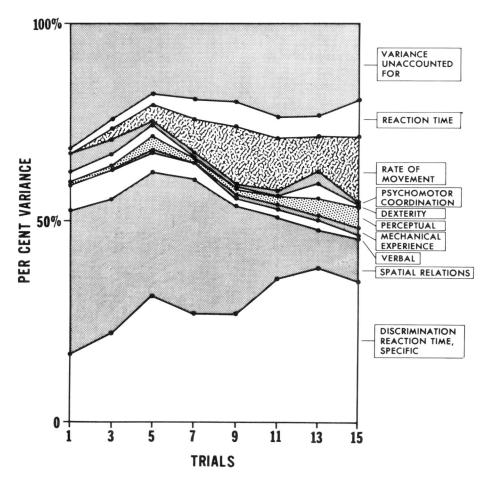

Figure 10. Percentage of variance represented by each factor at different stages of practice on the Discrimination Reaction Time Task. (Percentage of variance is represented by the *area* shaded in for each factor.) After Fleishman and Hempel (1955).

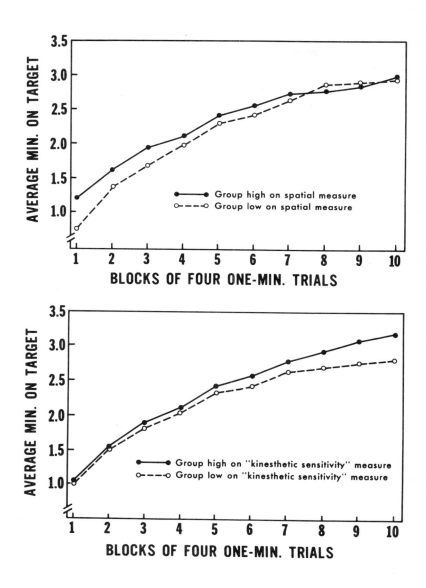

Figure 11. Comparison of Two-Hand Coordination acquisition curves for groups high and low on spatial ability and kinesthetic sensitivity. Data from Fleishman and Rich (1963).

creasingly a function of habits and skills acquired in the task itself. But pre-task abilities play a role, too, and their interactions with learning phenomena are important sources of variance to be studied. Furthermore, it appears desirable to better define the variance now termed specific to individual tasks. I am optimistic that some of this variance is not really "specific"; rather, we may need to be more ingenious at teasing it out.

Much of our later work has been concerned with the pursuit of this variance now defined as specific to late stages of learning tasks. Hypotheses we have explored are that: (a) late stage measures of different practiced tasks have abilities in common not found in early stages of the same tasks (Fleishman, 1957); (b) the ability to integrate component abilities represents a separate individual difference variable not found in early stage learning, but is critical in late stage learning; (c) kinesthetic ability factors play an increasing role in psychomotor learning relative to spatial-visual abilities. Figure 11 shows the confirmation of this latter hypothesis in a recent study (Fleishman and Rich, 1963). In this study we first had to develop a measure of "kinesthetic sensitivity" on which subjects differ reliably. Performance in this measure was a good indicator of late learning in a two-hand coordination task, but not of early learning. In this connection, it is useful to point out that the exploitation of individual differences allowed us to test a principle of motor learning which had only been assumed before. (Fitts, 1951.)

Use of the paradigm in training settings. Lately our findings and methods have been extended to more complex tasks studies over lengthy periods of time. In one study (Parker and Fleishman, 1960), we developed a simulation of an air intercept mission on which subjects learned a highly complex tracking task over a seven-week period. The same 203 subjects received one of the most extensive battery of perceptual-motor and cognitive tests ever assembled. The design allowed for the identification of 15 abilities factors and the specification of their contribution to tracking performance at different stages of learning over this lengthy learning period.

In a later study (Parker and Fleishman, 1961), we attempted to make use of our analytical information about ability requirements of this task, in designing a skill training program. In terms of our integrated error measure of performance during the last three training sessions, the experimental group showed a 39 per cent increase in proficiency over the second best training condition investigated.

We have also studied the relation of ability variables to learning in a reàl training environment (Fleishman and Fruchter, 1960). In this latter case, we were able to identify abilities underlying the acquisition of skill at different stages of Morse Code learning, in an Air Force radio telegraphy school. Specifically, early learning depended on two auditory-perceptual abilities (auditory perceptual speed and auditory rhythm discrimination), and later learning was increasingly a function of "speed of closure," representing an ability to unify or organize an apparently disparate field into meaningful units. This study extended our findings on learning and individual differences to perceptual learning.

Individual differences and part-whole task relationships. A recent study (Fleishman, 1965) investigated the relations between individual differences in performance on task components and subsequent performance on the total task. Two hundred and four subjects practiced the components of a complex multidimensional compensatory pursuit task, singly and in combination. These components involved discrete display-control relationships. The total task, which was practiced last, requires an integration of these components; that is, the subjects must operate the multiple controls in order to minimize error indications on all displays simultaneously. The problems investigated were (a) the extent to which performance on task components, individually practiced, is predictive of subsequent total task performance; (b) the extent to which practice on combinations of components is predictive of total task performance; (c) the interrelationships among component performances; and (d) the relative contribution of various component performances to total and subtask performances. The analysis provided some tentative principles of part-whole task relationships relevant to the understanding of skilled performance. The results pointed up the over-simplification of explanations based on simple S-R concepts. The level of description which provided the "best" explanation of the observed relations among the components and with the total task were in terms of "common ability" requirements.

A related study (Fleishman and Fruchter, 1965) examined the differences in factor structure of two criterion measures (time on target and integrated error) taken from the same task. It was found that individual differences in proficiency, as represented by the factor structure of these scores, differed at different stages of learning. Also demonstrated was the differential contribution of the task components to each kind of total score measure. The study underscores the need to better understand the performance measure selected for study in learning experiments with particular tasks. Both studies indicated how an approach through the study of individual differences could contribute to the understanding of part-whole task relationships.

Individual differences in retention. I should not like to leave the topic of individual differences and skill learning without mentioning our studies on retention (Fleishman and Parker, 1962). Very little is known about individual differences in retention. We were able to give people extended (seven weeks) practice on a highly complex perceptual-motor skill and obtain matched groups of subjects back after periods of no practice of one, four, nine, fourteen, and twenty-four months. Thus, we varied retention intervals, as well as type of initial guidance and level of original learning. The main points of interest in the results of this study are that there was virtually no loss in skill regardless of the length of the retention interval, and that the most powerful variable operating was individual differences in the level of original learning. The prediction of retention from original learning was independent of the length of the retention interval. Thus, for all intervals, even up to two years, individual differences at the end of learning correlated in the .80's and .90's with subsequent performance after periods of no practice. Our design also allowed us to say that this prediction was not accounted for by the subject's pre-task abilities, but rather was explainable in terms of individual differences among subjects in the specific habits acquired in practicing the original task.

Individual differences and other learning phenomena. We have also investigated the relation between individual differences and a variety of learning phenomena, including associative interference and transfer, reminiscence, and performance during massed versus distributed trials (Fleishman and Ellison, unpublished). Space does not permit me to summarize these studies here, except to say that knowledge about the subjects' previously developed abilities helped us predict these phenomena. We also introduced "personality" variables, which were unsuccessful in predicting associative interference, but certain of these measures did predict the performance decrement which occurred during a massed-practice period.

Lewis and associates (1953) were unsuccessful in identifying any general trait of "susceptibility to interference," despite a notable programmatic attempt to do so. The trait was hypothesized to account for variance at the shift points between tasks which reversed the display-control relationships. Our results also failed to identify such a trait, but did indicate why associative interference effects appeared specific to the tasks in question. It appeared that the particular combinations of abilities, measured by external reference tasks which predict such interference effects, depended on the tasks studied. This study also attempted to relate personality variables such as "rigidity-flexibility," "anxiety," and "extroversion" to "associative interference," without success. Since certain of these measures did predict individual differences in decrement during massed practice, we have at least some encouragement. This result confirms earlier work by Eysenck (1960).

Changes in Abilities with Task Requirements

We have obtained other results which indicate that it is possible to build up a body of principles regarding task requirements through systematic studies of ability-task interaction in the laboratory. The approach is to develop tasks which can be varied along specified physical dimensions, to administer these tasks systematically varied along these dimensions, to groups of subjects who also receive a series of "reference" tasks, known to sample certain more generalized abilities (e.g., "spatial orientation," "control precision," certain "cognitive abilities"). Correlations between individual differences on these reference tasks and scores on variations of the criterion task specify the ability requirements (and changes in these requirements) as a function of task variations.

In several studies (e.g., Fleishman, 1956) we have been able to show systematic changes in the abilities required to perform certain tasks, as the display-control relations in these tasks were systematically varied. In one task, the subject was required to press a button within a circular arrangement of buttons on the response panel, in response to a light which appeared in a circular arrangement of lights on the display panel. In all cases subjects received a battery of reference measures prior to experiencing the task manipulations. Progressive rotations of the display panel were shown to change the ability requirements of the task from "perceptual speed" to two other factors, "spatial orientation" and "response orientation" (Table 11). Thus, individual differences along known dimensions were used to explore the relations between tasks and the characteristics of people who could perform the tasks most effectively. Of course, these are problems faced every day by personnel, engineering, and systems psychologists as well.

Other task dimensions which have been varied in certain of our studies include: the predictability or non-predictability of target course or response requirements; the extent to which the task allows the subject to assess the degree of coordination of multiple-limb responses; the degree of stimulus-response compatibility in display-control relationships; whether there is a constant "set" or changing "set" from one stimulus presentation to the next; whether or not certain kinds of additional response requirements are imposed in a visual discrimination reaction task; whether or not certain kinds of feedback are provided.

TABLE 11

FACTOR LOADINGS OF RESPONSE MEASURES FOR DIFFERENT CONDITIONS OF DISPLAY ROTATION[a]

	Factor		
Display Rotation	*Perceptual Speed*	*Response Orientation*	*Spatial Orientation*
0° (↟)	.47	—	—
45° (↗)	.40	—	.34
90° (→)	—	—	.69
135° (↘)	—	.37	.48
180° (↓)	—	.40	.40
225° (↙)	—	.30	.35
270° (←)	—	—	.30
315° (↖)	.36	—	—

[a]From Fleishman, E. A. (1957). Loadings below .30 omitted.

The results of such studies have shown that certain variations did make a difference in what abilities were measured, but others did not. Hopefully, a program of such research should make it possible to look at new tasks, operational or otherwise, and specify the ability requirements.

The Problem of Task Standardization

Are ability categories, derived in the manner described, useful as a means of task standardization and for generalizing research results to new tasks? At present no ready answer is available, but the problem is being worked on. Let me at least mention a few studies in which tasks designed to represent generalizable task dimensions have been used. These studies have included research on the effects of stress or fear (Gorham and Orr, 1957), diet (Brozek *et al.*, 1955), and drugs (Elkin, Freedle, Van Cott and Fleishman, 1965). Recently, we (Parker *et al.*, 1965) developed a console to provide measures of independent perceptual-motor factors for evaluating effects of the space environment.

In our drug work we hope to make an approach to checking on the generalizations possible from standardized tasks. We are observing the effects of a variety of drugs and dosages on measures of a variety of reference measures. These measures sample the perceptual, motor, sensory, and cognitive areas. We are getting differential effects; that is, some abilities within each area are more affected than others by drug administrations. The question is whether we get parallel results with other tasks representing the same factors. A further phase of the work includes the development of complex tasks and the testing of these drug effects on such tasks. The question is whether our laboratory results, using component ability measures, could have predicted the drug effect on the complex tasks.

Melton and others have underscored the lack of task standardization in learning research. It remains to be seen whether an approach which defines tasks in terms of abilities required to perform them, can provide an avenue to such standardization.

Concluding Statement

In this chapter I have attempted to show how certain classes of individual differences can be studied to gain insights into perceptual-motor learning. The subjects' pre-task abilities become major treatment variables with significant interactions with learning trials and with other learning phenomena. I have tried to show some of the problems which need to be faced, some of the strategies and methods which have been used, and have described the kinds of individual difference variables found useful so far. I have also emphasized many unresolved questions.

It appears to me that there is much to be gained in the study of individual differences and learning, within the same conceptual framework, through combinations of correlational and experimental methods.

REFERENCES

Adams, J. A. *The prediction of performance at advanced stages of training on a complex psychomotor task.* Lackland Air Force Base, Texas: USAF Research Center, 1953. Research Bulletin 53-49.

Brown, J. S., and Jenkins, W. O. An analysis of human motor abilities related to the design of equipment and a suggested program of research. In P. M. Fitts (ed.), *Psychological research on equipment design.* AAF Aviation Psychology Research Report No. 19. Washington, D. C.: Government Printing Office, 1947.

Brozek, J., Fleishman, E. A., Harris, S., Lassman, F. M., and Vidal, J. H. Sensory functions and motor performance during maintenance of survival rations. *Amer. Psychologist,* 1955, *10,* 502.

Cronbach, L. J., and Meehl, P. E. Construct validity in psychological tests. *Psychol. Bull.,* 1955, *52,* 281-302.

Elkin, E. H., Freedle, R. O., Van Cott, H. P., and Fleishman, E. A. *Effects of drugs on human performance: The effects of scopolamine on representative human performance tests.* Washington, D. C.: American Institutes for Research, 1965.

Eysenck, H. J. *Experiments in personality.* London: Routledge and Kegan Paul, 1960.

Ferguson, G. A. On learning and human ability. *Canad. J. Psychol.,* 1954, *8,* 95-112.

Ferguson, G. A. On transfer and the abilities of man. *Canad. J. Psychol.,* 1956, *10,* 121-131.

Fitts, P. M. Engineering psychology and equipment design. In S. S. Stevens (ed.), *Handbook of experimental psychology.* New York: John Wiley & Sons, Inc., 1951.

Fleishman, E. A. A factor analysis of intra-task performance on two psychomotor tests. *Psychometrika,* 1953, *18,* 45-55. (a).

Fleishman, E. A. Testing for psychomotor abilities by means of apparatus tests. *Psychol. Bull.,* 1953, *50,* 241-262. (b).

Fleishman, E. A. Dimensional analysis of psychomotor abilities. *J. exp. Psychol.,* 1954, *48,* 437-454.

Fleishman, E. A. Psychomotor selection tests: Research and application in the U. S. Air Force. *Personnel Psychol.,* 1956, *9,* 449-467.

Fleishman, E. A. A comparative study of aptitude patterns in unskilled and skilled psychomotor performances. *J. appl. Psychol.,* 1957, *41,* 263-272.

Fleishman, E. A. Factor structure in relation to task difficulty in psychomotor performance. *Educ. psychol. Measmt.,* 1957, *17,* 522-532.

Fleishman, E. A. An analysis of positioning movements and static reactions. *J. exp. Psychol.,* 1958, *55,* 13-24. (a).

Fleishman, E. A. Dimensional analysis of movement reactions. *J. exp. Psychol.,* 1958, *55,* 438-453. (b).

Fleishman, E. A. The description and prediction of perceptual-motor skill learning. In R. Glaser (ed.), *Training research and education*. Pittsburgh: University of Pittsburgh Press, 1962.

Fleishman, E. A. *The structure and measurement of physical fitness*. Englewood Cliffs, New Jersey: Prentice-Hall, Inc., 1964.

Fleishman, E. A. The prediction of total task performance from prior practice on task components. *Human Factors*, 1965, *7*, 18-27.

Fleishman, E. A., and Ellison, G. D. A factor analysis of fine manipulative performance. *J. appl. Psychol.*, 1962, *46*, 96-105.

Fleishman, E. A., and Fruchter, B. Factor structure and predictability of successive stages of learning Morse Code. *J. appl. Psychol.*, 1960, *44*, 97-101.

Fleishman, E. A., and Fruchter, B. Component and total task relations at different stages of learning a complex tracking task. *Percept. mot. Skills*, 1965, *20*, 1305-1311.

Fleishman, E. A., and Hempel, W. E., Jr. Changes in factor structure of a complex psychomotor test as a function of practice. *Psychometrika*, 1954, *18*, 239-252. (a).

Fleishman, E. A., and Hempel, W. E., Jr. A factor analysis of dexterity tests. *Personnel Psychol.*, 1954, *7*, 15-32. (b).

Fleishman, E. A., and Hempel, W. E., Jr. The relation between abilities and improvement with practice in a visual discrimination reaction task. *J. exp. Psychol.*, 1955, *49*, 301-312.

Fleishman, E. A., and Hempel, W. E., Jr. Factorial analysis of complex psychomotor performance and related skills. *J. appl. Psychol.*, 1956, *40*, 96-104.

Fleishman, E. A., Kremer, E. J., and Shoup, G. W. *The dimensions of physical fitness—A factor analysis of strength tests*. New Haven: Yale University, 1961. Office of Naval Research Contract Nonr 609(32), Technical Report No. 2.

Fleishman, E. A., and Ornstein, G. N. An analysis of pilot flying performance in terms of component abilities. *J. appl. Psychol.*, 1960, *44*, 146-155.

Fleishman, E. A., and Parker, J. F. Factors in the retention and relearning of perceptual-motor skill. *J. exp. Psychol.*, 1962, *64*, 215-226.

Fleishman, E. A., and Rich, S. Role of kinesthetic and spatial-visual abilities in perceptual-motor learning. *J. exp. Psychol.*, 1963, *66*, 6-11.

Fleishman, E. A., Thomas, P., and Munroe, P. *The dimensions of physical fitness—A factor analysis of speed, flexibility, balance, and coordination tests.* New Haven: Yale University, 1961. Office of Naval Research Contract Nonr 609(32), Technical Report No. 3.

Gagné, R. M., and Fleishman, E. A. *Psychology and human performance: An introduction to psychology.* New York: Holt, Rinehart & Winston, Inc., 1959.

Gorham, W. A., and Orr, D. G. *Research on behavior impairment due to stress.* Washington, D.C.: American Institutes for Research, 1957.

Greene, E. B. An analysis of random and systematic changes with practice. *Psychometrika,* 1943, 8, 37-53.

Guilford, J. P. Psychological measurement. In G. Seward and J. Seward (eds.), *Current psychological issues.* New York: Holt, Rinehart & Winston, Inc., 1958.

Harlow, H. F. The formation of learning sets. *Psychol. Rev.,* 1949, 56, 51-65.

Hempel, W. E., Jr., and Fleishman, E. A. A factor analysis of physical proficiency and manipulative skill. *J. appl. Psychol.,* 1955, 39, 12-16.

Herbert, M. J. Analysis of a complex skill: Vehicle driving. *Human Factors,* 1963, 5, 363-372.

Hull, C. L. *Essentials of behavior.* New Haven: Yale University Press, 1951.

Lewis, D., McAllister, E. E., and Bechtoldt, H. P. Correlational study of performance during successive phases of practice on the standard and reversed tasks on the SAM complex coordinator. *J. Psychol.,* 1953, 36, 111-126.

Locke, E. A., Zavala, A., and Fleishman, E. A. Studies of helicopter pilot performance: II. The analysis of task dimensions. *Human Factors,* 1965, 7, 285-302.

Loevinger, J. Objective tests as instruments of psychological theory. *Psychol. Rep.,* 1957, 3, 635-694.

McCorquodale, K., and Meehl, P. E. On a distinction between hypothetical constructs and intervening variables. *Psychol. Rev.,* 1948, 55, 95-107.

Nicks, D. C., and Fleishman, E. A. *What do physical fitness tests measure?—A review of factor-analytic studies.* New Haven: Yale University, 1960. Office of Naval Research Contract Nonr 609(32), Technical Report No. 1.

Osgood, C. E. *Method and theory in experimental psychology.* New York: Oxford University Press, Inc., 1953.

Parker, J. F., and Fleishman, E. A. Ability factors and component performance measures as predictors of complex tracking behavior. *Psychol. Monogr.*, 1960, *74* (Whole No. 503).

Parker, J. F., and Fleishman, E. A. Use of analytical information concerning task requirements to increase the effectiveness of skill training. *J. appl. Psychol.*, 1961, *45*, 295-302.

Parker, J. F., Reilly, R. E., Dillon, R. F., Andrews, T. G., and Fleishman, E. A. *Development of tests for measurement of primary perceptual-motor performance.* Washington, D.C.: Biotechnology, Inc., 1965. NASA Contractor Report CR-335.

Reynolds, B. The effect of learning on the predictability of psychomotor performance. *J. exp. Psychol.*, 1952, *44*, 189-198.

Spence, K. W. Nature of theory construction in contemporary psychology, *Psychol. Rev.*, 1944, *51*, 47-68.

9

THE RELATION OF
IQ AND LEARNING[1]

DAVID ZEAMAN and BETTY J. HOUSE
University of Connecticut

The relation of learning and intelligence is a textbook problem of long tradition, but not one marked by clarity of theory or data. As we have noted earlier,

> "Theories of intelligence are often vague or inconsistent about whether MA, IQ, or both, should be related to learning. According to one view, it is MA score that is related to learning, because MA is a measure of the *developmental level* of the organism, and it is this level which limits learning ability. In these terms, IQ is *not* a measure of present learning ability, but rather a mathematical statement of the rate at which learning ability will change in time. An alternative view classifies the intelligence test as an achievement test of universally taught subject material. The MA score is then a measure of how much has been learned. If training is assumed to go on uniformly in time, the ratio MA/CA is the slope of a life-time learning curve, characteristic of the organism and recoverable in new, miniature learning situations. Consequently, IQ is the measure of present learning ability" (House and Zeaman, 1960).

[1] The preparation of this paper was supported in part by Grants M1099 and K6-MH-HD-20,325 from the U. S. Public Health Service.

It would seem that the MA-IQ issue might in part be resolved experimentally: which of these two subject variables does in fact correlate with learning? Relevant data are available, of course, which we will review, but we plan to concentrate on just half the problem, the relation of learning and IQ, because our prime concern is with retardate learning.

The relation of retardation and learning can be translated in psychological terms to be the relation of a process (learning) and a trait (intelligence), or more specifically, learning and IQ, since it is IQ rather than MA that defines retardation. Despite the fact that intelligence is among the most frequently measured of all traits, and that learning is surely the most popular target of research on basic behavioral processes, the conjunction of these two areas has been surprisingly underinvestigated. This may simply be the result of an arbitrary division of labor: trait psychologists and process psychologists tend to live in different skins. But the class of swinging psychologists (trait *and* process), while relatively small, is neither null nor idle. Consequently, the research literature on the IQ-learning relation has grown sufficiently of late to warrant a look at the current status of this traditional problem.

Two excellent reviews on IQ and learning appeared in 1963; Denny (1963) and Lipman (1963) each have book chapters covering the retardation literature on intelligence and learning. It is unnecessary to redo the job, so we shall restrict ourselves to an outline, a boxscore, and an evaluation of positive and negative findings, including about 20 new studies that have appeared in the last few years.

Delimiting the Problem

MA, CA, and IQ. If we wish to reason to the influence of IQ on learning, it is necessary to control other relevant subject factors correlated with IQ. MA and CA are the most likely relevant correlates. Theoretically, IQ is independent of CA, but in a population of equal MA's, IQ is negatively correlated with CA. And within a single age group, IQ correlates positively with MA.

It is impossible, of course, to control both MA and CA simultaneously and allow their ratio (IQ) to vary; but if CA were found to be irrelevant for learning, the problem would be reduced to the influence of two separable psychological variables, MA vs. IQ. Since the logic of our later arguments depends upon the assumption that CA is indeed an irrelevant variable for learning, this might be the best juncture at which to present some supporting evidence. Learning studies correlating per-

formance with CA have reported unreliable, zero, and negative correlations, unless accompanied by large MA differences. Instances include
Ellis and Sloan (1959), Stevenson (1965), Harter (1965), and House and
Zeaman (1960). Multiple correlations of learning with combined MA
and CA measures are not higher than those with MA alone (Harter,
1965); and the partial correlations of learning and MA with CA constant are not appreciably less than the first order correlations of MA
and learning (House and Zeaman, 1960). The evidence on this matter
is not overwhelming, and may be variously interpreted, but we do wish
to suggest that our basic assumption of the irrelevance of CA is not
without empirical support.

To separate the effects of IQ and MA on learning (assuming CA
irrelevant), three research strategies have been employed. (1) The simplest design compares the performance of two groups varying in IQ,
but matched in MA. Comparisons of retardates with equal-MA normals
are usually arranged for this. (2) Statistical control of MA has been
employed using correlational techniques with populations having wide
variability in IQ either in normal or retarded ranges. (3) Studies in
which IQ and MA are confounded may fail to show relations with performance in learning tasks. These are relevant studies as negative instances, since it appears safe to assume that if IQ has no effect when
correlated with MA, it would have no effect were it not. The usual
source of this kind of negative evidence is from comparisons of normals
and retardates of equal CA. All three sources of data will be considered.

LEARNING TASKS AND LEARNING MEASURES

A relation of intelligence to learning, unqualified with respect to
task, implies some generality of learning ability across tasks. Woodrow
(1946) reviewed the literature two decades ago and concluded that
many observed low correlations between measures of learning in different tasks meant that no unitary learning ability existed. If the measures of learning were reliable and a wide range of individual differences observed, this would make a relation between general learning
ability and intelligence impossible. The kinds of learning measures
(gain scores) used by Woodrow have been criticized by other writers
(Ruch, 1936; Ruch, 1961; Tilton, 1949) for unreliability and attenuation
of range, and for poor control of individual differences in starting level.
Subsequent investigators have turned up moderate correlations between learning measures within certain task domains, such as discriminative learning (Stevenson, 1965; House and Zeaman, 1960).

With the task-to-task consistency of individual differences in learning in doubt, it may be instructive to collate the evidence on each of several broad classes of tasks separately, not only to describe more precisely the empirical boundaries of the IQ-learning relation, but also to provide tests of theories predicting task differences (we have proposed such a theory).

The broad classes of learning tasks to be considered are (a) classical conditioning, (b) discriminative learning, (c) verbal learning, and (d) learning set. We chose these classes because they are broad and conventional classes with IQ-relevant experiments reportable on each.

To minimize the intrusion of processes other than learning, some further restrictions have been placed on the studies to be covered. Acquisition is the target variable here rather than extinction. Schedules of reinforcement give rise to motivational effects, so only 100 percent schedules are considered. Transfer designs may introduce complex mediating processes, so only the original learning phases of such experiments are counted. Similarly, for studies whose prime focus is on retention, we include only original learning data.

While it would be naive to believe that such restrictions will guarantee unique theoretical interpretations of the process or processes underlying performance on learning tasks, we hope these will narrow things down a bit. It will turn out that there is complexity enough in the data even with these restrictions, and that despite them we end up inferring the intrusion of some other process than learning.

Classical Conditioning

There is no relation between IQ and acquisition of simple, classically conditioned responses. The research literature (in English) is unequivocal on this point. The Russian literature, on the other hand, led one reviewer to quite the opposite conclusion. Razran (1961), after an extensive review of the large Russian literature on classical conditioning, concludes, "Other things equal, the more intelligent the child, the more readily he forms the CR." Not all Russian evidence is consistent with this view, however, since Razran (1933) earlier reviewed an experiment by Osipova in which retardates *exceeded* a group of equal CA normals in speed of conditioning finger-withdrawals with shock US. Whatever the balance of truth on this issue in the Russian literature, there have been half a dozen publications in English weighing heavily on the invariance side of the issue, i.e., conditioning is invariant with respect to IQ.

Let us look at the English literature. Six articles have appeared recently in which IQ was included as a parameter. Half of the studies conditioned in GSR with shock US: Birch and Demb (1959), Grings, Lockhart, and Dameron (1962), and Baumeister, Beedle, and Urquhart (1964). The remaining three studies conditioned the eyelid response: Cromwell, Palk, and Foshee (1961), Behrens and Ellis (1960), and Franks and Franks (1962). All of the studies used retarded subjects to represent the lower ranges of intelligence, and most had normal control subjects. Reliable over-all differences in CR acquisition between normals and retardates were not reported in any study, nor did IQ correlate with conditioning performance within the retardate range.

These studies cover a wide range of intelligence. Cromwell, Palk, and Foshee report a correlation of .03 between IQ and CR frequency for a population of 61 retardates ranging from IQ 15 to 68. Grings, Lockhart, and Dameron concluded, "Apparently, autonomic conditioning is unaffected by intelligence over the IQ range employed (20-78)." Add to this the absence of normal retardate differences for both autonomic and non-autonomic (eyelid) conditioning and a more general invariance can be asserted.

A suggestion of contrary evidence is reported in a very early study by Mateer (1918) who measured anticipatory mouth-openings of children given candy on signal. But the *instrumental* features of this procedure are so obvious as to make it doubtfully classifiable (as it often is) as a classical conditioning study. The candy reinforcement was, after all, contingent upon opening the mouth, and this is the defining condition for instrumental conditioning.

None of the six studies mentioned above made equal MA comparisons at different IQ levels. The negative findings make such controls unnecessary. If subjects varying in both MA and IQ do not differ in conditioning, then it is a reasonable inference that IQ alone would be an ineffective variable.

Among the six published papers, of suggestive theoretical significance is the fact that only one measured *discriminative* classical conditioning (Grings, Lockhart, and Dameron), as well as simple conditioning, and with the discriminative procedure there were some IQ differences favoring higher IQ subjects. This study confounds MA and IQ, so we cannot count it as positive evidence for IQ alone, but if the effect were replicable with equal MA controls, the finding would fit well with a theoretical interpretation (in terms of attention) that we will present later.

We have similar comparisons of lower and higher IQ retardates undergoing classical oculomotor conditioning in our laboratory at the Mansfield State Training School. In his dissertation research, R. Ramsey finds differences in performance corresponding to IQ for retardates classically conditioned to make eye movement anticipations of the occurrence of a peripheral light. The oculomotor response we regard as a peripheral correlate of attention.

Summary. Intelligence and simple conditionability are unrelated (at least for English-speaking subjects) over a wide range of intelligence. When discriminative features enter the classical conditioning procedures, however, a suggestion of a relation with intelligence appears.

Simple Discriminative Learning

In the area of discrimination learning, we have found 18 studies relating IQ to performance with MA controlled. Twelve of these report positive results, with better performances from the higher IQ subjects (Baumeister, Beedle, and Urquhart, 1964; Ellis, Hawkins, Pryer, and Jones, 1963; Hoffman, 1963; House and Zeaman, 1958; House and Zeaman, 1960; Kass and Stevenson, 1961; Martin and Blum, 1961; Rieber, 1964; Ross, Hetherington, and Wray, 1965; Rudel, 1959; Stevenson and Iscoe, 1955; and Stevenson and Zigler, 1957), and nine report negative results with no reliable differences among the various IQ groups (Hetherington, Ross, and Pick, 1964; Kass and Stevenson, 1961; Martin and Blum, 1961; Milgram and Furth, 1964; O'Connor and Hermelin, 1959; Sanders, Ross, and Heal, 1965; Schusterman, 1964; Stevenson, 1960; and Stevenson and Zigler, 1957). Three studies (Kass and Stevenson, 1961; Martin and Blum, 1961; Stevenson and Zigler, 1957) report both negative and positive results for different comparisons. With such discrepant results, the obvious question is how the two groups of studies differ. On the average, those with positive findings have higher IQ differences, and tend to include subjects of lower MA and IQ, but there is much overlap in these respects with the studies reporting negative findings. The big difference between the positives and negatives lies in the *difficulty of the task.* Six of the nine studies with negative findings had discrimination learning tasks which were far from optimally difficult, having been found too easy or too hard.

On the easy side were the following: An experiment by Hetherington, Ross, and Pick (1964) reports almost no errors at all for their equal MA comparisons, using "junk" stimuli in a 2-choice visual discrimination. Recognizing the possibility of a ceiling effect, these investigators increased the difficulty of their task in a later study (Ross, Hetherington, and Wray, 1965) of size discrimination and obtained positive results.

Studies by Milgram and Furth (1964) and Schusterman (1964) included 2-choice position discriminations which proved not only easy, but easier for retardates than normals. There are at least two other experiments in the literature (Weir and Stevenson, 1959; Osler and Trautman, 1961) which also show that for certain very easy discriminations, subjects of lower intelligence do better than brighter subjects.

On the hard side, the study by Martin and Blum (1961) used 3-choice oddity and the middle-sized problem, both of which turned out to be highly difficult for subjects of low developmental level. A 3-choice size discrimination by Stevenson and Zigler (1957) was even more difficult. Out of 81 subjects starting their second experiment, only eight learned the problem. Since a significantly greater proportion of retardates than normals were non-learners, we have classified this experiment as positive; it also appears in the negative list because reliable differences did not appear between the learners differing in intelligence. Floor effects may have been operating in the study by Stevenson (1960) with two complex discriminative tasks (a 3-choice size discrimination and a 7-item, non-verbal paired-associate discrimination). Here again, a majority of the subjects failed, both normal and retarded. Such studies are important in showing the complex interaction of task difficulty with the IQ-learning relationship (see Figure 12).

High task difficulty cuts down on the size of the population contributing non-chance data and enhances the possibility of a Type II Error. In the study by Stevenson (1960), the normals in one of his experiments were superior to retardates of equal MA, but the p level was between .10 and .20. Such outcomes do not inspire confidence in the null hypothesis. A similar interpretation may also be likely for a study by O'Connor and Hermelin (1959), in which ten imbecile children required 25 percent more training trials to reach criterion than did 10 normal children of equal MA—a difference falling short of statistical reliability. To the degree that the correlation between IQ and performance in learning tasks deviates from unity, outcomes of this sort tend to be likely.

In summary, the bulk of the negative evidence may be the result of extreme levels of difficulty with consequent attenuation in the range of performance. The entire assemblage of data, both positive and negative, can be handled by the following assumption: *at least a low positive correlation exists between IQ (with MA controlled) and performance in visual discrimination tasks when a wide range of IQ's is sampled and tasks of intermediate difficulty are used.*

The posited relations of performance and IQ for tests of varying difficulty are shown in Figure 12. The ceiling and floor effects represented

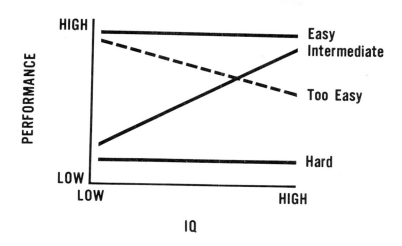

Figure 12. Expected effects of IQ on performance in tasks at four levels of difficulty.

by the "easy" and "hard" tests are obvious enough in principle, but often hard to avoid in practice. The paradoxical inverse relation of IQ and performance for the "very easy" condition has been observed by several investigators; a theoretical interpretation of this finding is considered later.

The magnitude of the correlation of IQ with visual discrimination learning has not been measured over the entire range of intelligence. A partial correlation of −.28 (p < .05) has been reported by House and Zeaman (1960) relating IQ (with MA constant) and log errors on a visual discrimination task. The population for which this relation held included 71 retarded children ranging in IQ from 17-67. A reasonable assumption would be that the −.28 correlation suffers from attenuation due to range and that a higher—moderate—correlation exists between IQ and intelligence for an unrestricted range of IQ's.

Verbal Learning

The two major subdivisions of verbal learning, for which IQ-relevant data exist, are paired-associate (PA) and serial-position (SP) learning. In all, there are 11 studies either having equal-MA controls or showing no differences despite the lack of such control. More of the evidence in these studies is negative than positive. Nevertheless, we give less weight to the negative findings because these so frequently occur when either very hard or easy tasks are examined. As in the case of discriminative learning, a bias in favor of negative results may be caused by restrictions in the ranges of the independent variable (IQ) and the dependent variable (learning).

Let us list first the studies showing positive and negative results before evaluating them. The PA and SP articles are considered separately.

Paired-Associate Learning. Ten PA studies could be found with relevant findings; three of them contained positive evidence of a direct relation of IQ and performance in a PA learning task (Iscoe and Semler, 1964; Jensen, 1965; Johnson and Blake, 1960), seven of them contained negative evidence (Akutagawa and Benoit, 1959; Berkson and Cantor, 1960; Cantor & Ryan, 1962; Eisman, 1958; Girardeau and Ellis, 1964; Ring and Palermo, 1961; Vergason, 1964. Of the latter group, three were equal CA comparisons with no accompanying differences (Berkson and Cantor, Eisman, and Vergason). All of the studies used variations on standard PA verbal learning techniques, and all of them used visual stimuli (pictures, words, or nonsense syllables) to be associated with verbal responses.

Serial-Position Learning. Only four SP studies supply pertinent data, three of them presenting positive evidence (Cassell, 1957; Girardeau and Ellis, 1964; Jensen, 1965), and two containing negative (Cassell, 1957; Johnson and Blake, 1960). As in the PA studies, the stimuli were all visual and the responses spoken.

Evaluation. Intelligence, or that aspect of it measured by IQ, can be varied over a wide range, and the greater the range of IQ in a particular study, the greater the likelihood of detecting a relation with verbal learning. The range of IQ differences in the set of 11 experiments above was from 12 points to 55. As might be expected, the study featuring only a 12 point IQ difference (Akutagawa and Benoit) reports negative findings; the study with 55 IQ points difference (Iscoe and Semler) yielded positive findings. This is not an arbitrary selection of cases. A bi-serial correlation of IQ differences versus positive-negative outcome for all the studies was computed at .86, showing a highly reliable tendency for the studies with higher IQ differences to yield positive results.

Restriction of range of the dependent variable may account for many of the negative results. Performance on verbal learning tasks will certainly be restricted if subjects who fail to learn at all are excluded in the analysis. Two of the studies (Cantor and Ryan, Berkson and Cantor) found normals and retardates not different in PA learning after having dropped failing subjects. In each case more retardates failed than normals—a finding hardly consistent with the conclusion that normals and retardates are not different in PA learning. These studies do establish the weakness, or absence, of an IQ-learning relation among normal and retardate *learners*, but do not permit generalization to the intact population, including nonlearners.

A similar limitation can arise in studies which must set other entrance requirements closely related to verbal learning ability. Girardeau and Ellis (1964) and Cassell (1957) had to drop subjects not able to read, since they were using visual verbal stimuli. Cassell was forced to drop 100 subjects from a population of 152 retardates (but none from his normal group) as non-readers, and found marginal evidence (i.e., some positive, some negative) of a difference in SP learning between the normals and retardates remaining. Why should groups presumably equal in verbal learning be so different in ability to read?

In fairness to these experimenters, it should be recognized that if verbal stimuli are to be used in comparisons of this kind, it is difficult to think of alternative procedures. If the results of these experiments had been positive, there would have been no difficulty in interpretation.

A third way to restrict the range of the dependent variable is to have the learning task turn out to be too easy. In the studies of Eisman (1958) and of Vergason (1964), subjects learned in about six trials with group SD's in the neighborhood of two or three trials. The effects of intelligence on learning may not be strong enough to show up with so little room.

Our reinterpretations of the negative results of the studies discussed are not intended as hindsight criticisms of experimental designs. It is much easier to know the boundary conditions of an empirical relation (such as IQ learning) *after* the research is done than before.

Of the ten PA studies listed above, four seem relatively free of the difficulties discussed. Ring and Palermo (1961) matched for MA a group of normal children (mean IQ 102) and retardates (mean IQ 76) and found no reliable differences in performance on a moderately difficult PA task. Johnson and Blake (1960) had similar matched groups (mean IQ's 70 vs. 102) and found normals better on two PA tasks, reliably so for one, but not the other. Varying IQ over a wider range, Jensen (1965) provided an equal-MA comparison for two groups of IQ 58 and 105 on two PA tasks and reported marked normal-retardate differences in both tasks in the expected direction. Finally, Iscoe and Semler (1964) arranged normal-retardate comparisons (mean IQ's 109 vs. 54, with

MA controlled) using four PA tasks ranging in difficulty. A clear over-all difference in favor of the normals was reported for this large IQ difference.

Of the four SP studies listed earlier, two provided clear tests of the underlying hypotheses. Johnson and Blake (1960) found no reliable differences in performance between groups of IQ 70 vs. 100, while Jensen (1965) found normals (IQ 105) far better than equal-MA re-tardates (IQ 58).

Summary. IQ and verbal learning performance are positively re-lated, in both paired-associate and serial-position tasks, for subjects of equal MA. The strength of this relation is dependent upon the magni-tude of IQ difference. With differences of 40 or more points, a clear difference emerges between normals and retardates. With differences of 20-30 points, performance differences are marginal or absent. The effects of IQ can easily be obscured by restrictions on the range of vari-ation of verbal learning performance, either by subject selection pro-cedures or unhappy choice of task difficulty level.

Learning Set

The relation of IQ to discrimination learning set has been investi-gated in five studies. While a larger number of experiments report on the relations of MA (and CA) to learning set, only five publications provide IQ comparisons with some control of MA. Three of these yield clearly positive findings (Girardeau, 1959; Harter, 1965, Wischner and O'Donnell, 1962), and two yield negative findings (Levinson and Reese, reported by Reese, 1963; Plenderleith, 1956).

It is not easy to explain the negative cases. Levinson and Reese had IQ differences restricted to the normal range, but Plenderleith did not. She used a wide range of IQ's (53-112) and an MA level (6 yrs.) approx-imating that of the positive studies. There is some question of the rep-resentativeness of her retardate sample, however. The levels of per-formance achieved by her retardates were astonishingly good compared with higher level subjects (cf. Harter, 1965).

A clear boundary condition on the IQ-learning set relation was es-tablished in a well-designed study by Harter (1965). She had subjects at three levels of IQ: 70, 100, and 130, at each of three MA levels: 5, 7 and 9 years, learning a series of 2-choice object discriminations. Learn-ing-set performance was positively related to IQ at the MA 5 and 7 year levels, but the relation was weak at the MA 9 level due to a ceiling effect. Wischner, Braun, and Patton (1962) observed similar limitations with object-quality learning-set tasks. Presumably, more difficult learning-set tasks could be found to provide adequate tests of the IQ-learning set relation at the higher MA levels. Despite the ceiling effects at the high MA levels, Harter reports the correlation of IQ and learning set (problems to criterion) as −.57 with MA controlled. The multiple correlation of combined IQ and MA with learning set was a surprisingly high .73. The first order correlation of performance with MA was −.47.

In summary, this modest package of learning-set evidence is consistent with the view that between IQ and learning-set formation there exists a positive relation of a magnitude approximating that observed with simple discriminative and verbal learning.

SOME RELATIONS WITH THEORY

Learning Theory

To show that intelligence is related to performance on some learning tasks is not sufficient to prove that intelligence is related to learning, if we mean by learning something like habit acquisition or growth of associative strength. Virtually all modern learning theorists distinguish learning and performance, and explicit theories provide rules for inferring learning from the data of learning experiments. A theorist such as Hull postulates that individual differences may occur in rate of growth of habit strength (his parameter, i), but no simple relation exists between i and the appearances of empirical learning curves. The reason is simple. Performance is theorized to be a function not only of habit strength but of other constructs such as drives and inhibitions as well. Individual differences can affect these. Which ones are responsible for individual differences observed in a particular set of empirical learning curves? A program of research is necessary to find out. Hull's theory is sufficiently explicit to permit such a program, and at least one serious attempt has been made to do this with some motor learning data (Zeaman and Kaufman, 1955).

Not enough data on the relation of motor learning and intelligence exist to make a Hullian analysis possible, but we have made a beginning on a similar program in the area of visual discrimination learning.

Attention Theory

We have published a theory of discrimination learning to account for the performances of retardates learning to solve 2-choice visual discriminations (Zeaman and House, 1963; House and Zeaman, 1963). The theory is formal and quantitative, and postulates a chain of two responses for problem solution: the first, an attention response to the relevant stimulus dimensions; and the second, a correct instrumental response to the positive cue of the relevant dimension. The theory is an extension and elaboration of Wyckoff's (1952) observing response model. Equations are written for the underlying processes of attention and habit acquisition, and parameters in these equations may in principle vary from subject to subject. The pertinent question here is, can we tell from the data of our experiments whether observed individual differences in empirical learning curves are attributable to individual differences in rate of habit acquisition or some other underlying process such as attention? The answer is, we think we can.

Among our retardates wide individual differences are observed in their learning curves, with the higher IQ subjects doing better than the lower. The general form of the learning curves is S-shaped or ogival (if plotted properly in the form of backward learning curves). Differences between brighter and duller subjects are observed to be not in the *slopes* of the rising portions of ogives, but in the length of the initial plateau.

Figure 13 conveys the point. It is not the rate of improvement, once it starts, that distinguishes bright and dull, but how long it takes for improvement to begin. Improvement is uniformly fast once it begins.

Theoretically, this result could come about in a variety of ways, but the main contenders in this theoretical contest were two classes of parameters: (1) the θ parameters controlling individual differences in rate of acquisition and extinction, and (2) the $Po_{(i)}$ parameters controlling individual differences in initial probabilities of paying attention to the various (i) dimensions of stimuli. It was shown by computer simulation that θ differences would have tended to produce the kind of function depicted by D_2 in the figure—with low slopes in the transition zone. Differences in initial probability of attending to the relevant dimension ($Po_{(i)}$) would produce the differences exhibited by B and D_1—the kind that were observed empirically.

The tentative conclusion was reached that intelligence level was associated with differences in attention (Po) rather than learning, in the sense of rate of habit acquisition (θ). The argument did not end there.

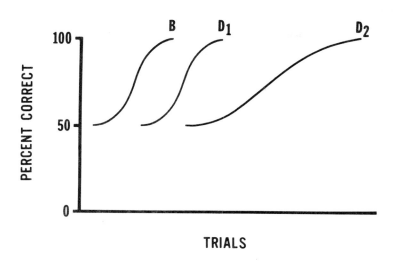

Figure 13. Idealized forms of the empirical discrimination learning curves for brighter subjects (B) and two groups of duller subjects (D₁ and D₂). The data resemble the B and D₁ functions but not D₂.

Other consequences followed from this notion (which we called the "θ-invariance hypothesis"). If dull subjects had the same θs as bright, this meant that conditions might be found in which the two groups would do equally well. It would depend upon Po, or what the subjects attended to when they entered the discrimination task. This means that if we could engineer their attention, that is, get them to focus on the relevant dimension, we could get fast learning and wash out the effects of intelligence.

Transfer designs such as intradimensional shifts and reversals are capable of producing high speed solutions of discrimination problems by retardates, and these are just the designs that theoretically produce high Po's (House and Zeaman, 1963).

Moreover, the theory receives support in providing a possible resolution of the paradoxical effects of very easy problems shown in Figure 12. If subjects of low intelligence do badly in visual discrimination problems because they have a low initial probability of attending to the dimensions the experimenter has chosen as relevant, then the same retarded subjects ought to do better than normals if the experimenter should choose as relevant, those dimensions the retardates *are* paying attention to. Analyses of error scores reveal that subjects of low developmental level tend strongly to respond to *position* in 2-choice tasks. If position is what retardates attend to, then our theory says that they should do better than normals on position discrimination learning, as Figure 12 suggests, and some studies have shown. The limitations or boundary conditions of the intelligence-learning relation set by task difficulty are translated in our theory as an attention phenomenon. A difficult task is one the relevant dimensions of which have a low probability of being attended to at the start of training. For an easy task, all subjects, both bright and dull, have a high probability of relevant attention. Instrumental learning starts immediately, and under the θ-invariance hypothesis, all subjects will do equally well. The kinds of findings described by Figure 12 are thus not unfriendly to attention theory.

To tidy up some of the other loose ends of data presented in our survey, let us ask whether the kinds of tasks which show and do not show IQ variation are at all consistent with theory.

Classical conditioning was the one area which most consistently failed to show IQ variations. All but one of these studies used non-discriminative classical conditioning. The experimenter presents a CS not in competition with other new stimuli, but in competition with a stable background. He turns on a light or sound. With only the adapted stimulation of a background as competition, such stimuli may reasonably be expected to have high attention value—for all subjects. If this analysis is true, the θ-invariance hypothesis says that no differences in conditioning should be observed between high and low IQ groups.

The one study which contained a suggestion of an IQ difference included a discriminative classical conditioning procedure (Grings, Lockhart, and Dameron, 1962). These authors reason along lines similar to ours—they say:

> "Certain results indicate a possible relation between intelligence and perception, if one includes orienting responses as perceptual behavior. The following observations bear on the nature of this relation. If GSR response during the delay interval is used as an indication of orienting behavior, the two IQ groups differ in the number of orienting responses to test and control stimuli" (p. 27).

Extreme conditions are often regarded by methodologists as carrying special probative weight. Suppose we could show that subjects of low intelligence could regularly learn discriminations in a single trial. No one can do better. Hence, there is no room for an IQ-learning relation. We have arranged a set of experimental conditions in which retarded subjects have a fairly high probability of attending to the relevant dimensions (either color or form) of the discriminative problems. We make the theoretical assumption that instrumental learning is complete in a single trial ($\theta=1$) and try, then, to fit their learning functions with equations that make this assumption. Their empirical learning functions do not get to unity in a single trial because their $Po_{(i)}$, while high, is not 1.0. Theoretically, once they look at the relevant dimension, they learn immediately. The data of a coordinated series of six experiments were handled quantitatively by such assumptions (House and Zeaman, 1963). We were led to the amusing conclusion that retardates were slow learners who learned in one trial.

Our one-trial learning assumption has not been found inapplicable even for the verbal learning of retardates. House (1963) has shown that the retardate data of serial-position verbal learning task can be quantitatively described by a postulate set including a one-trial learning assumption. A doctoral dissertation by Kusmin (1963) has added further empirical support.

As in discrimination learning, the empirical verbal learning curves do not asymptote at unity in a single trial, but the items that are selected by the subject for learning on each trial are learned in one trial.

House (1963) has presented in detail evidence for a dual process of retardate verbal learning, following the Miller and McGill model, and has identified two parameters of the model with the process of learning and with the process of retention. Individual differences in intelligence were found to correspond with one but not both parameters. The interpretation was made that retardates vary in immediate memory ability as a function of intelligence but not learning ability.

The parallelism in our theoretical treatments of discriminative and verbal learning is close but not complete. Dual processes are inferred for both (attention and learning in discriminative tasks, learning and retention in verbal tasks), individual differences are found in only one of the component processes corresponding to intelligence, and in neither case is the process that of learning.

REFERENCES

Akutagawa, D., and Benoit, E. P. The effect of age and relative brightness on associative learning in children. *Child Developm.*, 1959, *30*, 229-238.

Barnett, C. D., Ellis, N. R., and Pryer, M. W. Serial position effects in superior and retarded subjects. *Psych. Rep.*, 1960, *7*, 111-113.

Baumeister, A. A., Beedle, R., and Hawkins, W. F. Transposition in normals and retardates under varying conditions of training and test. *Amer. J. ment. Defic.*, 1964, *69*, 432-437.

Baumeister, A., Beedle, R., and Urquhart, D. GSR conditioning in normals and retardates. *Amer. J. ment. Defic.*, 1964, *69*, 114-120.

Behrens, R. and Ellis, N. R. Simultaneous and trace eyelid conditioning in normals and defectives. *Abstracts of Peabody Studies in Mental Retardation*, 1960-1962, *2*, No. 20.

Berkson, G., and Cantor, G. N. A study of mediation in mentally retarded and normal school children. *J. educ. Psychol.*, 1960, *51*, 82-86.

Birch, H. G. and Demb, H. The formation and extinction of conditioned reflexes in "brain-damaged" and mongoloid children. *J. nerv. ment. Dis.*, 1959, *129*, 162-170.

Blue, Milton, C. Performance of normal and retarded subjects on a paired-associate task. *Amer. J. ment. Defic.*, 1963, *68*, 228-234.

Cantor, G. N. and Ryan, T. J. Retention of verbal paired-associates in normals and retardates. *Amer. J. ment. Defic.*, 1962, *66*, 861-865.

Cassel, R. H. Serial verbal learning and retroactive inhibition in aments and children. *J. clin. Psychol.*, 1957, *13*, 369-372.

Cromwell, R. L., Palk, B. E., and Foshee, J. G. Studies in activity level: V. The relationships among eyelid conditioning, intelligence, activity level and age. *Amer. J. ment. Defic.*, 1961, *65*, 744-748.

Denny, M. R. Learning. In R. Heber and H. Stevens (eds.), *Review of research in mental retardation*. Chicago: University of Chicago Press, 1963.

Eisman, B. S. Paired associate learning, generalization, and retention as a function of intelligence. *Amer. J. ment. Defic.*, 1958, *63*, 481-489.

Ellis, N. R., Hawkins, W. F., Pryer, M. W., and Jones, R. W. Distraction effects in oddity learning by normal and mentally defective humans. *Amer. J. ment. Defic.*, 1963, *67*, 576-583.

Ellis, N. R., Pryer, M. W., Distefano, M. K., Jr., and Pryer, R. S. Learning in mentally defective, normal and superior subjects. *Amer. J. ment. Defic.*, 1960, *64*, 725-734.

Ellis, N. R. and Sloan, W. Oddity learning as a function of mental age. *J. comp. physiol. Psychol.*, 1959, *52*, 228-230.

Franks, V., and Franks, C. M. Conditionability in defectives and in normals as related to intelligence and organic deficit: The application of a learning theory model to a study of the learning process in the mental defective. In B. W. Richards (ed.), *Proceedings of the London Conference on the Scientific Study of Mental Deficiency.* Dagenham, Eng.: May & Baker, 1962, pp. 577-583.

Gardner, L. P. Responses of idiots and imbeciles in a conditioning experiment. *Amer. J. ment. Defic.*, 1945, *50*, 59-80.

Girardeau, F. L. The formation of discrimination learning sets in mongoloid and normal children. *J. comp. physiol. Psychol.*, 1959, *52*, 566-570.

Girardeau, F. L., and Ellis, N. Rote verbal learning by normal and mentally retarded children. *Amer. J. ment. Defic.*, 1964, *68*, 525-532.

Grings, W. W., Lockhart, R. A., and Dameron, L. E. Conditioning autonomic responses of mentally subnormal individuals. *Psychol. Monogr.*, 1962, *76* (Whole No. 39).

Harter, Susan. Discrimination learning set in children as a function of MA and IQ. *J. exp. child Psychol.*, 1965 (in press).

Hetherington, E. M., and Banta, T. J. Incidental and intentional learning in normal and mentally retarded children. *J. comp. physiol. Psychol.*, 1962, *55*, 402-404.

Hetherington, E. M., Ross, L. E., and Pick, H. L., Jr. Delay of reward and learning in mentally retarded and normal children. *Child Develpm.*, 1964, *35*, 653-659.

Hoffman, D. T. (with House, B. J., and Zeaman, D.). Miniature experiments in the discrimination learning of retardates. In L. P. Lipsitt and C. C. Spiker (eds.), *Advances in child development and behavior.* Vol. I. New York: Academic Press Inc., 1963.

House, B. J. Recalls versus trials as factors in serial verbal learning or retardates. *Psychol. Rep.*, 1963, *12*, 931-941.

House, B. J., and Zeaman, D. A comparison of discrimination learning in normal and mentally defective children. *Child Develpm.*, 1958, *29*, 411-416.

House, B. J., and Zeaman, D. Visual discrimination learning and intelligence in defectives of low mental age. *Amer. J. ment. Defic.*, 1960, *65*, 51-58.

House, B. J., and Zeaman, D. Miniature experiments in the discrimination learning of retardates. In L. P. Lipsitt and C. C. Spiker (eds.),

Advances in child development and behavior. Vol. I. New York: Academic Press Inc., 1963.

Iscoe, I., and Semler, I. F. Paired-associate learning in normal and mentally retarded children as a function of four experimental conditions. *J. comp. physiol., Psychol.,* 1964, *57,* 387-392.

Jensen, A. R. Rote learning in retarded adults and normal children. *Amer. J. ment. Defic.,* 1965, *69,* 828-854.

Johnson, G. O., and Blake, K. A. *Learning performance of retarded and normal children.* Syracuse University Press, 1960.

Kass, N., and Stevenson, H. W. The effect of pretraining reinforcement conditions on learning by normal and retarded children. *Amer. J. ment. Defic.,* 1961, *66,* 76-80.

Kusmin, A. Verbal learning and retention of retardates at varying IQ, MA and CA levels. Unpublished Doctoral dissertation, University of Connecticut, 1964.

Lipman, R. S. Learning: Verbal, perceptual-motor, and classical conditioning. In N. R. Ellis (ed.), *Handbook of mental deficiency.* New York: McGraw-Hill Book Company, 1963.

Martin, W. E., and Blum, A. Interest generalization and learning in mentally normal and subnormal children. *J. comp. physiol. Psychol.,* 1961, *54,* 28-32.

Mateer, F. *Child behavior.* Boston: The Gorham Press, 1918.

Milgram, N. A., and Furth, H. G. Position reversal vs. dimension reversal in normal and retarded children. *Child Develpm.,* 1964, *35,* 701-708.

O'Connor, N., and Hermelin, B. Discrimination and reversal learning in imbeciles. *J. abn. soc. Psychol.,* 1959, *59,* 409-413.

Osler, S. F., and Trautman, G. E. Concept attainment: II. Effect of stimulus complexity upon concept attainment at two levels of intelligence. *J. exp. Psychol.,* 1961, *62,* 9-13.

Plenderleith, M. Discrimination learning and discrimination reversal learning in normal and feeble-minded children. *J. genet. Psychol.,* 1956, *88,* 108-112.

Prysiazniuk, A. W., and Wicijowski, P. J. Learning sets in mongoloid children: A replication. *Amer. J. ment. Defic.,* 1964, *69,* 76-78.

Razran, G. H. S. Conditioned responses in children: A behavioral and quantitative critical review of experimental studies. *Arch. Psychol.,* 1933, No. 148, 1-120.

Razran, G. H. S. The observable unconscious and the inferable conscious in current Soviet psychology: Interoceptive conditioning, semantic conditioning, and the orienting reflex. *Psychol. Rev.*, 1961, *54*, 81-147.

Reese, H. W. Discrimination learning set in children. In L. P. Lipsitt and C. C. Spiker (eds.), *Advances in child development and behavior.* Vol. I. New York: Academic Press Inc., 1963.

Rieber, M. Verbal mediation in normal and retarded children. *Amer. J. ment. Defic.*, 1964, *68*, 634-641.

Ring, E. M., and Palermo, D. S. Paired-associate learning of retarded and normal children. *Amer. J. ment. Defic.*, 1961, *66*, 100-107.

Ross, L. E., Hetherington, M., and Wray, N. P. Delay of reward and the learning of a size problem by normal and retarded children. *Child Develpm.*, 1965 (in press).

Ruch, F. L. The method of common points of mastery as a technique in human learning experimentation. *Psychol. Rev.*, 1936, *43*, 229-234.

Ruch, F. L. Measuring gain from a common point of mastery. *Psychol. Rep.*, 1961, *9*, 234.

Rudel, R. G. The absolute response in tests of generalization in normal and retarded children. *Amer. J. Psychol.*, 1959, *72*, 401-408.

Sanders, B., Ross, L. E., and Heal, L. W. Reversal and non-reversal shift learning in normal children and retardates of comparable mental age. *J. comp. physiol. Psychol.*, 1965, *1*, 84-88.

Schusterman, R. J. Strategies of normal and mentally retarded children under conditions of uncertain outcome. *Amer. J. ment. Defic.*, 1964, *69*, 66-75.

Stevenson, H. W. Learning of complex problems by normal and retarded Ss. *Amer. J. ment. Defic.*, 1960, *64*, 1021-1026.

Stevenson, H. W. Interrelationships in children's learning. *Child Develpm.*, 1965 (in press).

Stevenson, H. W., and Iscoe, I. Transposition in the feeble-minded. *J. exp. Psychol.*, 1955, *49*, 11-15.

Stevenson, H. W., and Zigler, E. F. Discrimination learning and rigidity in normal and feeble-minded individuals. *J. Pers.*, 1957, *25*, 699-711.

Tilton, J. W. Intelligence test scores as indicative of ability to learn. *Educ. psychol. Measmt.*, 1949, *9*, 291-296.

Vergason, G. A. Retention in retarded and normal subjects as a function of amount of original training. *Amer. J. ment. Defic.*, 1964, *68*, 623-629.

Weir, M. W., and Stevenson, H. W. The effect of verbalization in children's learning as a function of chronological age. *Child Develpm.*, 1959, *30*, 143-149.

Wischner, G. J., Braun, H. W., and Patton, R. A. Acquisitions and long-term retention of an object quality learning set by retarded children. *J. comp. physiol. Psychol.*, 1962, *55*, 518-523.

Wischner, G. J., and O'Donnell, J. P. Concurrent learning set formation in normal and retarded children. *J. comp. physiol. Psychol.*, 1962, *55*, 524-527.

Woodrow, H. The ability to learn. *Psychol. Rev.*, 1946, *53*, 147-158.

Wyckoff, L. B., Jr. The role of observing responses in discrimination learning. Part I. *Psychol. Rev.*, 1952, *59*, 431-442.

Zeaman, D., and Kaufman, H. Individual differences and theory in a motor learning task. *Psychol. Monogr.*, 1955, *69*.

INDIVIDUAL DIFFERENCES IN RETARDATE LEARNING

GEORGE J. WISCHNER
University of Pittsburgh

I could take my cue from a previous discussant and proceed to a consideration of our own research on retardate learning.[1] Although there may be occasion to refer to some of this work along the way, let me try to attend, and I use the term advisedly, to some of the dimensions of the paper by the Zeamans.

The authors, acknowledging recent excellent reviews on IQ and learning, provide us with an updating of findings, reviewing the most recent studies, in many of which a primary objective has been a comparison of the performance of retardates and normals in a variety of situations, including classical conditioning, discrimination learning, learning set and verbal learning. With CA disposed of as an irrelevant variable, the presumed differentiating factor is IQ. That MA is a relevant variable is accepted (otherwise, why match for MA?), but as the authors say, concerning the MA-IQ issue, "we plan to concentrate on just half of the problem, the relation of learning and IQ, because our primary concern is with retardate learning."

In view of the extensive literature reviews that have appeared recently the authors choose to employ a box-score technique—the categorization of studies on IQ and learning into either a positive or a negative column. The primary purpose is to demonstrate that by and large the evidence favors an IQ-learning relationship in retardates, and further, to show how this evidence can be systematized within the attention theory framework developed by the authors. The authors

---

[1] Some of the research referred to in this chapter is supported by Grant M-1290 from the National Institute of Mental Health, U. S. Public Health Service.

are to be congratulated on a nice job of rationalizing the findings to support their theoretical position.

The box-score results, taken at face value, however, don't always appear to be supportive of the position held by the authors. For example, in their evaluation of the area of discrimination learning, eighteen studies are considered which relate IQ to performance, with MA controlled. Twelve are classified as positive, and nine as negative. The authors probe a little deeper into the negative studies and appear to be able to integrate in a satisfactory manner the negative findings in terms of a task difficulty parameter, which assumes general importance in their paper.

It seems to me that negative findings are too readily discounted by the authors, or else considered primarily in terms of factors which apparently fit in with their theoretical position. It may be noted in this regard that some of the negative findings on the IQ-learning relationship possibly could be explained in ways other than that proposed by the present authors. Denny (1963), in his recent review, considers some of the same studies cited by House and Zeaman and points up certain procedural variables that might account for negative findings. It may be relevant to note that one study (Stevenson and Zigler, 1957) cited by Zeaman and House, appears in both the positive and negative columns. The dual placement seems to be a function of the particular measure that is employed. Of relevance here, also, is the seeming casualness with which the authors dispose of the CA variable, upon which the logic of their position depends. They state: "The evidence on this matter is not overwhelming, and may be variously interpreted, but we do wish to suggest that our basic assumption of the irrelevance of CA is not without empirical support." A further reflection of the approach to data is to be found in a reference to one of our learning-set studies (Wischner and O'Donnell, 1962). The authors correctly place this study in the plus column. This is correct, however, only for the learning-set data. The authors fail to note that on the very first learning-set problem, paradoxically, there was no difference between retardates and normals; in fact, the retardates were slightly, although not significantly superior to the normal children.

I should like now to comment on the authors' attention theory, which they specify is an extension of Wyckoff's (1952) observing response model. The authors believe that they can infer from their empirical data whether performance differences are attributable to a habit acquisition factor or to a more fundamental process such as attention. (I might say, parenthetically, that I don't believe it wise to accept the word "attention" and the term "observing response," in

Wyckoff's sense, as synonyms.) Their conclusion is that attention is the determining process or mechanism.

According to the authors, the relatively poorer performance of retardates in many situations is due to a low initial probability of making an observing response. If retardates are deficient in observing response behavior, the question remains, "Why?" I don't think this is an idle question. If it is assumed that observing responses obey the same laws of learning as do other responses, then we are still faced with the problem of why retardates are poorer at acquiring or initially manifesting observing response behavior. It seems to me that we may still be faced with the possibility of a learning deficit rather than an attention deficit. It may be noted that in experiments with animals the attempt has been made to define observing response behavior operationally so as to provide for its independent and objective measurement. I would suggest that we need studies with both normal and retarded children which parallel those which have employed lower animals. Several interesting questions arise. Are retarded children more deficient in developing observing response behavior than appropriate normals? Are retarded children able to successfully utilize acquired observing responses in subsequent discrimination tasks? My guess would be that if observing responses do in fact obey the same laws as other responses, then we may find that in certain experimental arrangements retarded children may be poorer than normals in the development of such behaviors. May we then find ourselves in the position of having to conclude that retardates are deficient in acquiring observing ("attention") responses because they already have an attention deficit?

I turn now to a few more general remarks. In terms of the focus of the present conference on individual differences, there would seem to be as much reason to emphasize and evaluate performance differences *within* a population (sample) of retardates as there is to focus on differences *between* groups of retardates and normals (IQ differences). Retardates, like college students, may vary widely in performance on a given task and these individual differences are not necessarily attributable to variables such as MA and IQ. Wischner, Braun, and Patton (1962), for example, found that 32 retarded subjects differed quite markedly in rate of acquisition of an object-quality learning set. In fact, twelve (38 percent) subjects showed relatively little evidence of learning-set formation over the ten-day experimental period. A comparison of these non-criterion subjects with the twenty criterion subjects indicated no significant differences in IQ between the two groups.

An individual difference factor that might help us understand such intra-retardate differences was suggested by an examination of the school records of the children participating in the study. There appeared to be a relatively high incidence of central organic involvement among the non-criterion subjects, with little indication of this kind of involvement among the criterion subjects. The obvious study comparing the learning-set performance of subjects with and without evidence of central organic involvement was done by Hall (1959), but he found no performance differences between these two groups. Examination of the characteristics of the subjects in the involved group now suggested the need for further refinement of the organic category and the investigation of the learning-set performance of subgroups representing different retarded organic diagnostic classifications. Such a study showed quite clearly that among institutionalized retarded children with organic involvement, a cerebral palsy subgroup was superior in learning-set performance to other organic subgroups, with cerebral birth trauma subjects showing practically no learning-set formation within the experimental period employed. It is relevant that the diagnostic subgroups in this study did not differ significantly on CA, IQ, or MA, although the poorest cerebral birth trauma subgroup tended to have the lowest mean IQ. It would appear that there is a need for better delineation or categorization of groups within the retardate population which might focus attention on individual difference factors in addition to IQ.

I should like to mention, finally, two variables which we have found to exert a rather dramatic positive effect on the performance of retardates. James O'Donnell and I have completed a study which showed that an old friend, a distributed practice condition, improved the concurrent learning-set performance of retarded children to a level comparable to that of equal MA normals run under massed practice. Under the latter condition, it is significant that retardates showed no learning at all on the initial concurrent problem and this condition had to be discarded from the experiment. We have also found that certain pretraining procedures, particularly those involving verbal labeling of significant stimulus elements in a Weigl-principle discrimination task, markedly improves the discrimination performance of retarded children (Gerben and Wischner, 1965). Of particular interest is the finding that analogous motor pretraining procedures were relatively ineffective. In their paper, House and Zeaman state that IQ effects could be washed out if one could engineer the attention of retardates. Some of our studies have been stimulated by concepts derived from frameworks other than attention theory. This is not to say, of course, that our manipulations and findings could not be fitted by them into their attention conceptualization. In any event, there remains the possibility that many variables and training procedures not readily incorporated within attention theory may affect the performance of retardates on a variety of tasks.

REFERENCES

Denny, M. R. Learning. In R. Heber and H. Stevens (eds.), *Review of research in mental retardation*. Chicago: University of Chicago Press, 1963.

Gerben, M. J., and Wischner, G. J. A comparison of the effects of motor and verbal pretraining on the learning of a single Weigl discrimination by normal and retarded children. Paper presented at Annual Meeting, Eastern Psychological Association, Atlantic City, April 1965.

Hall, R. Object-quality discrimination learning-set formation by children with and without central organic involvement. Unpublished Master's thesis, University of Pittsburgh, 1959.

Stevenson, H. W., and Zigler, E. F. Discrimination learning and rigidity in normal and feeble-minded individuals. *J. Pers.*, 1957, 25, 699-711.

Wischner, G. J., Braun, H. W., and Patton, R. A. Acquisition and long-term retention of an object-quality learning set by retarded children. *J. comp. physiol. Psychol.*, 1962, 55, 518-523.

Wischner, G. J., and O'Donnell, J. P. Concurrent learning set formation in normal and retarded children. *J. comp. pyhsiol. Psychol.*, 1962, 55, 524-527.

Wyckoff, L. B., Jr. The role of observing responses in discrimination learning. Part I. *Psychol. Rev.*, 1952, 59, 431-442.

10

SIMULATION OF COGNITION AND LEARNING: THE ROLE OF INDIVIDUAL DIFFERENCES

PAUL M. KJELDERGAARD

University of Pittsburgh

I should like to start by discussing the parameters which I have imposed upon my topic and to relate some of my biases, definitions, and assumptions in order to communicate more effectively later on. First, let me list what this paper will not attempt: I will not survey the considerable accomplishments in the area of simulation of learning and cognition by the Carnegie Tech Group, by Feigenbaum, Feldman, Uhr, Hovland, Hunt, Selfridge, and others. Nor will I play the role of critic and point out that a man is not a machine and that machines are not human; ergo, the task that the simulators have set for themselves is impossible [Tabue (1961); Neiser (1963); and Kendler (1961)]. Neither will I rebut these critics for this has already been eloquently accomplished [Armer (1960); Laing (1962); Reitman (1962); and Reitman (1964)].

Rather, I will talk about two programs: The first as an exemplar of what I consider to be some general problems in the area of simulation; the second, an illustration of a simulation strategy which, where applicable, will help overcome some of these basic difficulties.

Before talking about specific programs, however, I should like to make some general comments about the simulation area. Frequently,

218

one encounters a distinction between artificial intelligence and simulation, treating these areas as if they were dichotomous. A more fruitful approach, I think, is to view this as a continuum with artificial intelligence (AI), emphasizing the product, at one end, and simulation, emphasizing the process, at the other. The end point for artificial intelligence would be defined by the most parsimonious procedures to achieve some goal, for example, the correct solution to a problem. The simulation end of the continuum would represent the generation of "complex" behavior by processes which *parallel at some level* the processes involved in a human subject.[1] To increase the utility of the previously mentioned conceptualization, I would like to add a dimension which represents the potential of individual differences, which is presumed to increase as one moves from one end of the above continuum to the other. This conceptualization is presented in Figure 14. Since there is only one "most" parsimonious or optional solution to a problem, the AI end of the continuum precludes any consideration of individual differences. As an example, one might consider the way in which a computer adds two numbers. As the behaviors or problems under consideration become more complex, an algorithm or unique practical solution does not exist. Thus, a solution, even by computer, necessitates strategies or heuristics which in turn vary according to the programmer. Chess playing programs, several of which have been described in the literature, document this point (cf. Kister, *et al.*, 1957; Berstein and Roberts, 1958; Newall, Shaw, and Simon, 1958). Since all possible moves and countermoves cannot be considered, decisions must be made as to how to proceed.

As one attempts to produce, via computer, behavior that looks like human behavior, and especially when one initiates simulations with general instructions such as learn a list, find a concept, solve a problem, the discussion in the last two days leads one to believe that the human counterparts being simulated differ from one another. To produce a successful simulation, therefore, the programmer must take these human differences into account and reproduce them. Thus far, few simulation programs have attempted to consider individual differences in any depth.

The fundamental purpose of simulation is to enable the scientist to

---

[1] The computer hardware and the programming languages impose restrictions on how operations are simulated. As we deal with higher order (or special purpose) languages and develop general purpose subroutines, we tend to move away from hardware restrictions. Nevertheless, the Whorfian hypothesis probably holds at the programming language level: the problem conceptualization and solution are, in part, a function of the language being used.

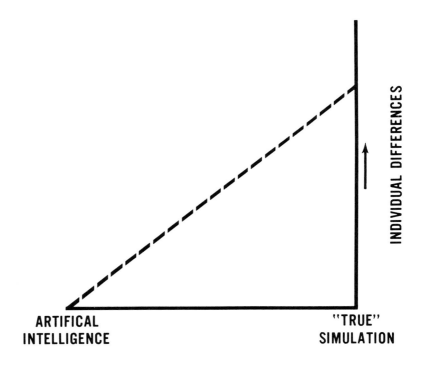

Figure 14. The relationship between degree of involvement of individual differences and the artificial intelligence—"true" simulation continuum.

build models (a computer program) which in turn reflect theories or portions of theories. The models can be manipulated and tested, thereby providing a basis for evaluating the underlying theoretical assumptions. Since the experimental conditions can be precisely controlled, simulations can provide a rigorous test of the theory; the model and theory can be modified until they provide an adequate description *and explanation* of observed phenomena. If one inquires about the extent to which the simulation of cognition and learning has contributed to the psychological theory of behavior, one is forced to conclude, very little. The emphasis thus far has been upon creating models which produce an adequate match of the human counterpart; modifications have involved changing the models (programs) to provide better descriptions. New constructs have not been uncovered, nor has simulation led us to new experiments which in turn have revealed behavioral phenomena previously unobserved.

The major contributions of previous efforts has been: first, a demonstration that the digital computer is not limited to arithmetic operations; second, that a wide variety of complex human behavior is capable of simulation on a digital machine; third, an interest in simulation and artificial intelligence has led to the development of new programming languages, first IPL, and subsequently a variety of symbolic or list-processing interpreters and compilers which decrease the programming effort required to simulate complex processes and increase the flexibility of the kinds of mechanisms which can be programmed; fourth, the early efforts have provided simulation techniques or heuristics which have been adopted by programmers working on other problems. The bootstrap effects due to capitalizing on the work of the pioneer simulators in part accounts for the considerable achievements in the field.

The major problem in the area of simulation, as I view it, is the problem of how to evaluate the product of a simulation effort. I would like to discuss this problem by selecting one example from the literature and examining it in depth. Following this, I will report on a simulation effort which is amenable to quantitative evaluation and represents a simulation technique which presumably could be paralleled in many other areas.

I turn first to EPAM (Elementary Perceiver and Memorizer), which was devised by Feigenbaum (1959) to simulate verbal learning, both serial and paired-associate. It has, in fact, been used to simulate learning under a variety of conditions (Feigenbaum, 1961; Feigenbaum and Simon, 1961; Feigenbaum and Simon, 1962).

A recent article by Simon and Feigenbaum (1964) describes a comparison of EPAM with the outcome of several previously published studies. I would like to review a portion of that article to illustrate the problem mentioned above. Table 12 is a reproduction of Simon and Feigenbaum's table showing a comparison of the results of EPAM with Underwood's (1953) study of intralist similarity.

EPAM learned the same lists of nonsense syllables as had Underwood's subjects. The first row in Table 12 represents the relative effects of stimulus and response similarity as reported by Underwood, with the low stimulus similarity, low response similarity condition, (L-L), set equal to 100. The second row represents the relative effects of the similarity when EPAM learned the lists in its normal mode. In an attempt to explain the discrepancy between the simulation and the actual results, particularly for the stimuli which were of a medium degree of similarity and responses were low similarity, (M-L), Simon and Feigenbaum hypothesized that subjects recode nonsense syllables aurally into a consonant-vowel unit and a consonant unit. (This hy-

TABLE 12[a]

COMPARISON OF EPAM WITH UNDERWOOD'S (1953) DATA
ON INTRALIST SIMILARITY (RELATIVE NUMBER OF TRIALS
TO CRITERION, L-L = 100)

Data	Condition of stimulus and response similarity				
	L-L	L-M	M-L	L-H	H-L
Underwood	100	96	109	104	131
EPAM — III ("visual only")	100	88	141	91	146
EPAM — III ("aural only")	100	100	100	100	114
EPAM — III ("visual" and "aural" mixed, 1:1)	100	94	121	96	130
EPAM — III ("visual" and "aural" mixed, 1:2)	100	96	114	97	125

[a]From Simon, H. A., and Feigenbaum, E. A. An information-processing theory of some effects of similarity, familiarization, and meaningfulness in verbal learning. *J. verb. Learn. verb. Beh.*, 1964, 3, 389, with permission of the authors and the copyright owner.

pothesis seems counter to Espers' (1925) findings that subjects treat trigrams as units and find it nearly impossible to break this set.) The segmentally recoded syllables would make Underwood's syllables more dissimilar to one another than they appear by a graphemic analysis; thus, they are easy to learn for EPAM and for subjects who recode. The results of an EPAM simulation after the materials had been physically recoded to conform to the hypothesis are presented in the third row of Table 12. All conditions then yielded equal effects except the high stimulus similarity list which was too easy relative to the other conditions. The authors then computed the average of EPAM predictions, "assuming that some subjects are processing in the 'visual-literal' mode and some in the 'aural' mode." Since, in three out of the four relevant comparisons, the "aural simulation" produced a constant equal to the initial arbitrary base, the average prediction had to be better than the original prediction ("visual mode") unless the original prediction had been between the base and the actual data, which it never was. In the fourth condition, Underwood's (H-L), when the two EPAM estimates straddled the true value, the averaging also automatically improved the prediction. The multiplier which was applied to produce the fourth row, one part "visual" learners to two parts "aural" learners, is, to the best of my knowledge, unsupported anywhere in the literature. Also, I know of no research which suggests that subjects segment trigrams in the hypothesized way.

I would like to relate the results of one more EPAM simulation before discussing the implications of these findings. I used EPAM to simulate the learning of a paired-associate list made up of materials which were first used by Horton and Kjeldergaard (1961). These materials consisted of low-frequency English words selected from the Thorndike-Lorge (1944) list, words such as DELFT, PRAWN, VENAL, CAIRN, etc. The words were selected and paired in such a way as to produce a list of eight pairs which were low in intralist similarity on both the stimulus and response sides. The comparison data was gathered from 30 Harvard and Radcliffe undergraduates.

Although these materials were devised and paired in such a way as to represent a relatively homogeneous list in terms of difficulty, an analysis by PAVLOV (Kjeldergaard, 1965), a retrieval program designed to perform clerical searches of learning data, indicated that the individual pairs were quite heterogeneous, varying from very easy to very difficult.

My limited knowledge of EPAM indicated that it too would consider the list heterogeneous and relatively easy. The simulation supported this conclusion. EPAM learned rather quickly, so that trial comparisons are not meaningful. If, however, one examines the item analysis data, the pairs which EPAM learned first turn out to be those pairs which the subjects found most difficult. Table 13 presents several comparisons of difficulty measures between the four pairs EPAM learned first (all on a single trial) and the four pairs which it learned last. Whether one looks at the number of correct anticipations, the trial on which a given pair was first correctly anticipated, or the number of trials to a criterion of one perfect trial, the four pairs which EPAM found easiest were, relatively, much more difficult for human subjects. Although the three measures are very highly correlated, a statistical test of any one of these measures is significant according to the usual standard. I then examined the "protocols" of the individual subjects and could not find a single subject who learned the list in any way comparable to the way EPAM had.

My purpose here is not to point out that EPAM as a model is incomplete, for I am sure its authors would concur. Instead, I have attempted to show that such discrepancies would not be detected if only global performance measures are examined with a simulation designed to simulate a group effect. This is particularly true where only relative

TABLE 13

LEARNING BY HARVARD AND RADCLIFFE
STUDENTS OF PAIRED ASSOCIATES FOUND
EASY AND DIFFICULT FOR EPAM

Group		EPAM Easy Pairs	EPAM Difficult Pairs
10-Trial Group N = 15	Mean trials to criterion	9.46	7.67
	Mean 1st correct anticipation	6.63	5.12
	Mean correct anticipations	5.45	7.80
15-Trial Group N = 15	Mean trials to criterion	9.93	7.13
	Mean 1st correct anticipation	7.15	4.83
	Mean correct anticipations	7.22	9.93

group comparisons are made such as with the Underwood data. Only a microscopic comparison, a point by point analysis, will provide sufficient information for a proper evaluation of the simulation.

Evaluation of Simulations

I should point out before proceeding, that I have selected EPAM for detailed discussion only as matter of convenience and because I felt that I knew more about its subject matter area than about most other simulations. The problem of evaluation is a general one, and the results of many simulations could be questioned in terms of "goodness of fit." Typically, evidence supporting a simulation effort takes one of the three following forms:

1. Subjective Judgment. A qualitative statement is made by the simulator, frequently with anecdotal evidence to support the conclusions. Although some evidence is better than none, it is difficult to decide how much of the simulation-data match is specific to the program or to the case, and how much is general.

2. Program-problem generality. The extent to which a program is capable of simulating a variety of behaviors, or the extent to which it can be applied to a given behavior under various conditions, is sometimes offered as evidence favoring a model. EPAM, as mentioned previously, has been shown to simulate both serial and paired-associate phenomena under a variety of experimental conditions. Although I would concur that this is positive evidence, it should be noted that programs written in a general format with respect to input-output, and with parameters that can be externally manipulated, will generally be applicable to problems other than the ones for which they are specifically written. Thus again the question of adequacy of the simulation remains unanswered.

3. Curve fitting. The acceptability of curve fitting as evidence depends upon the number of points being fitted as well as statistical considerations such as the sample size and variability of the data being simulated. Statistically, one can only prove lack of fit, and failure to reject the null hypothesis does not prove the converse. Usually, in simulation studies, only a visual comparison is offered, without any statistical test.

An alternative which is at least theoretically feasible, but which has rarely been implemented in simulation studies, is to acknowledge individual differences and take them into account in the simulation. Those programs which are already sensitive to individual differences need to simulate more subjects so that hits and misses may be tabulated and tested with frequency-test statistics. Others need to incorporate individual differences into their model and then simulate according to these parameters. Simon and Feigenbaum (1964) seem to suggest this when they assume that some subjects are processing in the "visual-literal" mode and some in the "aural" mode. Their task is to demonstrate that this is so, and that EPAM can simulate either kind (or perhaps even a mixture), rather than an average of their effects. By way of illustrating that this kind of simulation is feasible and informative, I would now like to describe a recent simulation effort which I have undertaken in an attempt to simulate free association behavior. The program, called APE (Association Producing Engine) is based upon the following theoretical assumptions:

1. Common language background or common language experience establishes certain language habits which, although they may differ in strength from one individual to another, exist at some strengths for all individuals who have even remotely comparable experiences.

2. The above habits are reflected in a general way in normative data, such as the Minnesota Norms (Russell and Jenkins, 1954).

3. Each individual has a set of verbal habits that include the normative responses (other than the very rare ones).

Evidence for the first three assumptions is contained in the work of Jenkins (1959), Storms (1958), Horton, Marlowe, and Crowne (1963), and Rosen and Russell (1956).

4. Individuals have certain response tendencies (or sets) such that certain classes of responses are more probable than others.

5. These response tendencies vary from individual to individual.

The last two assumptions have been supported in part by the finding of Carroll, Kjeldergaard, and Carton (1962), and by Kjeldergaard and Carroll (1962).

6. These response tendencies vary within an individual over time.

APE simulations can be viewed only as tests of assumptions four, five, and six.

In addition to the above assumptions about an individual's verbal habits, the program is dependent upon a classification scheme which places the responses of free-association experiments into five categories, as follows:

Class I (Contrast-Coordinate).—This category includes logical opposites such as *black-white*, *slow-fast*, as well as coordinate pairs that are frequently used in a contrasting way, and/or coordinate pairs that frequently occur together in the same "frame" connected by "and," e.g., *table-chair*, *man-woman*, *salt-pepper*.

Class II (Superordinate—Adjective-Noun).—This includes logically superordinate response terms, e.g., *dog-animal*, as well as adjective-noun pairs, e.g., *black-night*, noun-adjective pairs, e.g., *woman-lovely*.

Class III (Subordinate—Noun-Verb, Verb-Adverb).—This class includes logically subordinate responses, e.g., *animal-dog*, as well as noun-verb, e.g., *house-build*, verb-adverb, e.g., *simulate-well*.

Class IV (Synonym—Coordinate).—A category including logical synonyms, e.g., *beautiful-pretty*; and coordinates (same class) that are not ordinarily contrasting pairs, e.g., *table-desk*, *dog-fox*, etc.

Class V (Idiosyncratic).—This class contains response words which bear no obvious semantic relationship to stimuli, and appear to be a function of the individual's particular conditioning history. In classifying the normative data, the frequency cut-off point was too high to include idiosyncratic responses; the category is included in the scheme since it may be useful to predict that the subject will give an unpredictable response.

APE works in the following way: For each stimulus word, the program makes two predictions, the category of the subject's response and the actual word within the category. Each category has associated with it a weight which may be viewed as the probability that the subject will respond with a word contained in that category. In a similar way, each word within a category has a weight, derived from normative data, which may be viewed as the probability that a particular word within the selected category will be the subject's response.

The dictionary was derived from the Minnesota Norms (Russell and Jenkins, 1954) and all responses in the norms with a frequency equivalent to 0.5 percent or greater were classified according to the previously described scheme. The normative frequencies are used to arrive at the word weights. The dictionary for each stimulus term is read into the computer as data. Similarly, subjects' responses are read in as the data to be compared with the computer predictions. Subjects for this experiment were psychology graduate students who were given the Kent-Rosanoff list with the same instructions used in the normative study.

For each stimulus word, the program predicts a response category and one of the dictionary words contained in that category. The category prediction is made by normalizing the product of the momentary category weights and the proportional frequency of all of the words in a given category. If all categories had equal weights and the sum of the response frequencies within each category were equal, all categories would be equally likely. As the weights favor one category or as one category has a higher proportion of the normative response frequencies, that category has a higher probability of being selected. Once the normalized weights are derived, actual selection is done via a random number generator.

The word prediction within a category also uses the random number generator. The probability that a given word will be predicted is a simple function of the proportional response frequency associated with that word compared to all words in the category.

The initial category weights are read in as data. So far, they have been set equal to the total proportion of responses in a given category over all stimuli in the norms. The values are as follows:

Class I   (Contrast—Coordinate) .33
Class II   (Subordinate, adjective—noun) .30
Class III   (Superordinate, noun—verb) .16
Class IV   (Synonyms—coordinate) .19
Class V   (Idiosyncratic) .02

The category weights are adjusted after each response; the response class of the subject's response is incremented and the remaining classes are decremented. The magnitude of the adjustment is a function of two parameters, one of which is to be read in as data and a second which is a measure of the program's success. Preliminary experiments indicate that the magnitude of adjustment, within very broad limits, has little effect.

Summarizing what has been said about the theory and the model to this point, it is assumed that subjects in a free association situation have, for each stimulus item, a set of possible responses. Which response is actually made is a function of a number of variables—two of which are availability (reflected in the normative frequency) and response biases or sets (reflected in the category weights). Since a number of other non-specified factors help determine which response is emitted, a random selection device is included to account for the effect of these variables. The program simulates one response at a time, based in part on an analysis of the kind of response that a subject has been making.

A first attempt at an evaluation may be made by referring to Table 14 and by applying the famous test suggested by Turing (1950). Looking at the pairs of columns under responses, one may try to decide which is the person, A or A', B or B', C or C', and which is the product of the simulation. It should be noted that this is a selected subset of the 26 S's who have been simulated, and that the program does not uniformly perform this well. The real people, incidentally, are A, B', and C'.

Since Turing's test (or more precisely, this shifty modification of it) lacks rigor, one can turn to statistics. Table 15 presents the results of a typical simulation run and some comparative data for the 26 subjects who have been simulated. The statistics are reported in terms of proportions. Since APE has not been completely deloused, there are a number of minor dictionary errors, e.g., singular-plural distinctions, which would unfairly handicap the program if absolute frequencies

TABLE 14
RESPONSES AND APE SIMULATED RESPONSES TO THE LAST
20 WORDS ON THE KENT-ROSANOFF WORD ASSOCIATION TEST

Stimulus	Responses A	Responses A'	Responses B	Responses B'	Responses C	Responses C'
Butter	Buttermilk	Bread	Bread	Soft	Bread	Bread
Doctor	Nurse	Nurse	Nurse	Medicine	Dentist	Lawyer
Loud	Soft	Soft	Soft	Soft	Soft	Soft
Thief	Robber	Robber	Steal	Steal	Steal	Steal
Lion	Cub	Wolf	Tamer	Roar	Animal	Cub
Joy	Sorrow	Sorrow	Sad	Happiness	Sorrow	Sorrow
Bed	Room	Room	Sleep	Sleep	Sleep	Chair
Heavy	Light	Coat	Hard	Light	Light	Light
Tobacco	Smoke	Smoke	Chew	Smoke	Cigarette	Cigarette
Baby	Sitter	Cute	Cry	Child	Blue	Boy
Moon	Sky	Bright	Earth	Glow	Full	Stars
Scissors	Cloth	Cut	Cut	Cut	Sharp	Thread
Quiet	Noisy	Loud	Rest	Shout	Noise	Soft
Green	Water	Grass	Color	Color	Red	Blue
Salt	Pepper	Sea	Eat	Pepper	Water	Sugar
Street	Avenue	Sign	Walk	City	Lane	Road
King	Queen	Queen	Queen	Queen	Throne	Queen
Cheese	Spread	Cracker	Food	Cake	Bread	Bread
Blossom	Flower	Flower	Rose	Fruit	Flower	Flower
Afraid	Danger	Courage	Shake	Fear	Brave	Scared

were used; consequently, responses which were not found in the dictionary were ignored in terms of reweighting and tabulating hits and misses.

The second column of Table 15 presents the statistics for commonality scores as used by Jenkins (1959). Each of these represents the proportion of times a subject responded with the most popular response for a given stimulus. Practically, though not technically, it might be viewed as an upper limit in terms of word prediction for APE; the expected value would be less than this. The third column lists the statistics for word hits for the program. Column four relates to the category hits in the simulation run. The program fairly consistently predicts the correct category about half of the time. Columns five through eight give the words and category hits for non-simulation comparative runs with the weights held constant, according to the total normative category frequency (Column 5–6) or with weights equal for all categories (Column 7–8).

TABLE 15

MEANS, RANGES, AND STANDARD DEVIATIONS OF COM-
MONALITY SCORES AND OF PROPORTION OF WORD AND
CATEGORY HITS WHEN APE WAS PROGRAMMED WITH
SELF-ADJUSTING WEIGHTS, WITH CONSTANT WEIGHTS
BASED UPON NORMS, AND WITH EQUAL CONSTANT
WEIGHTS (N = 26)

Statistic	Common-ality	Simulation		Norm Weights		Equal Weights	
		Word	Category	Word	Category	Word	Category
Mean	.41	.25	.51	.24	.49	.22	.45
Range	.26-.55	.12-.38	.38-.61	.11-.37	.42-.58	.14-.30	.37-.55
SD	.08	.07	.05	.07	.05	.06	.05

Even a casual inspection indicates that a frequency-weighted random selection from the same dictionary does as well as the simulation
based upon an analysis of the subject's performance and a dynamic
weighting scheme. This holds for all individuals. Where the simulator
does well, frequency prediction does well. To account for the total
failure, since there was at least some justification for thinking that it
might work, the three most plausible explanations would seem to be
as follows: (1) The model is inappropriate and people do not respond
to this test in the way that has been assumed. There is evidence cited
earlier that people do tend to behave consistently, at least with respect to contrast-coordinates (Carroll, Kjeldergaard, and Carton;
1962). It may be, however, that the situation is so dynamic that general tendencies have little effect on momentary response. (2) The
dictionary may be in error; the classes may lack homogeneity. Accordingly, weighting according to this classification scheme may work
against the general model, or produce, at best, random effects. Other
than contrast-coordinates, the classes lack empirical support. (3) There
may be mechanical programming errors which work against the model.
I can think of at least one which would have a detrimental effect,
although it alone would not account for the gross failure.

Rather than pursue a lengthly post-mortem, let me return to some
general implications from this study. By itself, it provides a strong
argument in favor of simulation and for careful attention to individual
differences. If I had not tested the model on the computer, if I had
not tested it against a number of subjects, I might have persisted for
years with this model and with this classification scheme. Looking

at one subject, as many simulators have done, I might have concluded success. There were runs in which the program achieved 65 percent category hits and 38 percent word hits for a single subject.

I remain confident that I could have written a program to simulate one subject, as some others have done, and been successful, but such a program would lack generality. Only by attempting to write a general program and match it against multiple subjects was I able to fail so summarily.

In terms of the general programming strategy, APE simulated one item at a time and was presumably self-correcting. This may not always be possible or desirable. It is difficult, however, to conceive of a cognitive process which can be simulated, but which cannot incorporate individual differences either in the program or as a basis for evaluation.

REFERENCES

Armer, P. Attitudes towards intelligent machines. 1960, Tech. Rep. 60-600, p. 3-19.

Bernstein, A., and Roberts, M. Computor vs. chess-player. Scient., 1958, *198*, 96-105.

Carroll, J. B., Kjeldergaard, P. M., and Carton, A. S. Number of opposites versus number of primaries as a response measure in free-association tests. *J. verb. Learn. and verb. Behav.*, 1962, *1*, 22-30.

Esper, E. A. A technique for the experimental investigation of associative interference in artificial material. *Lang. Monogr.*, 1925, *1*, 1-46.

Feigenbaum, E. *An information processing theory of verbal learning*, Santa Monica, Calif.: The RAND Corporation, 1959. (Report P-1817.)

Feigenbaum, E. *The simulation of verbal learning behavior.* Washington, D. C.: Spartan Books: Proc. of *W. J. C. C.*, 1961, 121-132.

Feigenbaum, E., and Simon, H. A. Forgetting in an association memory. A.C.M., 1961, *16*, 202-205.

Feigenbaum, E., and Simon, H. A. A theory of the serial position effect. *Brit. J. Psychol.*, 1962, *53*, 307-320.

Horton, D. L., and Kjeldergaard, P. M. An experimental analysis of associative factors in mediated generalizations. *Psychol. Monogr.*, 1961, *75* (Whole No. 515).

Horton, D. L., Marlowe, D., and Crowne, D. P. The effects of instructional set and need for social approval on commonality of word association responses. *J. abnorm. and soc. Psychol.*, 1963, *66*, 67-72.

Jenkins, J. J. Effects on word-association of the set to give popular responses. *Psychol. Rep.*, 1959, 5, 94.

Kendler, T. S. Concept formation. In P. R. Farnsworth (ed.), *Annual Review of Psychol.*, Vol. 12, 1961.

Kister, J., Stein, P., Ulam, S., Walden, W., and Wells, M. Experiments in chess. *Assoc. for Comp. Machinery*, 1957.

Kjeldergaard, P. M. An information retrieval program for learning studies. Unpublished paper, 1965.

Kjeldergaard, P. M., and Carroll, J. B. Two measures of free-association response and their relation to scores on selected personality tests. *Psychol. Rep.*, 1962, *12*, 667-670.

Laing, R. A review of "Computers and Common Sense" by M. Taube. *Behav. Sc.*, 1962, 7, 238-240.

Neisser, U. The imitation of man by machine. *Science*, 1963, *139*, 193-197.

Newell, A., Shaw, H. C., and Simon, H. A. Chess-playing program and the problem of complexity. *IBM Journal*, 1958, *2*, 830-835.

Reitman, W. R. A review of "Computers and common sense, the myth of thinking machines." *Science*, 1962, *135*, 718.

Reitman, W. R. Information processing models in psychology. *Science*, 1964, *144*, 1192-1198.

Rosen, E., and Russell, W. A. *Frequency characteristics of successive word association.* Tech. Rep. No. 12, 1956, University of Minnesota.

Russell, W. A., and Jenkins, J. J. *The complete Minnesota norms for responses to 100 words from the Kent-Rosanoff Word Association Test.* Tech. Rep. No. 11, 1954, University of Minnesota.

Simon, H. A., and Feigenbaum, E. An information-processing theory of some effects of similarity, familiarization, and meaningfulness in verbal learning. *J. verb. Learn. and verb. Behav.*, 1964, *3*, 385-396.

Storms, L. H. Apparent backward association. A situational effect. *J. Exp. Psychol.*, 1958, *55*, 390-395.

Taube, M. *Computers and common sense, the myth of thinking machines.* New York: Columbia University Press, 1961.

Thorndike, E. L., and Lorge, I. *The teacher's word book of 30,000 words.* New York: Columbia, University Press, 1944.

Turing, A. M. Computing machines and intelligence. *Mind*, 1950, 59, 433-460.

Underwood, B. J. Studies of distributed practice: VII. Learning and retention of paired nonsense syllables as a function of intralist similarity. *J. exp. Psychol.*, 1953, 45, 133-142.

SIMULATION MODELS AND HUMAN DIFFERENCES

LEE W. GREGG

Carnegie Institute of Technology

The dual intent of Kjeldergaard's paper—to bring to light some problems of simulation and to illustrate a strategy for evaluating theories—is only partially fulfilled. He has certainly pointed up the difficulties one encounters in trying to construct a model of human behavior at the level of detail that demands close attention to the unique moment-by-moment responses of the individual. He has not, I think, made clear the real issues in evaluating computer simulation models. Let me return to the question of evaluating computer models after commenting more generally on a few of the points Kjeldergaard has made.

Role of Individual Differences

In the first place, it is true that a successful simulation must take into account human differences. As a result, and contrary to Kjeldergaard's statement, most computer simulation models *have* attempted to account for individual differences in great depth. The very nature of the technique demands that decisions about what a particular subject in an experimental situation will do at a particular time must be made. Individual differences are represented in the several successful simulation programs that have been produced. For example, the EPAM program makes explicit use of the fact that different verbal materials are more or less familiar to the subject and exist in memory for that subject at the outset of the experimental run. An attention-directing mechanism is also a part of EPAM and determines which

234

items will be considered in the short-term memory of the simulated learner. Feldman's (1963) binary choice program was capable of being reorganized in ways that matched individual subject protocols. The several hypothesis selection mechanisms that were incorporated in that program could be arranged independently for different response sequences. Although the general problem solver of Newell and Simon (1963) is much more toward the artificial intelligence end of the continuum that Kjeldergaard has proposed, there is, nevertheless, provision for differentially representing the cues the particular subjects might associate with the operators for producing action. My own sequential problem-solving program (Laughery and Gregg, 1962) is one that considers in detail individual differences in perceptual encoding. The initial state of that program contains symbolic representations of concepts and strategies. These comprise the assumed repertoire of the subject at the time he comes into the experimental situation. Obviously, the repertoire can vary as a function of what we know or think we know about the knowledges and skills of a particular subject.

I do not wish to be placed in the position of defending any particular simulation model, especially one written by others. That EPAM failed to learn a list in any way comparable to Kjeldergaard's individual subjects does not surprise me. But I would like to make the point that there exists no alternative theory that will provide a precise trial-by-trial, item-by-item prediction for serial or paired-associate learning tasks. An encouraging thought is that while psychologists often fail to communicate their ideas by word of mouth, perhaps at some future time we can tell one another precisely what we mean by exchanging computer programs.

Nature of Individual Differences in Simulation Models

What are the individual differences that are treated in simulation models of the sort that describe the information processes of man? First, it is clear that structural properties of the information store—the concepts, the remembered facts, and the previously acquired strategies for perceiving, identifying, and naming—are different from one individual to another, and can be represented in various ways. These, then, are the data from which behavior is generated. Second, there are the functional rules that describe manipulations and transformations of the data store. They can be organized differently for different individuals. These are the processes that Glanzer has spelled out in great detail in his statement of the requirements for an adequate theory of behavior (see Chapter 7). Together, the structural properties of memory and the functional rules for organizing the sequence of responses form a complex system. Most of us in trying to organize our own thinking about human behavior are capable of handling only parts of the total system at one time. The computer's role is to generate the consequences of our assumptions about what the subject knows when he comes into the experiment and what he is doing during the course of it.

Kjeldergaard's Model

But what about Kjeldergaard's model of controlled association? He has presented it as an illustration of how the psychologist might gain an understanding of a particular aspect of human behavior. The particular ideas incorporated in that program failed to predict association tendencies any better than prediction based on random selection from group norms. The mechanisms that underlie the operation of the Association Producing Engine (APE) are themselves probabilistic selection mechanisms that are modified by incrementing and decrementing the possibility that a particular category of the classification scheme will be selected.

Insofar as the model assumes that there are "random" variables over which the experimenter has no control, the use of random selection seems justified. The controlled association task is probably one of the most difficult of all the tasks we might propose for modeling. There is a very large set of possible responses; there is very little opportunity to observe whatever cognitive mechanisms produce the response. However, there are a few things that we can be sure of about an individual subject's behavior in such a task. Most important is that subjects do not and cannot select anything randomly.

Kjeldergaard's model is based on normative data that are themselves abstractions of behavioral results. As such, it is a theory about how data should behave, not about people. This, then, becomes the crux of the problem of evaluating simulation models.

Strategy for Simulation Models

Models that purport to be theories of human cognitive behavior must specify what people do. The goal of the research is to identify processes that can be implemented in a central nervous system. Although the simulation is implemented through the computer, the fact that physical isomorphism does not hold for computer and man is irrelevant. The issue is whether or not we can show a functional correspondence between the proposed cognitive processes and the behavior of the subject.

To do this requires a research strategy based on developing experimental techniques that bring to public view more of the usually covert cognitive events. We have used verbal protocols of subjects "thinking aloud" during the course of problem-solving tasks. We have designed tasks so that more intermediate steps intervene between problem statement and solution, and these must be signaled by the subject via switch throws or verbal responses. We are currently using correlative measures such as eye movements to increase points of contact between theory and observable behavior.

Within the framework I have outlined, each computer simulation is a model of a single individual, responding in the dynamic context of his environment. It is perfectly possible, however, to create in theory a number of individuals and examine the usual kinds of statistics generated in an experimental group of subjects. The point that Kjeldergaard makes, namely that microscopic comparisons or point by point analysis should provide information for proper evaluation of the simulation, is a good one. That this should be done for many subjects rather than one is also obvious, for only then will we be able to understand which interactions among the structural and functional properties of the model are fundamental. Only then can we argue that the information processes incorporated in the model are, in fact, general enough to account for the behavior we are investigating.

REFERENCES

Feldman, J. Simulation of behavior in the binary choice experiment. In Feigenbaum, E. A. and Feldman, J. (eds.), *Computers and thought*, New York: McGraw Hill Book Company, 1963, 329-346.

Laughery, K. R., and Gregg, L. W. The simulation of human problem solving behavior. *Psychometrika*, 1962, 27, 265-282.

Newell, A., and Simon, H. A. GPS, a program that simulates human thought. In Feigenbaum, E. A. and Feldman, J. (eds.), *Computers and thought*, New York: McGraw Hill Book Company, 1963, 279-293.

11

INDIVIDUAL DIFFERENCES AND THEORETICAL PROCESS VARIABLES: GENERAL COMMENTS ON THE CONFERENCE [1]

ARTHUR W. MELTON
University of Michigan

Each one of the principal papers and discussants' commentaries speaks informatively to the issue of this conference, and so deserves some mention in my general comments. However, this is impossible. Therefore, I will confine my remarks to the reiteration and examination of a proposition about research on individual differences in learning that seems to me to be of fundamental importance for future progress.

The central theme in a number of papers is that research on individual differences in learning must be guided by theories of human learning and performance. It is not enough that we measure individual dif-

[1] The preparation of this paper was supported in part by the Advanced Research Projects Agency, Department of Defense, and monitored by the Air Force Office of Scientific Research, under Contract No. AF 49(638)-1235 with the Human Performance Center, Department of Psychology.

ferences in performance in learning tasks as a function of the almost infinite variety of operationally defined variables in those tasks. Nor is it enough—although we may gain some guidance from rigorous factor-analytic studies—to know that such-and-such performance is heavily weighted with whatever is measured in a reference test of "immediate memory" as defined by Games (1962), or others. *What is necessary is that we frame our hypotheses about individual differences variables in terms of the process constructs of contemporary theories of learning and performance.*

This italicized statement is the basic theme on which Jenkins, Glanzer, Fitts, Jensen, Zeaman, and Maltzman play variations. These deserve a brief review in order that there may be no uncertainty about the theme. Jenkins concludes by saying: "Individual differences can be looked at by the experimentalist as a way of adding information to his description of important constructs developed in his concern with the process of learning" (p. 56). Glanzer makes the point in his insistence that "R-R theory" be the approach to individual differences theory, after specifying that the first R is an intervening process or mechanism and the second R is the output response or performance. He goes on to say that such R-R theory requires the specification of a manipulable process within the individual. Fitts has no quarrel with the meta-theory of Glanzer, and in fact says that "[he] would give *even greater emphasis* to Glanzer's point that R-R theory must deal with sequential psychological processes . . ." (p. 163); his critical comments merely point out that Glanzer has not been as refined in his process analysis as he should be. Jensen clearly concurs in this emphasis on process variables that derive from general behavior theory when he lists (p. 131) "genotype" processes of behavior theory such as trace decay, trace consolidation, reactive inhibition, stimulus satiation, etc. Finally, the theme seems to show through clearly in Maltzman's emphasis on the "orienting reflex" and in Zeaman's conclusion that IQ affects the attention processes in discrimination tasks and the immediate memory process in verbal tasks, but in neither case does it affect the rate of gain in S-R strength from repetition.

This is an impressive consensus, even if there are those who prefer the sophisticated empiricism of a factor-analytic approach, and others who remain suspicious of theories that employ process or mechanism constructs. Perhaps the latter (who might well include the former) have a point when they remain aloof from these speculative processes and mechanisms that characterize some of the "cognitive" and information processing theories that are around today. Such speculations sometimes read as though behavior is the product of a team of homunculi operating according to the principles of group dynamics, and one wonders whether our neo-behaviorism has gone down the drain. However, I shall not be distracted from allegiance to the main theme by these slips-of-the-tongue, be they diagnostic in the Freudian sense or merely colloquialisms. I agree with Glanzer when he says that the most significant development in theoretical and experimental psychology in recent years is acceptance of the need for theoretical statements about processes or mechanisms that intervene between stimuli and responses. The argument is no longer about whether such intervening processes occur and have controlling effects on behavior, but about their defining properties, their sequencing, and their interactions.

Where does this conclusion leave us in our new strategy for examining the relations between individual differences and learning and performance? It leaves us with a program, but without a ready-made, agreed-to process-theory of behavior. We cannot at this time ask well-directed questions about the individual differences in Process X without risking the discovery that our process is quite a complicated affair that is, in fact, a compound of other more fundamental processes. Although this discovery may give heart to those with factor-analytic leanings, it should sink the individual differences theorist even more deeply in the process-variable approach, and contribute to a more adequate process theory of behavior. As I see it, this contribution to process theory will happen in two ways. First, our interest in manipulating and finding individual differences in the hypothesized process will refine our analysis of the process and contribute to a *taxonomy of processes*. Second, research on individual differences in hypothesized process factors will be a double-edged sword in process validation: if there are observable individual differences in performance that can be traced directly to individual differences in a process that is identified in a theory, then the theory gains greatly in predictive power and acceptability; if, on the other hand, the process does not vary between individuals, or if it varies without significant correlated performance effects, there is probably something wrong with the process construct.

In the last paragraph, the term "taxonomy of processes" was used. I should like to elaborate on the meaning I attach to it, because I suspect that many taxonomic ambiguities will be involved in carrying out this program of research on individual differences in processes. One of our recurring difficulties is with the term "process" which is used to describe everything within the scope of our taxonomic interest from "the learning process," which means any instance of adaptive behavior that influences later adaptive behavior, through "the learning processes" which means conditioning, rote learning, skill learning, problem solving, concept attainment, etc., to various levels of inferred processes such as stimulus recognition, response integration, S-R association, attentional filtering, a variety of information transforming processes, stimulus trace process, memory trace process, central inhibition, neural recruitment, etc., etc. It should be clear that neither I nor those with whom I am agreeing are using the term "process" so loosely. Instead, they make a distinction between a task taxonomy and a process taxonomy. This distinction is very well described by Jensen in his contrast of phenotype and genotype taxonomies, the former having to do with combinations of operationally defined task variables and the latter having to do with inferred processes within the organism. These are the processes or classes of events—some theorists like the term "mechanisms"—within the organism that are properly inferred after one has tested them by what Garner, Hake, and Eriksen (1956) call "converging operations."

This important distinction between a task taxonomy and a process taxonomy does not, however, relieve us of taxonomic problems in the study of individual differences in processes. There is no magic whereby the "processes" that should be examined with respect to individual differences can be identified. The process concepts to be examined will depend on the level of analysis that our theoretical-experimental approach has achieved and on the level of analysis and range of task variables that the theoretical model attempts to encompass.

These dependencies are clearly illustrated in the papers in this conference. First, we always have with us a primitive taxonomy of learning processes, by which I mean the classification of learning processes as conditioning, rote learning, selective learning, skill learning, problem solving, concept attainment, etc. Although these classes of learning situations may be identified as major classes in a task taxonomy, our early theoretical insights also arranged them in a process taxonomy. Thus, conditioning and rote learning were thought to be heavily weighted by a process of simple associative learning (S-R connection formation and strengthening) and selective learning, concept attainment, skill learning, and problem solving were thought to be heavily weighted by a process of discovery and selective strengthening of S-R associations, or perhaps (among theorists of an anti-S-R bent) by "understanding" or "organization." These process distinctions that we originally thought to be strongly correlated with the task distinctions of our primitive taxonomy are now seen to be relative at best, and sometimes downright false (Melton, 1964). A prime example is rote verbal learning, which was originally thought to be a matter of simple associative learning, but is now seen to involve "raw" associative learning only rarely and discovery of a "good" mediator very often (Underwood, 1964).

My point is not that the process distinction between simple associative learning (through contiguity) and selective learning (through differential reinforcement), and the primitive taxonomy of tasks that was thought to reflect this process distinction, should be discarded in our research on individual differences. The process distinction and the task taxonomy live on into the present, and you will see that they have been appropriately observed as boundary conditions by participants in this conference, perhaps through the urging of the Chairman. Also, it is noteworthy that a very important recent treatment of the conditions and management of human learning (Gagné, 1965) uses only a slightly more analytic classification of learning processes. What is being urged is that the focus of studies of individual differences be shifted to more analytic levels of process specification, as reflected in contemporary theories of learning and performance.

So, research on individual differences should emphasize process variables that reflect the most advanced levels of analysis of our contemporary theories of human learning and performance. But this approach is no panacea. It is merely a way to increase the likelihood of significant advances in the understanding of individual differences. As everyone knows, we have at this time no general theory of human learning and performance. Therefore, we have no necessary and sufficient list of process constructs or variables that can serve as the foci of individual-differences research. Even though the number of genotype process variables may eventually be found to be relatively small, as Jensen suggests, at present the number that must be considered is quite large, and the necessity and sufficiency of each is quite unclear, as Cofer suggests. One has merely to identify and list the process variables referred to by Jenkins, Jensen, Zeaman, Maltzman, Glanzer, Fitts, Cofer, and others in this conference, to recognize the problem we have when we set forth to analyse individual differences in such process variables. And it may well be, as Cofer states, that highly specific task characteristics interact with highly specific individual "propensities and abilities" to produce major portions of the observed variance in performance of most learning tasks.

These are pessimistic thoughts, and theory is always an expression of optimism. I believe our optimism can be recovered in this instance by a closer look at contemporary theories of human learning and performance, especially those having to do with verbal learning and behavior, and the intellectual performance that depends so heavily on verbal skills. At this point in time, it seems to me that we have two competing theoretical approaches to human learning and performance, both of which use a process language to describe what is going on within the organism between input stimulus and output response. These are the S-R Association and Information Processing theoretical approaches that have been mentioned earlier. Their proponents are well-known and frequently referenced in this conference: Underwood (1964), Underwood and Schulz (1960), Postman (1961, 1964), Kendler (1964) and Gagné (1965) are representative of the S-R approach; Broadbent (1958), Miller, Galanter, and Pribram (1960), Bruner, Goodnow, and Austin (1956) and Hunt (1962) are representative of the IP approach.

Characteristically, Information Processing theories of behavior emphasize "mechanisms" or "acts" that process information as it enters and passes through the nervous system. They have process constructs such as pre-perceptual sensory storage, attentional filtering, perceptual coding, perceptual and memorial scanning and search, and a collection of states or processes associated with statistical (probabilistic) decision-making. Great emphasis is placed on cognitive sets, rules, and strategies. All of these "central" processes have the common characteristic that they are ways in which the control of response by antecedent events, conceived as stimuli, is overridden or replaced by control by the processing activity. In contrast, S-R Association theories seek an explanation of the sequencing of these intervening events and the determination of the output response in terms of relations between antecedent (stimulus) and consequent (response) events that reflect learning (S-R association formation) and transfer of learning (based on principles that relate transfer to stimulus similarity).

These two approaches are not incompatible, and there are some signs that they are moving toward a common process language; in fact, if psychology should be blessed with a truly great theorist in the next 20 years, his theoretical tour-de-force may well be the systematic integration of these two approaches. One reason for optimism in this regard is that the two approaches have been principally concerned with, and applied to, quite different problems in the analysis of behavior causation. The S-R Association theory has been concerned with the formation and strengthening of S-R relations and the rules for transfer of such relations when antecedent conditions (stimuli) are changed, and characteristically it minimizes the attentional, perceptual, and central processing (rules, strategies, concept utilization) factors. The major portion of S-R Association theory as we know it today has been developed in experiments on classical conditioning and "rote" learning, with discrimination learning and concept attainment as the principal extensions into selective learning processes. On the other hand, Information Processing theories have been principally concerned with selective processes in behavior, and especially intellectual performances (e.g., vigilance, visual search, selective listening, choice reaction, decision making) that involve attentional, perceptual, memorial, information transforming and collating, and decision-making processes. The structural basis of a change in behavior has not been a principal concern; rather, the analysis is that appropriate to the performance of man in intellectual and perceptual-motor skills in which the limits of learning have been approximated and in which the repertoire of codes for specific input information (stimuli or instructions) has been well-established.

The theoretical contrast I have described is, of course, an exaggeration. Broadbent bridged the two approaches at several points in his book on *Perception and Communication* (1958), Shepard, Hovland, and Jenkins (1961) adopted an IP approach although well-versed and frequent contributors to the S-R Association approach, and Fitts (1964) has explicitly bridged the two approaches in his thinking about skills. Perhaps of greater importance, however, is the fact that research results seem to be leading to a convergence of these approaches. For example, IP theorists now recognize that the process characteristics of some performances, such as choice reactions, are dramatically altered by the degree of learning of the S-R associations (the "S-R compatibility") involved (Broadbent, 1964; Fitts and Switzer, 1962). As a movement from the other direction, S-R theorists now recognize that the process of formation of S-R associations, such as in "rote" paired-associate learning, involves selective processes of attention and coding (Underwood, 1963, 1964). Finally, there is a bi-directional movement in research that centers around the problems of short-term memory, because it now appears that the processes involved in short-term memory are keystones in both the S-R and IP superstructures. For this reason, I have the hunch that agreement between S-R and IP theorists about the fundamental nature of short-term memory may be the needed giant step toward molding these approaches into a unified process theory of human behavior.

In order to illustrate this rapprochement of S-R and IP theories, and at the same time give a little substance to the prescription that theoretical processes should be the focus of research on individual differences, a look at some theoretical notions about "rote" serial and paired-associate learning, and short-term memory, may be helpful. My reason for this selection of examples is not only my greater familiarity with data and theory on these "kinds" of learning, but also my conviction that these may be productive of understanding of learning and performance in a wide variety of tasks that go under other names. This conviction derives from the judgment that these kinds of learning and performance offer the most fertile contexts for the manipulation of the conditions of simple association formation and utilization, i.e., of *memory*. If these things are true—some agree and many disagree—then these tasks should be appropriate as foci for individual differences studies, as has already been suggested by Jenkins and Jensen.

A defense of rote verbal learning and memory as productive of principles and processes of broad generality is not intended at this time. Nevertheless, the conditions that affect the entrance of stimulus information into memory, the storage of that information, and its retrieval at a later time are clearly fundamental to all information processing activities of the organism and all learning. Attention and other cognitive set factors influence what is perceived, but perception appears to be a sufficient condition for storage in memory. It remains to be seen whether perception is a necessary condition for entrance into the memory store, although such is implied by the data on incidental learning, as cited by Jenkins, and also by the doctrine of serial processing of input information through the perceptual system of IP theory (Broadbent, 1958). Storage between time n and some later time may or may not be affected by autonomous consolidation and/or autonomous decay, but some residue of the perception is a necessary condition for retrieval on which the inference of learning is based. Finally, the retrieval process, as indexed by recognition, reinstatement, or saving in repetitions in relearning is now well-known to be greatly influenced by the characteristics of the perceived unit (especially its complexity and organization) and the characteristics of the preceding and interpolated events (Postman, 1961, 1964; Melton, 1963). These principal components of the process theory of memory for verbal materials—perception, storage, retrieval—are, it seems to me, obvious places to look for individual differences, as Jensen has suggested.

These subprocesses of memory (or remembering) have been examined in "list" learning, with multiple presentations to achieve mastery, and more recently in short-term memory for single events with or without embedding in a series of similar events. At the level of list learning we now have a well-formed, intermediate-level process theory which takes into consideration not only the events associated with a single "stimulus" event and a single "response" event, but also the relations between the multiple perceptions (of stimulus and/or response terms) that must be integrated into a higher-order memory or

habit. This theoretical model, which was succinctly described and
tested by McGuire (1961), has been mentioned by both Jenkins and
Jensen, but I wish to use the slightly expanded version of the model
shown in Figure 15.

The basic notion in this model is that all paired-associate learning,
and perhaps all learning, involves a stimulus differentiation component,
a response integration (and perhaps differentiation) component, and a
"hookup" between the internal representation of the stimulus and the

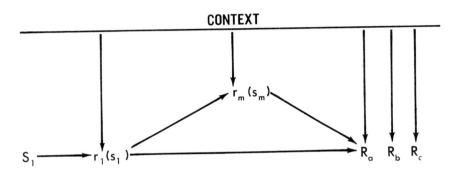

Figure 15. **A multi-process model of associative learning.**

integrated response or a segment of it. The stimulus differentiation
component $(S_1 \rightarrow r_1)$ is the organism's coding response to the physical
stimulus (S_1). It is the functional stimulus $[r_1(s_1)]$ in S-R associations;
it is reflective of the characteristics of the physical stimulus, but also
selective (Underwood, 1963) with respect to it, and this selection may
reflect learning, set, and identification and categorization factors. The
response integration component $(R_aR_bR_c)$ is the required output response, which may be a simple already learned unit (R_a) or a new combination of such units $(R_aR_bC_c)$. The new association or "hook-up" is
the connection $[r_1(s_1) \rightarrow R_aR_bR_c]$ between the stimulus-as-coded and
the required response. My first addition to the McGuire model (although it was implicit in his model) is an alternative mediational route
$[r_m(s_m)]$ for the connection of the internal representative of the physical
stimulus $[r_1(s_1)]$ and the required response $(R_aR_bR_c)$. My second addition is the associations between context stimuli, i.e., usually unspecified
but manipulable environmental and intra-organic stimuli, and *all* response elements $(r_1, r_m, R_a, R_b, R_c)$ involved in the S-R sequence.

This model has wide acceptance among S-R Association theorists
and is a far cry from the simplistic notions of what S-R theory is about.

It seems to me that our analysis of individual differences in such simple associative learning will be very productive of meaningful relations between individual differences and learning as well as refinements of the model. We know that we can manipulate experimentally the extent to which response integration, stimulus differentiation and coding, and a variety of mediational processes, may be involved in new learning. We also know that to look at any new learning without an attempt to assess the status of the habit systems of the learner with respect to the availability of these pre-established response integration, stimulus differentiation, and mediational habits, is to be blind to the nature of the processes that are under investigation. If this is so, then it seems self-evident that the analysis of individual differences variables must carry this multi-process analysis of the learning process to the analysis of individual performance differences. Jenkins has said this elegantly, and with a great deal more specificity than I am permitted, so that my statement is chiefly a strong reiteration of the desirability of his programmatic goal.

One point does, however, deserve further elaboration. This relates to the possibility that mediational (recoding) processes may be of fundamental importance in producing individual differences in simple associative learning (Cofer's discouraging data notwithstanding!). And in order to make this point, I must move into the recent data on short-term memory for to-be-learned units that are far below the memory span.

Consider, first, the results obtained when one tests for the recall of three-consonant trigrams of low association value after intervals of time filled with a rehearsal-preventing or rehearsal-minimizing activity such as counting backward by threes from a three-digit number which the experimenter has provided. We know from the work of Peterson and Peterson (1959) that the short-term retention function for such trigrams over intervals from 3 to 18 seconds looks very much like the Ebbinghaus forgetting function, with 90 percent correct recall at 3 seconds and only 10 percent correct recall at 18 seconds. Furthermore, we now know from experiments on the same or similar material that the degree of retention of the to-be-remembered unit will be a function of its length or complexity (Melton, 1963), the number of preceding units of the same type that have been presented to and recalled by the subject (Keppel and Underwood, 1962; Wickens, Born and Allen, 1963) and the nature of the activity that is used to fill the interval between the presentation and recall of a particular unit (Wickelgren, 1966). Thus, we have considerable evidence that the same interference factors that operate in the longer-term memory (Postman, 1961, 1964) also operate in short-term memory. This is not, however, my primary concern here.

We also know that the slope of the short-term memory function for 3-consonant trigrams is less steep the higher the meaningfulness of the trigrams (Peterson, Peterson, and Miller, 1961), and that the slope is less steep the greater the number of presentations (or readings) of the stimulus before the retention interval begins (Hellyer, 1962). But more important for my present purpose is the fact that one can, at least under some circumstances, eliminate the differences between high-meaningful and low-meaningful trigrams by providing to the subject a cue for recoding the trigram into a meaningful unit. Thus, the trigram TKR, which is a low-meaningfulness trigram, will be retained very well if you suggest to the subject that he remember it by thinking of the word "TinKeR" (Lindley, 1963; Lindley and Nedler, 1965). Alternatively, subjects may be trained to generate recoders for such trigrams, and in such experiments the trigrams become very well, if not perfectly, recalled over intervals comparable to those used in other studies of short-term memory (G. H. Bower, personal communication). Still further studies that are not yet published show that such recoding of a stimulus into a more meaningful unit is generally effective, varies with the memory value of the recoding response, and varies with the complexity and uniformity of the recoding rule, i.e., the rule required for the subject to generate the to-be-remembered stimulus once he has remembered what his recoding of the stimulus was.

I relate these observations to the topic of the conference by assuming that most memory for verbal materials is exceptionally sensitive to the mediational or recoding operations performed on it at the time of reception and storage. In fact, there may be, as Underwood (1964) suggests, very little "raw" memory for verbal materials operating in the usual verbal learning task. (It is possible that such "raw" memory does operate over a very brief interval, e.g., 2-3 seconds or 7-8 perceptual events, and is what Waugh and Norman (1965) describe as "primary" memory.) If one accepts the notion that most memory is based upon such mediational recoding operations, and also the notion that stimuli differ in the ease of recodability, then it seems probable that the principal factors in verbal learning may be the availability and efficiency of such recoding (and decoding) operations that the subject performs on the sequence of events that is being experienced.

The final step in the development of this thought is to assert that subjects differ in the speed and/or efficiency of recoding of input information, and there is ample evidence that this is the case. Some subjects recode trigrams by using single words, others do so by using strings of words (Bugelski, 1962), and we have the intriguing suggestion from Glanzer that the difficulty of remembering a perceptual object or a string of binary numbers is a function of the length of the string of words used by the subject to perform this recoding operation. I suspect that an equally important factor in the efficiency of the recoding process is the simplicity of the rule that must be used to get back from the recoder to the to-be-remembered input information. One of the simplest and most effective recoding rules is to employ an ordinal position tag ("first, second, third," etc.), even though using this same simple rule over and over again for the same kind of to-be-remembered elements will produce demonstrably high frequencies of erroneous intrusions from preceding recalled units into the recall of the last unit to be experienced (Peterson and Gentile, 1965).

If we assume that individuals differ in the speed and efficiency of such recoding processes, then it is clear that a valid theory for the interpretation of short-term memory functions must include individual differences measures of recoding processes employed in the storage of the information. For example, is the change in the slope of the short-term memory curve as a function of the meaningfulness of the trigram due to a change in the recoding process involved in a single subject, or is it due to a change in the frequency with which subjects use an efficient recoder? As another example, is the duration or frequency of repetition of a to-be-remembered unit effective in changing its rememberability because of a change in the process of recoding within the individual, or because of a change in the frequency with which subjects achieve an efficient recoder?

We cannot possibly have a good theory of the processes involved in remembering, either in a short-term or a long-term sense, unless we have procedures for assessing the status and change of such processes within individuals. As long as we throw possible within-individual and between-individual differences together in a measurement, we have no way to think clearly about the effects of the variables we employ in experiments on short-term memory. If, as I believe, the understanding of human short-term memory is essential for an understanding of the effects of repetition on long-term memory, there will be the same deficiency in the latter analysis.

These, then, are some of the lines of thought that lead me to the conclusion that the sooner our experiments and our theory on human memory and human learning consider the differences between individuals in our experimental analyses of component processes in memory and learning, the sooner we will have theories and experiments that have some substantial probability of reflecting the fundamental characteristics of those processes. When we are thus able to deal with the "genotypical" processes at the level of the individual learner, we will have the predictive efficiency we all seek. If the same concern guides the analysis of non-associative factors in learning and performance, an integration of the S-R Association and Information Processing approaches to behavior will be further encouraged. With the consensus on these points that seems to prevail at this conference, something may indeed be done about these ideas that so many of you have iterated and I have only reiterated.

REFERENCES

Broadbent, D. E. *Perception and communication.* London: Pergamon, 1958.

Broadbent, D. E. S-R compatibility and the processing of information. In *Proceedings of the XVII international congress of psychology.* Amsterdam, Netherlands: North-Holland, 1964. Pp. 325-327.

Bruner, J. S., Goodnow, J. J., and Austin, G. A. *A study of thinking.* New York: John Wiley & Sons, Inc., 1956.

Bugelski, B. R. Presentation time, total time, and mediation in paired-associate learning. *J. exp. Psychol.,* 1962, *63,* 409-412.

Fitts, P. M. Perceptual-motor skill learning. In A. W. Melton (ed.), *Categories of human learning.* New York: Academic Press Inc., 1964. Pp. 243-285.

Fitts, P. M., and Switzer, G. Cognitive aspects of information processing: I. The familiarity of S-R sets and subsets. *J. exp. Psychol.,* 1962, *63,* 321-329.

Gagné, R. M. *The conditions of learning.* New York: Holt, Rinehart & Winston, Inc., 1965.

Games, P. A. A factorial analysis of verbal learning tasks. *J. exp. Psychol.,* 1962, *63,* 1-11.

Garner, W. R., Hake, H. W., and Eriksen, C. W. Operationism and the concept of perception. *Psychol. Rev.,* 1956, *63,* 149-159.

Hellyer, S. Supplementary report: Frequency of stimulus presentation and short-term decrement in recall. *J. exp. Psychol.,* 1962, *64,* 650.

Hunt, E. B. *Concept learning: An information processing problem.* New York: John Wiley & Sons, Inc. 1962.

Kendler, H. H. The concept of the concept. In A. W. Melton (ed.), *Categories of human learning.* New York: Academic Press, 1964. Pp. 211-236.

Keppel, G., and Underwood, B. J. Proactive inhibition in short-term retention of single items. *J. verb. Learn. verb. Behav.*, 1962, *1*, 153-161.

Lindley, R. H. Effects of controlled coding cues in short-term memory. *J. exp. Psychol.*, 1963, *66*, 580-587.

Lindley, R. H., and Nedler, S. E. Further effects of subject generated recoding cues on short-term memory. *J. exp. Psychol.*, 1965, *69*, 324-325.

McGuire, W. J. A multiprocess model for paired-associate learning. *J. exp. Psychol.*, 1961, *62*, 335-347.

Melton, A. W. Implications of short-term memory for a general theory of memory. *J. verb. Learn. verb. Behav.*, 1963, *2*, 1-23.

Melton, A. W. The taxonomy of human learning: Overview. In A. W. Melton (ed.), *Categories of human learning.* New York: Academic Press Inc., 1964. Pp. 325-339.

Miller, G. A., Galanter, E., and Pribram, K. H. *Plans and the structure of behavior.* New York: Holt, Rinehart & Winston, Inc., 1960.

Peterson, L. R., and Gentile, A. Proactive interference as a function of time between tests. *J. exp. Psychol.*, 1965, *70*, 473-479.

Peterson, L. R., and Peterson, M. J. Short-term retention of individual verbal items. *J. exp. Psychol.*, 1959, *58*, 193-198.

Peterson, L. R., Peterson, M. J., and Miller, A. Short-term retention and meaningfulness. *Canad. J. Psychol.*, 1961, *15*, 143-147.

Postman, L. The present status of interference theory. In C. N. Cofer (ed.), *Verbal learning and verbal behavior.* New York: McGraw-Hill Book Company, 1961. Pp. 152-179.

Postman, L. Short-term memory and incidental learning. In A. W. Melton (ed.), *Categories of human learning.* New York: Academic Press Inc., 1964. Pp. 145-201.

Shepard, R. N., Hovland, C. I., and Jenkins, H. M. Learning and memorization of classifications. *Psychol. Monogr.*, 1961, *75*, Whole No. 517.

Underwood, B. J. Stimulus selection in verbal learning. In C. N. Cofer and B. S. Musgrave (eds.), *Verbal behavior and learning: Problems and processes.* New York: McGraw-Hill Book Company, 1963. Pp. 33-38.

Underwood, B. J. The representativeness of rote verbal learning. In A. W. Melton (ed.), *Categories of human learning.* New York: Academic Press Inc., 1964. Pp. 47-78.

Underwood, B. J., and Schulz, R. W. *Meaningfulness and verbal learning.* Chicago: J. B. Lippincott Co., 1960.

Waugh, N. C., and Norman, D. A. Primary memory. *Psychol. Rev.,* 1965, *72,* 89-104.

Wickelgren, W. A. Phonemic similarity and interference in short-term memory for single letters. *J. exp. Psychol.,* 1966, *71,* 396-405.

Wickens, D. D., Born, D. G., and Allen, C. K. Proactive inhibition and item similarity in short-term memory. *J. verb. Learn. verb. Behav.,* 1963, *2,* 440-445.

INDEX

INDEX

Locke, E. A., 178, 190
Lockhart, R. A., 196, 206, 209
Loevinger, J., 170, 190
Lord, F. M., 6, 17, 76, 88
Lorge, I., 223, 233
Luria, A. R., 96, 98, 111
Lykken, D. T., 47, 57

Machover, K., 159
Mackay, G. W. S., 25, 39
Mackworth, N. H., 110, 111
Magoun, H. W., 108, 111
Malmo, R. B., 108, 111
Maltzman, I., 70, 88, 91, 93, 97, 104, 111
Man, variability, 19
Mandler, G., 12, 17, 35, 39
Manning, W. H., 6, 17
Morgenau, H., 13, 16
Marlowe, D., 226, 232
Martin, W. E., 197, 198, 210
Mateer, F., 196, 210
McAllister, E. E., 190
McCarthy, J., 29, 39
McComas, H. C., 162, 164
McCorquodale, K., 170, 190
McGinnies, E., 145, 149, 158
McGuire, W. J., 49, 57, 246, 251
McNemar, O. W., 137, 140
McNemar, Q., 27, 39
Measurement
  behavioral change, 6-7
  reliability, 129
Mech, E. V., 93
Meehl, P. E., 170, 188, 190
Meissner, P, B., 159
Melton, A. W., 163, 164, 241, 245, 247, 251
Memory span, factor analysis, 128-129
Memory
  individual differences variables, 248
  law, 2
  mediating process, 247-248
  processes, 245-246

recoding, decoding, 248
rote, factor, 61, 62
short-term, 247-250
span, factor, 61, 62
Mental age
  classical conditioning, 196-197
  IQ, issue, 213-214
  learning, 192, 193-194
Mental retardation
  attention, observing response, 214-215
  attention theory, 204-207
  IQ vs. MA, 213-214
  learning theory, 203
Merrell, Margaret, 9, 17
Merrifield, P. R., 67, 88
Messick, S., 146, 158
Metlay, W., 110, 111
Milgram, N. A., 197, 198, 210
Miller, A., 248, 251
Miller, G. A., 243, 251
Miller, N. E., 143, 158
Motivation
  anxiety and instruction, 35
  compulsiveness and instruction, 35
  constructive, defensive, 34-36
Motor abilities, taxonomy, 172-178
Mowrer, O. H., 143, 158
Multiple regression, 41
Munroe, P., 173, 190

Nature, nurture controversy, 2
Nedler, S. E., 248, 251
Neisser, U., 218, 232
Newell, A., 219, 232, 235, 237
Newman, S. E., 49, 57
Neyman, J., 32, 38
Nicks, D. C., 173, 191
Nies, R., 105, 107, 112
Noble, C. E., 8, 12, 15, 17, 46, 56
Noble, Janet L., 8, 12, 17
Norman, D., 248, 252

O'Connor, N., 197, 198, 210
O'Connor, P., 35, 37